THE PSYCHOLOGY
OF THE
GIRL WITH THE
DRAGON TATTOO

OTHER SMART POP PSYCHOLOGY TITLES

THE PSYCHOLOGY OF THE GIRL WITH THE DRAGON TATTOO

Understanding Lisbeth Salander and Stieg Larsson's Millennium Trilogy

EDITED BY ROBIN S. ROSENBERG, PHD, AND SHANNON O'NEILL

An Imprint of BenBella Books, Inc.
Dallas, Texas

Smart Pop is an Imprint of BenBella Books, Inc.
10300 N. Central Expressway, Suite 400
Dallas, TX 75231
www.benbellabooks.com
www.smartpopbooks.com
Send feedback to feedback@benbellabooks.com

Printed in the United States of America
10 9 8 7 6 5 4 3 2 1

Library of Congress Cataloging-in-Publication Data
The psychology of the girl with the dragon tattoo : understanding Lisbeth
Salander and Stieg Larsson's millennium trilogy / edited by Robin S.
Rosenberg, PhD, and Shannon O'Neill.
    p. cm.
Includes Bibliographical references and index.
ISBN 978-1-936661-34-3
1. Larsson, Stieg, 1954—Criticism and interpretation.
2. Psychology and literature. I. Rosenberg, Robin S. II. O'Neill, Shannon.

PT9876.22A6933ZZ88 2011
839.73'8—dc23
                    2011036887

Copyediting by Cody Dolan
Proofreading by Michael Fedison
Cover design by Faceout Studio
Text design and composition by Neuwirth & Associates, Inc.
Printed by Bang

Distributed by Perseus Distribution
http://www.perseusdistribution.com/

To place orders through Perseus Distribution:
Tel: (800) 343-4499
Fax: (800) 351-5073
E-mail: orderentry@perseusbooks.com

Significant discounts for bulk sales are available. Please contact Glenn Yeffeth at glenn@benbellabooks.com or (214) 750-3628.

CONTENTS

INTRODUCTION

Reading a good book is like undertaking an investigation: as readers we comb through paragraphs and pages, linking pieces of plot and character together to build a coherent, compelling picture of a complete world. When we come to the end of a book and snap shut the cover, we often feel satisfied that our investigation is over. Our questions have been answered; the "case" is closed. But the books that truly affect us—whether thrillers, mysteries, or stories of unrequited love—often don't give us a complete sense of closure. They raise questions that linger long after the last page.

Stieg Larsson's books *The Girl with the Dragon Tattoo*, *The Girl Who Played with Fire*, and *The Girl Who Kicked the Hornet's Nest* whisk us away almost instantly with their spellbinding characters, fast-paced action, and dark, brooding mysteries. Larsson gives us a world in which we can lose ourselves, ignoring dirty laundry or dishes in the sink as we race through the streets of Stockholm on the back of Lisbeth Salander's motorbike to try and stop a serial killer. But instead of merely going along for a fictional ride, Larsson challenges us to look beneath the surface of things, to ask difficult questions, and to seek the truth for ourselves. We are driven to try to make sense of—or at least find our way through—the labyrinth of clues the books lay out.

It's not just his plots that have twists and turns and blind corners, however. Many of his characters are puzzle-boxes: difficult to pry open and hiding a wealth of secrets—some simply shocking, others downright dangerous. Many of these characters—for instance, investigative journalist Mikael Blomkvist and computer hacker Lisbeth Salander—are truth-seekers themselves, driven to unearth clues, solve complex cases, and hunt down dangerous criminals.

Unlike Mikael and Lisbeth, we aren't in the business of hunting down serial killers or unraveling cold cases of state-sponsored espionage. But that doesn't mean the cases we're challenged with solving as readers of the Millennium trilogy are any less complex. Stieg Larsson seems to want us to wonder much more than simply "whodunit." His books force us to question why we judge people by their appearances and why we so often unquestioningly accept authority. But for many of us, the central case to be cracked in the trilogy is that of Lisbeth Salander: who she truly is, what she really wants, and what she has to tell us about our world and ourselves.

Lisbeth is one of the most enigmatic and intriguing characters you'll ever come across—an astoundingly intelligent, prickly bundle of contradictions. We know about her unorthodox looks, her unslakable thirst for the truth, her fearlessness in the face of danger, and her . . . unusual relationships. But there's also a lot we don't know. What makes her tick? Is she a vulnerable young woman or a powerful hero? A crusader, a vigilante, a psychopath—or some combination?

Lisbeth relies on her brilliant skills of deduction to solve cases, but as a computer hacker her first step is breaking into data systems to access valuable, secret information. If we had Lisbeth's skills, we could find out more about her past and even her future by hacking into Stieg Larsson's computer; after all, we know the author had planned more books in the series before his death. Perhaps the answers to Lisbeth's true feelings and motivations, as well as her future path, could be found in the notes he supposedly left behind. Well, for better or worse, we can't work like Lisbeth. We don't have her skills or her daring, or possess her willingness to break the law. But we do have something else: the ability to "hack" Lisbeth herself. Unlike our heroine, our work doesn't involve getting inside a software system or a mainframe. Rather, we've chosen to delve into Lisbeth's psyche, using the tools of psychology to guide our way.

Our first step is to gather the clues on the trilogy's pages: what Lisbeth says and does; the way she portrays herself to the outside world; how others perceive her and react to her; and how she transforms the expectations of those she encounters. But collecting the clues as written by Larsson will only get us so far—an investigator ultimately must make *sense* of the clues. Consider Blomkvist, for instance. He assembled a lot of information about the Vangers in trying to solve Harriet's disappearance, but he needed Lisbeth's help to dig deeper into the case and piece it all together. Like Blomkvist, we've also recruited help in our quest to solve our case. We've asked psychologists and psychiatrists to take the clues they collected from the trilogy and use them to "crack the case" of Lisbeth Salander. Just as Salander can amass bits of data and make a coherent whole out of them, our contributors have taken the bits of intel Stieg Larsson has given us and used them to unearth meaning.

In this book, *The Psychology of the Girl with the Dragon Tattoo*, the contributors use all of the tools at their disposal—as readers, as investigators of psychology, as "mind-hackers"—to understand Lisbeth's inner world. Each essay in this book takes a facet of the Millennium story and examines it using a psychological lens, employing research and theory to better understand who Lisbeth Salander truly is. The conclusions our experts have drawn are not uniform; using the same clues, in some cases our investigators have come up with surprisingly different understandings of Lisbeth. That the findings range so widely says a lot about Lisbeth's complexity and richness as a character.

The appeal of the Millennium trilogy isn't solely due to Lisbeth Salander, of course. The novels raise questions about violence, about the nature of justice, and about the quest for truth and redemption. Those questions are essentially psychological in nature, addressing things like desires, motivation, resilience, and the psychological underpinnings and consequence of moral choices. Through examining Lisbeth, we also gain a broader understanding of these issues, and of ourselves.

The table of contents of this book is true to the process of investigating Lisbeth. We start with the most obvious clues we get from the Millennium series: Lisbeth is different *from* other people. From the moment we encounter her, Lisbeth looks, acts, and reacts differently than most of us, even as we may recognize elements of her character in ourselves. Part of her difference is her tough exterior—her many piercings and her unwelcoming attitude. Essays in the first section of this book, *The Girl with the Armored Façade*, help us better understand that armor. They explore the ways that Salander is different and what her differences might tell us about her.

Robert Young and Lynne McDonald-Smith help us understand Goths, and Rachel Rodgers and Eric Bui hone in on Lisbeth's tattoos and piercings. Misty Hook uses the psychology of gender to help us understand Lisbeth's unusual behavior and how people react to it. David Anderegg focuses on what at first glance might appear to be an absence of behavior—silence—and why Salander might choose to wield it as power. And Prudence Gourguechon highlights how and why Salander "does" relationships differently than most.

Once we—and others in her world—start to see how different Lisbeth is, we also begin to catch glimpses of what exactly is happening underneath her hardened exterior, and to wonder whether something is seriously wrong with her. We learn about the horrible trauma she suffered as a child and young adult, and we want to understand how these experiences shaped her. Essays in the second section, *The Girl with the Tornado Inside*, focus on the sources of her trauma and her response to it. Lisbeth is deeply troubled; she is mistrustful, angry, and guarded, and capable of harming certain people without remorse or regret. Is she dangerous enough that it warrants her being locked up, as the courts originally suggested?

Wind Goodfriend's essay starts us off by placing Lisbeth in context—that of a society steeped in sexism; her essay explores the ways that societal sexism has contributed to Lisbeth's behavior. Joshua Gowin examines Salander's use of (and seeming comfort with) violence, and the extent to which her use of violence might be rooted in her genes. Stephanie Mullins-Sweatt and Melissa Burkley consider whether Salander, who can be ruthless, is in fact a psychopath. Hans Steiner explains how Lisbeth's traumatic history has shaped who she is—and whether she's "abnormal." Forensic psychologist Marisa Mauro finishes the section with an evaluation of Salander, performed the way the courts in the trilogy should have.

Finally, we look at how Salander has taken trauma and transformed it into power. Essays in this final section, *The Girl Who Couldn't Be Stopped,* focus on what allows Salander to overcome the odds not only to save herself, but to help rescue others as well. These essays explore her strengths and abilities, and address whether Lisbeth's accomplishments are heroic . . . or something else. These essays also unearth another key theme of the series: the idea of (re)gaining power through knowledge, and using that power to seek justice.

First, Sandra Yingling explores what makes Lisbeth such a powerful and polarizing figure, as well as the power Lisbeth holds over us as readers. Pamela Rutledge explains Lisbeth's remarkable resilience, despite a childhood infused with trauma, neglect, and horrendous mistreatment. Bernadette Schell shines a light on Lisbeth's amazing hacking ability and compares her to real-world hackers. Robin Rosenberg proposes that Lisbeth is not just the hero of the series, but a bona fide *super*hero. In the book's final essay, Mikahil Lyubansky and Elaine Shpungin explore the costs of some of Salander's use of power—both to herself and to society.

In the end, Lisbeth is all of these things—damaged and resilient, victimized and powerful, terrifying and awe-inspiring. But in the end, too, she isn't quite as contradictory or as impenetrable as she initially seems. In giving us a character replete with incongruities and complexities, Larsson has made Lisbeth seem remarkably real. She is brought to life in three dimensions; her quirks and rough edges and aberrant behavior make her as frustrating and intriguing as an incredibly gifted but profoundly troubled friend. Understanding more about that complexity doesn't diminish the fascination she holds for us—it deepens it. We want to know even more. We want to figure her out.

Lisbeth is the true enigma at the heart of this blockbuster set of mysteries. To understand her, as well as her powerful effect on us, we'll need all the professional help we can get.

Let's get this investigation started.

Shannon O'Neill and Robin S. Rosenberg
August 2011

PART 1

THE GIRL WITH THE ARMORED FAÇADE

Lisbeth Salander crafts her appearance with thought and care, most strikingly when it comes to her Goth clothing and makeup. As a group, though, Goths are largely marginalized and ostracized. So why would Lisbeth intentionally choose to be one? Robert Young and Lynne McDonald-Smith use their own research to help us understand Goth identity, to correct our misconceptions (or confirm our existing views) about Goths, and also to show us how Lisbeth benefits from her Goth association.

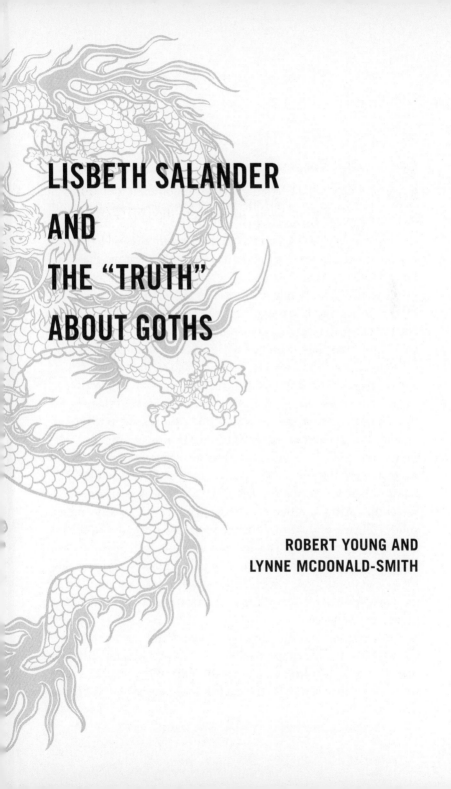

LISBETH SALANDER
AND
THE "TRUTH"
ABOUT GOTHS

**ROBERT YOUNG AND
LYNNE MCDONALD-SMITH**

One of the first things that we learn about Lisbeth Salander is that she stands out. Her dress and appearance are visually striking, and Stieg Larsson provides several vivid descriptions of her in *The Girl with the Dragon Tattoo*, the first book in the Millennium series. For example, we learn early on that Lisbeth "dressed for the day in a black T-shirt with a picture on it of E.T. with fangs, and the words I AM ALSO AN ALIEN. She had on a black skirt that was frayed at the hem, a worn-out black, mid-length leather jacket, rivet belt, heavy Doc Marten boots, and horizontally striped, green-and-red knee socks. She had put on makeup in a color scheme that indicated she might be colorblind." Despite her unique appearance, Lisbeth remains physically appealing: "She wore black lipstick, and in spite of the tattoos and the pierced nose and eyebrows she was . . . well . . . attractive."

Given this description, Salander appears to be a Goth—at least that's how the media and most book and film reviews portray her, although this is never explicitly confirmed in any of the books.[1] Even so, we can agree she belongs to at least one of the various tribes of alternative subcultures, be that generic alternative rock, punk, Goth, industrial, or something similar. There are real (sometimes subtle, sometimes distinct) differences between even these closely aligned youth cultures, and the uninitiated may have difficulty in distinguishing between them. This by itself is an illustration of our own psychological naiveté in understanding the subtleties of young people's social world. However, Lisbeth is clearly categorized as Goth in most people's eyes, so we will stick with that label and look for some supporting evidence.

But how much has Lisbeth's style to do with her character and identity? Is it really just chance that Larsson provides Lisbeth with such a striking identity? Of course not! Part of the success of Lisbeth as a popular heroine is the huge overlap between her character

[1] Voltaire, *What Is Goth?* (Boston: Weiser Books, 2004).

and our beliefs about what Goths "are," what Goths "do," and "what makes them tick." If you need to test this, try this brief thought experiment: write down the first five things that come to mind when you think about a Goth or alternative teenager. It's a fair bet that your list will contain at least two of the following words: gloomy, cynical, depressed, troubled, freak, odd, weird, loner, and possibly slutty, sexy, or even kinky. If Lisbeth is such a blatant stereotype, why then does she appeal to Goth and non-Goth readers alike?

The Role of the Goth in Literature and Popular Media

Lisbeth is far from the first Goth or alternative character in popular fiction (though she is one of the more famous). Larsson and other writers regularly tap into our latent beliefs about typical Goth behaviors and personalities in order to drive the plot and create believable and compelling characters. In order to understand what makes Larsson's treatment of Lisbeth and her Goth identity unique and different, it is revealing to take a brief look at how other Goth characters in popular media are treated. What traits are these characters purported to have, and what roles, common tropes, stereotypes, and themes are explored through them? Table 1 lists a selection of hit American TV shows that have featured Goth or "Gothed-up" characters and the themes explored in that particular episode.

Some of the most recognizable Goths are the Goth kids from the seventh season of *South Park*. *South Park* comically plays to every Goth cliché available; its Goth kids show deep cynicism, negativity, alienation, and a fixation with nonconformity—but nonconformity done together! A few of the Goth kids hint at a history of family and romantic discord, and this link is confirmed when Stan is dumped by his girlfriend Wendy and begins to hang around with the Goth kids in order to deal with the emotional and interpersonal trauma he suffers. As "another tortured soul" in pain, Stan is readily accepted.

Writers often use the Goth identity as a sign of transition (usually from childhood to teen independence) or of a significant and traumatic change in circumstances, or as a marker of a shift in core identity. This is illustrated in *The Simpsons* when Lisa Simpson, after a mix-up in IQ

TABLE 1: THE ROLE OF GOTH/ALTERNATIVE CHARACTERS AND THEIR ASSOCIATED THEMES WITHIN POPULAR FICTION

Source	Character	Character traits and commom themes
South Park (7-14)	The Goth kids; Stanley, who briefly becomes a Goth	Outsider, cynicism, depression, alienation, nonconformity, interpersonal trauma (Stan is dumped by Wendy), group identity
The Simpsons (15-13)	Lisa Simpson, who briefly identifies herself as "*Raven Crow Neversmiles*"	Intelligence, trauma (identity crisis), transition, rebellion, sexuality, alienation
Frasier (11-11)	Freddy (Frasier's son), who briefly becomes a Goth	Transition to independence, teen rebellion, rejection of parents, experimentation, developing sexually, interpersonal trauma (getting dumped)
Millennium trilogy	Lisbeth Salander	Traumatic & troubled past/present, psychiatric history, outsider, alienated, rebellious, defiant, intelligent, underestimated, sexually promiscuous/adventurous, cynical, distrustful, transition to independence and autonomy

test scores, can no longer claim the role of the "smart kid" so central to her character. This downgrade in status launches her into a spiraling identity crisis, in which she adopts a series of stock teenage identities—one of which is her Goth alter ego "Raven Crow Neversmiles." However, she quickly abandons this after Millhouse instantly picks up on the deviant and amorous potential, saying, "Cool . . .We'll go to the cemetery and summon the Dark Lord by kissing and junk."

The themes of transition, rebellion and interpersonal trauma are reiterated in an episode of *Frasier* where radio psychiatrist Frasier Crane's son Freddy briefly becomes Goth, thus signaling his transition into independence, teen rebellion, and the rejection of parental control. The interpersonal trauma comes at the end of the episode, when Freddy is dumped by his recently acquired Goth girlfriend.

Larsson explores these familiar themes of independence, interpersonal difficulties, and trauma within Lisbeth, who is also pessimistic (realistically so given her experience), sexually adventurous, and rebellious. As the Millennium series progresses, the theme of transitioning to adulthood and gaining autonomy comes to the foreground as Lisbeth transforms from someone who is controlled by others into an independent woman. As she shifts fully into her new identity, we see a fluctuation in her degree of Goth identification and clothing. Still, Lisbeth's Goth identity reemerges strongly when her autonomy is under threat, as exemplified by her reaction to legal authorities in *The Girl Who Kicked the Hornet's Nest*. Lisbeth seems to make a concerted effort to wear her most striking and inappropriate outfits to her many court appearances; as Larsson writes, "Even though Blomkvist was used to Salander's penchant for shocking clothing, he was amazed that his sister had allowed her to turn up to the courtroom in a black leather miniskirt with frayed seams and a black top—with the legend 'I am annoyed.'" Salander refuses to acquiesce to the expectations of others by modifying her appearance in court and appears instead in full Goth regalia.

We see this same set of themes emerging repeatedly in television and books whenever a Goth character appears, but the question remains: Do these stereotypes have any truth to them? In other words, in the "real world" can stereotypes ever provide information of practical use when it comes to understanding the psychology of the people behind them?

The Unbearable Truth about Stereotypes

The psychological literature that explores the "truth" of stereotypes, from both an insider and outsider perspective, and the importance of group and self-identity in understanding and defining ourselves and others is vast. But before we can attempt to understand someone like Lisbeth, we need to address an important question: Why do we have such a strong, almost compulsive need to stereotype distinctive social groups such as Goths?

The psychological reality we first need face is that the social world is complicated, and overloads us with conflicting information. There is far too much complicated data to deal with as we interact with others, and our minds require us to simplify it in some way. One of the cognitive shortcuts we tend to use is to create stereotypes—or in psychological terms, *social categories*. Although stereotypes can be highly inaccurate and stigmatizing, they can also contain some potentially useful information. In fact, when looked at objectively, some stereotypes are surprisingly accurate. It seems that, while we tend to view the world through our own particular set of biases, we are not completely blind to social reality.

Psychologist Lee Jussim and colleagues reviewed common stereotypes and found that most were fairly accurate.[2] For example, when it came to estimating the percentage of women employed in various occupations or guessing the income differences between women and men in the workplace, the general public made predictions that were surprisingly close to the actual figures. In fact, stereotypes can provide estimates that rival the accuracy of conventional psychological tests when guessing the characteristics of an individual. However, because of their simplistic nature, stereotypes are only good at predicting a limited range of people's characteristics and behaviors. Having demonstrated that reality and stereotypes can be surprisingly close, what are some of the common stereotypes about Goths—and how do they compare to what we know about Lisbeth and her life?

Goth Stereotypes: The Good, the Bad, and the Weird (But Mostly Just Bad and Weird)

Probably the single most common and most negative stereotype about Goths is that they are psychologically traumatized or damaged, invariably because of a troubled background. This is in line with Lisbeth's history; she has issues of parental abandonment, was

---

[2] L. Jussim, T. R. Cain, and J. T. Crawford, "The Unbearable Accuracy of Stereotypes," in *Handbook of Prejudice, Stereotyping, and Discrimination*, ed., T. D. Nelson (New York: Psychology Press, 2009).

brought up in a violent, abusive household, has been institutionalized in various psychiatric establishments, is prone to violent outbursts, and is (falsely) seen at risk of self-harm and suicide. It is also strongly hinted that she has some form of undiagnosed Asperger's syndrome (this might partially explain her lack of social skills).

Another Goth stereotype is that of the loner who is distrustful of people, society, and institutions. Lisbeth is a consummate loner: she's uncommunicative, far happier in her own company, and distrustful of groups. Her childhood and adolescence was spent in the care and under the scrutiny and repeated examinations of various psychiatrists, courts, and social workers who tried to control and contain her, so it's hardly surprising Lisbeth developed a strong distrust of authority. As we learn in *The Girl with the Dragon Tattoo*: "She was perfectly content as long as people left her in peace. Unfortunately society was not very smart or understanding; she had to protect herself from social authorities, child welfare authorities, guardianship authorities, tax authorities, police, curators, psychologists, psychiatrists, teachers, and bouncers."

What follows naturally from being distrustful of others is a sense of oneself as an outcast. A Goth identity seems almost synonymous with being deviant, weird, and an outsider. In Lisbeth's case we see that she is indeed a social outcast. Most of her associates are fellow Goths, punks, similarly deviant individuals, or computer hackers—another group portrayed as a loose clique of eccentric loners who enjoy flouting social and legal conventions and who are equally suspicious of mainstream culture. Few of her contacts are from mainstream society, and rarely come close to understanding her. Lisbeth is extremely socially alienated and only the most empathetic, nonjudgmental, and patient characters can get near her. This is part of her attraction to Blomkvist, who is described as having a liberal, tolerant, and accepting nature. Another part of the attraction is that Lisbeth instinctively recognizes a fellow rebel: Blomkvist himself doesn't fit in to the cozy complicit work of financial journalism and feels alienated from his own profession by its lack of integrity, lazy journalism, and barely concealed corruption.

Another Goth stereotype is their allegedly transgressive, pugnacious, defiant, rebellious, and stubborn disposition. Despite bullying, harassment, unwanted attention, coercion, and pressure to change from family, peers, and public, Goths seem unwilling to alter any facet of their style, attitude, or behavior. This describes Lisbeth to the core. Despite her diminutive size, Salander is described in *The Girl with the Dragon Tattoo* as fearless, "rarely afraid of anyone or anything." Further, she will simply not cooperate with the authorities despite intense pressure. An example of this can be found in her refusal to take a single psych assessment in her many years as ward of the court. What's more:

> All attempts by a teacher or any authority figure to initiate a conversation with the girl about her feelings, emotional life, or the state of her health were met, to their great frustration, with a sullen silence and a great deal of intense staring at the floor, ceiling, and walls. She would fold her arms and refuse to participate in any psychological tests. Her resistance to all attempts to measure, weigh, chart, analyze, or educate her applied also to her school work. *(The Girl with the Dragon Tattoo)*

The final trait repeatedly associated with Goths, and much exploited by the producers of low-budget horror flicks, is their supposed sexual promiscuity and transgressive or unconventional (in other words, kinky) sexuality. Lisbeth is from the start described as androgynous; she is also openly bisexual and has a history of sexual promiscuity, particularly with older men. She is sexually forward and adventurous, and is described as enjoying bondage and other sexual role play games with her occasional "S&M dyke" lover Miriam Wu. This is touched upon in the scene in *The Girl Who Played with Fire* when she first moves into Lisbeth's old apartment: "[Miriam] tied her T-shirt as a blindfold over Salander's eyes." In spite of her social awkwardness and personal experience of sexual violence, Lisbeth could never be described as inhibited, naïve, or remotely shy when it comes to sex—and ironically, this, too, fits in with the commonly held stereotypes of Goths.

The "Truth" about Goth Stereotypes

So how true are these stereotypes? Perhaps more importantly, is it "good" or "bad" to be Goth—and is there any way to measure this? Here the psychological literature is a bit sparse, which is unsurprising since few universities sport a Department of Goth Studies, but there are a few insights to be drawn from the scientific literature. In the early '90s psychologist Jeffrey Arnett published a book about heavy metal fans. Arnett interviewed over a hundred teenage fans, confirming that metal fans were more alienated compared to the average teen and exhibited signs that suggested a lower level of self-esteem.[3] A few in his sample mentioned thoughts about suicide, which occasionally translated into attempts. They were clearly more sensation-seeking than their peers and more rebellious (taking drugs, driving recklessly, or breaking rules), and had an unconventional outlook on life, rejecting social orthodoxy, prizing individuality, and staying "unpredictable".

More recent work by Robert Young (one of the authors of this piece) and colleagues at the MRC Social and Public Health Sciences Unit in Glasgow looked specifically at the relationship between psychiatric issues, attempted suicide, self-injury, and identity as a Goth or a member of many other contemporary youth subcultures.[4] The study found that, in a representative sample of 1,258 nineteen-year-olds, the more a participant identified as a Goth, the more likely he or she was to have attempted suicide. Only 5 percent of those who didn't identify as Goth had attempted suicide, while a staggering 47 percent who identified as Goth had. The pattern was the same for rates of self-injury, rising from 6 percent to 53 percent as the degree of identification increased. With the exception of a few of the more alternative subcultures (punk, nu-metal), none of the other youth cultures showed this trend. These findings *seem* to indicate a causal link between self-identifying as a Goth and exhibiting troubling behaviors.

Lisbeth certainly exhibits troubling behaviors, though attempted suicide does not seem to be one of them. The trauma that Lisbeth suffered was serious and long-standing, marked by an early history of

---

[3] J. J. Arnett, *Metalheads: Heavy Metal Music and Adolescent Alienation* (Boulder, CO: Westview Press, 1996).

[4] R. Young, H. Sweeting, and P. West, "Prevalence of Deliberate Self Harm and Attempted Suicide Within Contemporary Goth Youth Subculture: Longitudinal Cohort Study," *British Medical Journal* 332 (2006).

family violence and peer group and behavioral issues. Her formative experiences in childhood and adolescence are equally distressing, including her enforced custody by social services and culminating in her two-year stay at St. Stefan's Psychiatric Clinic for Children from age thirteen. She goes on to develop a history of negative assessments by a string of psychiatrists and psychologists. Is there something to this? Do Goths have more contact with mental health professionals than do other youth? Figure 1 shows the results of research that tested the association between the rate of contact with psychiatric services— that is, assessment or treatment by psychiatrists or psychologists—and the degree to which someone identified as a Goth. The answer to whether the two are correlated is a qualified yes. The rates of psychiatric care rise from 4 percent to 27 percent for those most strongly self-identified as Goth, as compared with the average teenage population. This lends further credibility to the troubled background stereotype, although this still means that in our study of young adults 73 percent of even the most clearly identified Goths never approach psychological or psychiatric services.

Figure 1: Proportion of psychiatric services used since age eleven and level of Goth identification (1258 young adults)

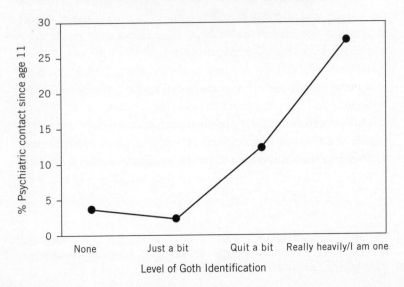

When looking at other Goth stereotypes, we have only unreliable and "anecdotal" evidence to call upon. Nursing professor Carolyn Rutledge and her colleagues reviewed some of this more anecdotal evidence, in an attempt to glean clearer conclusions from it. Rutledge reiterates that many of the common stereotypes link Goths to depression, negativity, sexual promiscuity, bisexuality, etc. She concludes that identifying as a Goth means participating in a "high-risk psychosocial (sub)culture" that reinforces depressive thoughts and encourages destructive behaviors.[5] This imitative or self-reinforcing behavior is known generically as the *social influence* or *social learning* model of behavior, and suggests that teen Goths imitate "destructive behaviors" from either Goth peers or music icons. Yet there is no solid evidence about the direction of cause and effect—for instance, rather than destructive behaviors being attributable to the social learning explanation, it could be that people who are drawn toward destructive behaviors start listening to Goth, metal, or alternative music during adolescence. Thus, without more reliable evidence, the social learning explanation for the high rates of "destructive behaviors" among Goth teenagers remains unproven and many other theories can readily account for such findings.

A more likely explanation of the link between Goth self-identification and the manifestation of troubling behaviors is a combination of two other psychological mechanisms: attraction to the subculture because of shared values and experience, and the *assortative friendships hypothesis*, more commonly understood by the phrase "birds of a feather flock together." To put it simply, troubled, angry, or disillusioned young people are attracted to Goth culture because the style and music reflects their experience of the world and gives them an opportunity to share their problems with like-minded friends and partners. To be fair, even in their generally negative assessment of Goth subculture, Rutledge and colleagues acknowledge both these alternative explanations. They also acknowledge the existence of more positive traits linked to people who identify as Goths, such as the

---

[5] C. M. Rutledge, D. Rimer, and M. Scott, "Vulnerable Goth Teens: The Role of Schools in this Psychosocial High-Risk Culture," *Journal of School Health* 78 (2008).

tendency for Goths to "possess above average intelligence" and to be "highly literate and creative."[6]

But how relevant are these findings to Lisbeth? Much of this research comes from either the United States or the United Kingdom, not Sweden. Nevertheless, because Goth is a worldwide youth sub-culture, most of the insights from the research are probably applicable. Further, when interviewing Goths from Germany, the UK, and America, German cultural researcher Dunja Brill found Goths share similar outlooks and experiences, irrespective of country of origin.[7] Most of the psychological research on Goths focuses on teens, while the sociological work tends to focus on young adults. Lisbeth is twenty-four when readers first meet her, but she could pass for fourteen as far as physical appearance is concerned and is arguably in many respects still a teenager, particularly in her degree of social skills and social identity. Either way, the typical age of those who participated in the research outlined here is similar enough to Lisbeth's life-stage—both physically and psychologically—that we can be reasonably confident that some of the conclusions we have drawn here would be relevant to her.

The Upside of Goth Identity: How Negative Goth Stereotypes Can Turn Into Positive Self-Identity

All of this begs the question: Given the largely negative reputation, why on earth would Lisbeth or any teenager choose to become a Goth? Social psychology and, more specifically, *social categorization* and *social identity theory* can address this. A good deal of our personal identity is shaped by the social groups we belong to, and sometimes even just the groups we aspire to belong to. Having first categorized the others around us, we then begin to self-categorize, automatically and almost unconsciously. But what possible benefit does self-labeling bring us? Social psychologists Henri Tajfel and John Turner, who

---

6 Ibid.

7 D. Brill, *Goth Culture: Gender, Sexuality and Style* (Oxford: Berg, 2008).

first developed social identity theory, suggest that the simple act of belonging to a group (even a stigmatized group, providing it has some redeeming features) can boost our self-esteem.[8] In other words, it is intrinsically important to us to have a positive social identity. Given that Goth culture is associated with depression and self-esteem issues, the benefits should be obvious.

Part of the advantage of group membership is the mutual social support such a network provides, even if this is just the knowledge that you are not alone in your views. In other words, even if you are going to be a loner or an outsider—or have a cynical and morbid worldview—it's better to do it with others. Paradoxically, it's better to be a loner or outsider with friends! Cultural researcher Paul Hodkinson's qualitative study of British Goths confirms this, with socializing cited as the number-one reason given by participants for their attraction to the Goth scene.[9] Larsson illustrates this lucidly when even the consummate outcast Lisbeth begins hanging out with hard rock band Evil Fingers, quickly finding it the only place she feels any sort of group loyalty and support. As Larsson tells us *in The Girl with the Dragon Tattoo*: "If there was one place where she felt any sort of group solidarity, it was in the company of the 'Evil Fingers' and, by extension, with the guys who were friends with the girls. 'Evil Fingers' would listen. They would also stand up for her."

Another insight as to the power of group identity can be gained from a series of psychological experiments looking at how ingroups (social groups one belongs to or identifies with, e.g., Goth, punk, Democrat, or Republican) tend to view outgroups (social groups one does not identify with) negatively, while promoting their own group and group characteristics. One study that powerfully illustrates this effect was conducted by Henri Tajfel. Tajfel randomly assigned adolescents into arbitrary groups (A or B) and asked them to allocate rewards to each of the two groups however they wanted. Even though each group only minimally functioned as such, participants strongly favored their

---

[8] H. Tajfel, and J. C. Turner, "An Integrative Theory of Intergroup Conflict," in *The Social Psychology of Intergroup Relations*, eds, W. G. Austin and S. Worche (Monterey: Brooks/Cole, 1979).

[9] P. Hodkinson, *GOTH: Identity, Style, and Subculture* (Oxford: Berg, 2002).

own group, giving their own group extra points.[10] In other words, people rewarded the group they had been randomly allocated to just minutes earlier. Similar experiments confirm this tendency to view your own group in a positive light, (over)emphasizing the similarity in characteristics that you all share and rationalizing reasons for favoritism. In essence, we all self-categorize or self-stereotype. This means that we all tend to overemphasize the characteristics that we share with members of a group, and overestimate the importance of our similarities. Self-stereotyping increases your sense of belonging and, at the very least, gives you something in common to start a conversation about!

But self-stereotyping, and stereotyping in general, can be a mixed bag. Although some Goth traits—such as intelligence and creativity—are unambiguously positive, most are not. Even being labeled with seemingly positive traits can have unintended negative consequences. As both Lisa Simpson and fellow class nerd Martin can attest, emphasizing one's intelligence and scholastic achievement does not necessarily boost your standing with your classmates.[11] One route to positive identity is to (re)interpret group traits in a positive light. Table 2 contrasts typical Goth views of common traits with how the mainstream observes them. While outsiders and mainstream culture may view Goths as rebellious and "not team players," the same trait can be viewed positively as being autonomous, individualist, or nonconformist. Lisbeth and other Goths can be viewed by non-Goths as stubborn, defiant, oppositional, and generally troublesome, but from an insider's perspective these same traits could be called courage, bravery, integrity, and being true to yourself. Although Lisbeth is an extreme example, her refusal to back down, even when the odds are stacked against her, is a large part of our attraction to her character and central to her role as heroine. Lisbeth's need to get even could be seen as aggressive and vengeful, or as a reflection

---

10 H. Tajfel, "Experiments in Intergroup Discrimination," *Scientific American* 223 (1970).

11 H. Sweeting, et al., "Dimensions of Adolescent Subjective Social Status Within the School Community: Description and Correlates," *Journal of Adolescence* 34 (2011).

of her desire for social justice. Weird becomes original or unique. The sexual slurs about Goths' promiscuity and deviancy can be viewed—equally validly—as attacks on sexual tolerance, attempts toward sexual equality, and thinly veiled instances of discrimination and prejudice. The same reversal can take place for traits seen as positive by the mainstream: being polite and following mannered social conventions can be viewed as being inauthentic, untrue, socially manipulative, or just dishonest.

Even the charge of nihilism, negativity, depression, and pessimism can be redeemed. A common Goth criticism of the mainstream, particularly mainstream American culture, is its unrealistic optimism and positive outlook. Goths see this attitude as naïve, gullible, or just plain delusional. Unfortunately, the evidence from psychology favors the Goth point of view! Results from numerous psychological experiments, examining everything from gambling to estimations of future career success, demonstrate that most humans have an inherent optimism bias—that is, they consistently inflate the likelihood of a favorable outcome, overestimate their level of control and competence, and

TABLE 2. GOTH/ALTERNATIVE VS. MAINSTREAM INTERPRETATIONS OF COMMON CHARACTER TRAITS AND STEREOTYPES.

Goth/alternative view		Mainstream view
Autonomous, individualistic, nonconformist	Vs.	Rebellious, not a team player, anticommunity
Courageous, brave, uncompromising, strong-minded, determined, principled	Vs.	Stubborn, wilful, defiant, oppositional, disobedient, trouble maker
Independent	Vs.	Solitary
Original, unique, distinct	Vs.	Weird, odd, freak, misfit
Inauthentic, untruthful	Vs.	Polite, mannered, adaptable
Sexually adventurous, tolerant	Vs.	Promiscuous, kinky, deviant
Spineless, weak-willed, corruptible, suggestible, manipulatable	Vs.	Agreeable, accommodating, reasonable, compromising
Realistic, nondelusional	Vs.	Negative, nihilistic, depressive
Gullible	Vs.	Distrusting

underestimate the likelihood of a negative outcome. There is a least one group who (on balance) seems resistant to this common delusion: the clinically or subclinically depressed. Psychologists Lauren Alloy and Lyn Abramson discovered that depressed people were less likely to have an optimism bias: depressed students in their study were more accurate than non-depressed students at judging when their actions (pressing a button) had a real influence on the outcome (making a green light flash). Non-depressed students thought they could "spot the system" and thereby influence the outcome. The button pressing had varying degrees of influence, but depressed students were far more accurate in predicting how much control they actually had.[12] In fact, it was the non-depressed students who were really deluding themselves!

In a postfinancial crisis world, the relevance of these findings to stock market trading (and other more reputable forms of gambling) should be obvious: most people are more optimistic than the situation warrants. So if you have some money to invest, it might not be wise to hand it over to a stockbroker if they appear overly cheerful. This phenomenon is known as *depressive realism*, or the "sadder but wiser" hypothesis. If the literature is true about Goths' negative disposition, we could probably add them to this "sadder but wiser" group since they are likely to be more in touch with reality than their mainstream counterparts. Lisbeth is sad but streetwise; she "knows" life is not fair and that the justice and social system will fail her and instead places her faith in her own abilities. She is for the most part correct: her ability to see the cold harsh reality of life and her caution in disclosing personal information is one of the reasons she survives. In contrast, the more open and vulnerable women in the Millennium series tend to have a shortened lifespan. Martin Vanger's victims are carefully selected from his detailed personal information database of contacts precisely because of their vulnerability and lack of social connection. As we learn in *The Girl with the Dragon Tattoo*, "His victims were often new arrivals, immigrant girls who had no friends

---

12 L. B. Alloy, and L. Y. Abramson, "Judgment of Contingency in Depressed and Nondepressed Students—Sadder but Wiser," *Journal of Experimental Psychology-General* 108 (1979).

or social contacts in Sweden." As Harriet Vanger knows, women who are distrustful of Martin and cautious with their personal details tend to live longer and happier lives.

So Is Lisbeth a Heroine, or Simply a Goth Stereotype?

Lisbeth conforms to almost all of the negative stereotypes about Goths. She is damaged, troubled, rebellious, cynical, and promiscuous. Yet she somehow remains a complicated and believable character. The secret Larsson uses to make Lisbeth compelling is to have her conform to these mainstream stereotypes about Goths while at the same time allowing us into her interior world, where we come to understand and respect her choices. Through the insight Larsson provides into Lisbeth's thinking, we begin to understand the world from a Goth-centric perspective like that listed in Table 2, as if we were a group insider. By contrasting how others view Lisbeth with Lisbeth's own personal narrative and behavioral motivations, Larsson subtlety reverses our understanding of Goth stereotypes, turning them from negative to positive traits. In fact, these traits, particularly Lisbeth's independence, brutal honesty, and indomitable force of will, are the key to her survival in an unjust and uncaring world. Her troubled nature has its genesis in the very real trauma she has suffered; it doesn't emerge as a result of imitating Goth culture. Her attraction to Goth and alternative culture is motivated by a search for a sense of belonging and an identity; only among other Goths can she feel any sense of group solidarity and make friends who understand and support her. Larsson is sympathetic to the often overlooked positive aspects such an identity brings, recognizing and valuing the intelligence, creativity, self-reliance, and tolerant attitude at its core.

Perceptively, Lisbeth's character also echoes the often-unnoticed Goth preoccupation with themes of truth, social injustice, and opposition to corporate, legal, and media manipulation. She shares a liberal but blunt and uncompromising attitude with Blomkvist, and their shared concerns and viewpoints form the basis for an ever-more trusting relationship and shape their understanding of each other. It's no coincidence that their jobs (private investigator and investigative journalist) share the common theme of uncovering truth and exposing deception, no matter the consequence. It's also no coincidence both Lisbeth and Blomkvist have regular run-ins with authority. Both to Lisbeth, a computer hacker, and to Blomkvist, a journalist, it is justice, and not simply "following the rules," that matters. This is a core part of their characters and a primary reason for the mutual attraction.

It's likely Blomkvist is at least in part a fantasy alterego of Larsson: they both just happen to be journalists with a strong libertarian streak who battle right-wing nationalists. Lisbeth, on the other hand, has been dubbed one of the most original heroines to emerge in crime fiction for years, and at least part of that originality is the way Larsson instinctively recognizes the reality of the Goth stereotype and understands the role identity plays in shaping Lisbeth's character. What all of this adds up to is one of the more believable Goth heroines in popular fiction.

ROBERT YOUNG, BSc (Hons), PgDip (IT), PhD (Cand.), is a research psychologist working at the MRC Social and Public Health Science Unit, University of Glasgow. His research focuses on the influence of peer group and youth culture on mental health. He was introduced to the Goth/Industrial scene over twenty years ago and self-identifies as "a bit of a Goth."

LYNNE MCDONALD-SMITH, MA (Hons) in film, television, and comparative literature, works for the Scottish Association for Mental Health and Choose Life, Scotland's national strategy to prevent suicide. Her dissertation in film, television, and comparative literature explored representation of Goths in British and American television programs. At University she self-identified as a Goth.

Neither author has a dragon tattoo.

L isbeth Salander's most famous characteristic, thanks to the title of the English translation of the Millennium trilogy's first book, is the dragon tattoo on her shoulder. Even more difficult to miss, when you consider her film incarnations, are her various piercings. Rachel Rodgers and Eric Bui share their understanding of and research into the psychology of body modification and explain the ways that Lisbeth is similar to—and different from—people with extensive body modifications in our world. After all, as the authors say, sometimes the body speaks louder than words. So what is Lisbeth saying with hers?

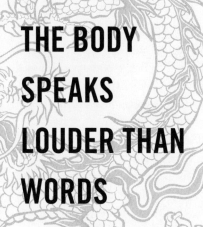

THE BODY
SPEAKS
LOUDER THAN
WORDS

WHAT IS LISBETH SALANDER SAYING?

RACHEL RODGERS AND ERIC BUI

n Western societies, and particularly among women, physical appearance is a central tenet of identity. Indeed, physical appearance is the first information we signal to others about ourselves. Hairstyle, clothes, makeup, and, of course, body art all contribute to tell other people who we are. Furthermore, as attractiveness is one of the most socially valued attributes, the way we perceive our body (our body image) is also linked to our self-esteem and mood.[1] In line with this, individuals who make choices about their appearance that do not adhere to what is socially accepted or considered attractive appear deviant or marginal. This is the case for multiple piercings and tattoos.

Throughout the Millennium trilogy, Lisbeth Salander speaks aloud remarkably little. She rarely initiates a conversation of her own accord or volunteers any information about herself. Furthermore, she very rarely defends herself when being criticized or accused of something and often becomes sullenly silent. This happens, for example, at school when she gets into an argument with a teacher over the correct answer to a problem and then later when in St. Stefan's clinic she pledges to never talk to a psychiatrist again after her thirteenth birthday. Her ensuing refusal to talk to authorities stems from her perception that speaking is ineffective, thanks to her failed attempt to explain her version of the attack on her father. Having talked to police officers, social workers, and hospital staff, she concludes that talking to authorities is ineffective and that her voice will never be heard. In view of this perceived failure to communicate with others using language, Salander seems to invest heavily in other means of nonverbal communication: her appearance in particular.

Salander cultivates a unique look and style of dress, and her clothes and general appearance can be interpreted as a means of communication. The extensive number of body modifications, including

---

[1] G. L. Patzer, *The Power and Paradox of Physical Attractiveness* (BrownWalker Press, 2006).

tattoos and body piercings, she displays (and sometimes chooses not to display) is also striking. In many ways Salander is an expert at manipulating her appearance according to her needs. However, her appearance also reveals more than she may know.

Given the importance of physical appearance, what are Salander's goals in presenting herself to the world in this way? As previously mentioned, Western societies often associate professional achievement, income, and psychological well-being with perceived attractiveness, and this is especially true for women. Girls, even at an early age, become highly aware that life is in many ways easier when attractive; as they enter adulthood, they often spend increasingly large amounts of time and money trying to resemble the mainstream ideal of beauty as closely as possible. This ideal, as presented by mainstream media, is generally acknowledged to be sexy yet fragile, and is embodied by a woman with a tall, very slender yet busty figure with shiny hair, wide eyes, and high heels.

The first description of Salander in *The Girl with the Dragon Tattoo* highlights her childlike physique, which contrasts strongly with the tough image she seems to cultivate. She is described as slender, small-boned, and girlish looking with childlike breasts, which gives some people the impression that she is much younger than she is, perhaps only fourteen. In many ways, she therefore fits in with the prevailing ideals of attractiveness, although she is perhaps a little flat-chested to match it perfectly. In defiance of this childlike and vulnerable appearance, Salander dyes her hair raven black, sometimes wears black lipstick, and has acquired a number of body modifications such as piercings and tattoos.

The Girl with the Dragon Tattoo, and Plenty of Other Body Modifications

What specifics can we glean about Lisbeth Salander through her chosen body modifications? She has nine tattoos and six body piercings, some of which are visible most of the time and some of which are generally hidden. These body modifications are central to her identity and tell a story: her story.

Tattoos, Identity, and Individuality

Tattoos and piercings can be used to signal a group identity. During her teenage years Salander became part of a hard rock band called "Evil Fingers" thanks to an introduction by a classmate dressed in a Goth style similar to that worn by both Salander and Evil Fingers' members. Although Salander felt that she was not fully included in the group, she did feel accepted. Her body modifications could be understood as symbols that marked her belonging to that group of people. Over time, however, her friends changed their style of dress and Salander began to feel more and more like an outsider. Her appearance no longer succeeded in identifying her as a member of the group. As the rest of her group moves on, Salander's body modifications appear increasingly deviant, marking her as the odd one out as opposed to a group member.

Tattoos and piercings can also help in creating a personal identity. This is particularly relevant in Salander's case as she has a twin sister, Camilla; developing a separate identity when one has a twin is known to be particularly challenging. Physical appearance is generally an important part of what distinguishes one person from another. Having a twin is a difficult exception to this rule, even in the case where the twins are fraternal, as with Salander and her sister. Salander may have been motivated to change her body so that it did not resemble her sister's as closely. Furthermore, Salander considers Camilla to be the "golden" twin: the prettier, more popular, more loved twin. As described in *The Girl Who Played with Fire*: "From the time they were little girls Camilla had been outgoing, popular and successful at school, while Salander had been ungiving and introverted, rarely responding to the teachers' questions." Lisbeth Salander's choice of body modifications to distinguish herself therefore serves to emphasize this difference, marking her as the deviant one and making her inner perception more visible.

Finally, tattoos can, through their content, be used to express things about oneself that may not otherwise be externally apparent, such as emotional attachment, personal beliefs, or, as noted above, group membership. For instance, Salander has a small wasp tattoo on her neck that symbolizes her pseudonym as a hacker. She is known as "wasp" among the hacker community, within which she is respected as one of the best hackers in the world. This high status within the hacker community is in sharp contrast with her real-world social identity: a single woman who has no contact with her remaining immediate family member, is reputed to have a psychiatric disturbance, and is under legal guardianship. Salander's wasp tattoo serves as a coded message of her other identity. Interestingly, people generally try to avoid getting to close to wasps. Wasps are small, but their sting can be very painful—just like Salander's, when she decides to avenge herself of something. The choice of the wasp tattoo could also be her attempt to signal to others that she can be dangerous.

Tattoos and Trauma

In the first book, Salander gets a narrow band tattooed on her ankle following her rape by Advokat Bjurman. The tattoo artist warns her that the tattoo is likely to be painful given its location, to which she replies that the tattoo is to be a "reminder." Salander seems to want a reminder of the fact that she had been victimized, perhaps to encourage herself to be more cautious in the future. Although this is the only piercing or tattoo that Salander acquires during the novels, what we learn of her rationale suggests a pattern for the acquisition of her other tattoos.

This is not an unusual rationale: using a tattoo to remember or commemorate a trauma is a relatively frequent motivation for victims of trauma. In the wake of Hurricane Katrina, for example, tattoo parlors in New Orleans noticed clients clamoring for tattoos related to the hurricane.[2] In this way tattoos can be a way of working through trauma or portraying a personal tragedy within a disaster. They can serve as visual aids or reminders, or be symbolic of a trauma overcome. The act of obtaining a tattoo can also be viewed as a way of regaining mastery of a violated body and reclaiming oneself. Instead of being subjected to physical pain, the person is choosing to seek it out. Salander chooses a particularly painful area of her body to

---

[2] K. Quillan, "Tattoo Business Is Booming in the Wake of Hurricane Katrina," *Times Picayune*, August 24, 2006.

place her commemorative tattoo, thus proving to herself that the pain inflicted upon her was not unbearable since she herself could choose to experience more pain. She is making the statement that her body is her own.

After the rape, Salander also inflicts a tattoo upon her aggressor, Advokat Bjurman, as a reminder. In this case, however, it is a reminder that such aggressions are punishable and meant to dissuade him from repeating his actions. In fact, the large tattoo—I AM A SADISTIC PIG, A PERVERT AND A RAPIST—aims to prevent him from any future sexual contact altogether. In the same way as she uses body modification to mark her own exterior with the signs of the life events she has experienced, Salander tattoos Advokat Bjurman's body with the sign of his crime. She seems to be saying that they will both carry the traces of the rape, both inside and out, for the rest of their lives. In Salander's world, as in ours, it seems that bodies tell the story of who you are and possess a clue to your identity.

Multiple Tattoos

While Salander's tattoos are far from meaningless individually and each forms an important aspect of her identity, it is also noteworthy that she has so many (nine total, including the dragon on her back, a loop around her ankle and one around bicep, a rose on her thigh, a wasp on her neck, and a Chinese symbol on her hip). She also has six body piercings. Research has suggested that undergoing tattooing and piercing has an addictive quality, possibly due to the release of chemicals including endorphins in response to the pain.[3] It is as if people get addicted to the "high" that comes with the pain. People with one tattoo or piercing often choose to get more body modifications, and individuals with numerous tattoos are known to sometimes end up with integral body tattoos that cover the whole of their skin.

Furthermore, possessing multiple body piercings has been associated with high risk behaviors such as substance use, risky sexual

---

[3] S. Wohlrab, J. Stahl, and P. M. Kappeler, "Modifying the Body: Motivations for Getting Tattooed and Pierced," *Body Image* 4 (2007).

activity, sensation seeking (pursuing novel and exciting activities that produce intense sensation but may be dangerous), manifestation of borderline personality disorder traits including impulsivity, evidencing unstable interpersonal relationships, difficulty in controlling anger, and possession of an unstable image of self,[4] all of which describe Salander to some extent. Her multiple tattoos and piercings may therefore indicate a global instability when it comes to relationships, self-image, and feelings. This combination of traits, though troublesome in real life, can make for interesting characters and is often found in fiction.

Now You See Me . . .

While Salander's appearance is very distinctive, she is also a master in the art of camouflage and is very effective at passing unnoticed when it suits her. The first time Salander disguises her appearance occurs in *The Girl with the Dragon Tattoo* when she goes to check out the apartment of Wennerström (the corrupt financier that Blomkvist is seeking to expose). She puts on warm winter clothes and matching gloves, scarf, and hat, removes her eyebrow and nose piercings, and puts on pale pink lipstick. Having done this, she feels as if she looks like "any other woman." This statement implies that Salander is aware that most of the time she has a very distinctive appearance and suggests that her choice to appear deviant is deliberate. It begs the question whether Salander might even exaggerate her usual appearance so as to be more likely to go unobserved when she strips herself of her piercings and provocative attire.

This willingness to use her appearance to achieve certain goals also emphasizes a lack of group affiliation expressed by her body modifications. Groups for whom body modifications are a central tenet of their identity are usually unwilling to divest themselves of their adornments. When they do, this often indicates a departure from

---

[4] E. Bui, R. Rodgers, Cailhol, P. Birmes, H. Chabrol, and L. Schmitt, "Body Piercing and Psychopathology: A Review of the Literature," *Psychotherapy and Psychosomatics* 79 (2010).

the group and a change of lifestyle.[5] While for a time Salander's body modifications identified her as an affiliate or member of Evil Fingers, as noted above, her friends moved on and the group dissolved. Having lost their symbolic meaning as a marker of belonging, the presence, or absence, of her body modifications is now used to other ends, such as occasional camouflage.

Salander modifies her appearance again in *The Girl with the Dragon Tattoo* on her trip to Zürich to steal Wennerström's money. She wears a wig, hides her tattoos under makeup, wears false eye lashes and latex breast enhancers, and puts on expensive clothes and jewelry. She does this as a disguise, yet she is extremely successful in mimicking the attire and appearance of a rich young woman who might come to Zürich for financial matters. This further supports the idea that she is equally aware of the effects of her usual appearance.

Another notable example of Salander's sense of choice and control as exhibited by her choices regarding appearance comes at the trial in *The Girl Who Kicked the Hornet's Nest*. Salander's outfit is unusual for the setting but ordinary for her, and obviously a deliberate choice considering her earlier ease in dressing "appropriately" when the circumstances demanded it. Her choice of courtroom attire includes a T-shirt—featuring the words "I am annoyed"—that fails to conceal her tattoos. Some of her piercings are visible and she wears a lot of black makeup, giving her a Gothlike appearance. This is clearly (as Blomkvist observes) a parody of herself and has been carefully thought out so as to be very clear about her rejection of what many of the people present at the trial stand for in society. Salander keenly feels misused by authorities and is eager to communicate her contempt wordlessly through her appearance.

Salander uses her appearance effectively to convey aspects of her personality. When she needs to convey other messages, she is an expert at changing her appearance to achieve what she needs. This high level of awareness as to how physical appearance is interpreted and the stereotypes and assumptions we associate with certain choices in attire and body decoration may have developed as a result of her difficulties

---

[5] L. E. Bazan, L. Harris, and L. A. Lorentzen, "Migrant Gangs, Religion and Tattoo Removal," *Peace Review* 14 (2002).

in verbal communication. Thanks to her control of her appearance, Salander can say a lot without having to say anything at all.

Lisbeth Salander Does NOT Want to Be Considered Attractive . . . or Does She?

Her appearance is designed not only to convey hostility, but also to show a rejection of society's codes and rules. She perceives that, when flaunting piercings and tattoos, she is placing herself in the margins of society. Far from an unintentional act, or one driven by personal preference, she goes out of her way to achieve this effect. This is the case not just when it comes to piercings and tattoos, but also when it comes to her clothing choices. Her style of dress, too, seems to have a provocative element; it's almost as if she is a defiant adolescent, seeing how far she can go without someone telling her to "go upstairs and change your clothes." Consider her attire: Salander often wears a combination of leather and rivets, frayed or used clothes, and heavy-duty boots. These types of clothes clearly indicate hostility; they form a kind of armor, warning people not to come too close. In case the message is not clear enough, she has a number of explicit T-shirts that emphasize the message. In *The Girl with the Dragon Tattoo* she wears a T-shirt that has a picture of ET with fangs and the words "I am also an alien," and another emblazoned with "I can be a regular bitch. Just try me." The trend continues in *The Girl Who Played with Fire*; one of her T-shirt reads "Consider this a fair warning." Like her tattoos and piercings, these shirts send out the message that she is trying not to fit in. While unsupported by any evidence, people with piercings and body modifications are perceived as different—as less open, agreeable, and conscientious than those with no body modifications.[6] It should also be noted that her clothing, body modifications, and makeup—the use of black makeup is frequently associated with Gothic trends—all contrast with cultural conceptions of attractiveness.

---

[6] G. B. Forbes, "College Students with Tattoos and Piercings: Motives, Family Experiences, Personality Factors, and Perception by Others," *Psychological Reports* 89 (2001).

All in all, Salander tries very hard to convey through her appearance that she is tough and unfriendly, and that she rejects society's expectations regarding female appearance. Interestingly, however, Salander is actually quite dissatisfied with her appearance. She is particularly bothered by her flat-chestedness, considers her figure to be "ridiculous," "repulsive," and "pathetic," and is uncomfortable showing herself naked (*The Girl with the Dragon Tattoo*, *The Girl Who Played with Fire*). While body dissatisfaction is very prevalent among young women of Salander's age, her apparent rejection of social norms makes her dissatisfaction seem surprising.[7] However, her exaggerated efforts to appear unattractive might in fact serve a defensive purpose against her fear of not, in fact, being found so. She preempts any negative judgments about her appearance by consciously distancing herself as much as possible from social standards of beauty. In other words, she prefers to make herself unattractive rather than be found so by others; she would prefer to be thought of as conventionally attractive, and is painfully aware that she might fall short should she try. This lack of confidence in her appearance and overly critical appraisal of her body may also stem from low self-esteem, a factor often associated with body dissatisfaction, and a trait that Salander exhibits in many ways. Her lack of faith in herself is visible, for example, in her incapacity to believe that she is lovable. Referring to Blomkvist at the end of *The Girl with the Dragon Tattoo*, she thinks, "It couldn't possibly work out. What did he need her for?"

Another possibility as to why Salander cultivates an intentionally alienating appearance is that she is trying to ward off any unwanted sexual attention. By adopting a hostile and unconventional appearance, she may be trying to ward off potential sexual advances and ensure that sexual encounters occur only because she chooses to initiate them. The explanation for this might be found in her experiences at the hands of Dr. Teleborian, the psychiatrist who treated her for several years at St. Stefan's clinic. While the psychiatrist was not openly sexually abusive to Salander, he took a perverse pleasure in tying her to her bed, allegedly for the sake of her mental health, and

---

[7] L. J. Heinberg, M. Altabe, S. Tantleff-Dunn, and J. K. Thompson, "Exacting Beauty," *American Psychological Association* (1999).

derived sexual pleasure from seeing her lying there restrained. These types of early experiences of unwanted sexual attention might easily have led Salander to seek to protect herself from such situations in the future by doing her best to distance herself as much as possible from the social codes of attractiveness.

Beauty Comes from Within

During the course of the story, Salander's personality changes thanks to important events and relationships in her life. During this time there are a number of changes in her appearance as well, changes that closely parallel her personal growth. In many ways, these inner and outer changes happen together so as to keep her appearance aligned with her inner self.

The Mirror of Her Inner Self

Salander's trauma and loss, as well as personal growth, are evidenced by exterior changes. One of the most notable changes in her appearance occurs at the start of her long trip abroad at the beginning of *The Girl Who Played with Fire*. It's on this trip that she visits a clinic in Genoa and has the wasp tattoo on her neck removed. She justifies this decision by concluding that the wasp is visible and distinctive and therefore makes her easily recognizable. However, removing the wasp is also very significant because the tattoo symbolizes her identity as a hacker. This could be interpreted as Salander refashioning her identity and starting over. Hacking is, by definition, an illegal activity, and therefore hackers place themselves outside society through their actions. Furthermore, it is essential that a hacker remain anonymous and work in secret to be successful. By removing the wasp tattoo, the visible sign of Salander's secret identity as a hacker, she seems to be effectively saying that her work no longer defines her. While it is true that the tattoo made her recognizable, removing it also means that she is no longer the same person socially. During this trip she also removes the piercing in her nipple and the one in her left labium. Upon her return to Sweden, she installs herself in her new apartment and removes the stud from her tongue. She notes that a "fundamental" change has taken place in her life. It seems that a fundamental change has not only occurred in her life, but also in her understanding of herself. This change is expressed physically by the removal of the tattoo and piercings.

It is interesting to note that, while the acquisition of multiple body modifications has been associated with dysfunctional personality traits, the removal of these modifications seems to coincide with a working through of these issues and a general increase in psychological well-being. Based on our research on body modification, it appears anecdotally that individuals who have acquired multiple body modifications tend to gradually remove them as they find meaning and purpose in their lives and curb involvement in risky behaviors. Other research documented that gang members and criminals who renounced violence often removed tattoos that may have served as markers or identifiers.[8] Individuals evolve as they grow and many aspects of their personalities can change. In Salander's case, a number of elements point to an increase in psychological well-being at this point. Firstly, and perhaps most importantly, Salander has formed a real, equal relationship with another person for perhaps the first time. By falling in love with Blomkvist, Salander sees herself as having let her guard down, and this is a very apt description. Salander has suffered many traumatic events in her life, starting as a child in her home. Her father abused her mother, Agneta, who was in turn unable to protect herself. Salander was therefore unable to feel secure in her relationships with her parents as a child, which may have resulted in difficulties in her forming trusting relationships as an adult. The relationships children form with their caregivers serve as templates for their adult relationships. In this way, her efforts to keep others at a distance—even when they were entirely well meaning—helped motivate her to build defensive armor around herself that included her rivets and piercings. This armor in turn formed a barrier to establishing relationships in which Salander could potentially be hurt and let down.

The capacity to form relationships is a good indicator of psychological well-being and, moreover, the act of doing so can be healing

---

8 Bazan et al. "Migrant Gangs, Religion and Tattoo Removal."

in and of itself. Salander's appearance evolves during her relationship with Blomkvist, first through a softening of her dress. For example when joining Blomkvist at his cottage on Hedeby Island in *The Girl with the Dragon Tattoo*, Salander dresses in a worn jeans skirt and a black camisole and remains barefoot, giving a much more feminine image than usual. This continues on a more significant level through the removal of some of her body modifications. These removals can be understood as an exterior expression of the lowering of her psychological defenses. Whereas in Salander's case this is in part a literary device to provide the reader with subtle cues regarding the character's development, the behavior being described is also seen in real life. Individual dress styles evolve with personality and inner states.

Salander's increased capacity to form relationships and blossoming awareness of her effect on others is also evident when she returns to Sweden after her trip and feels guilty about her lack of contact with her friend Mimi. It seems like a revelation when she realizes that her friend might have been concerned about her disappearance. But perhaps the most telling piece of evidence at the beginning of *The Girl Who Played with Fire* that Salander is evolving is the fact that she buys a new apartment—an investment she makes herself in a permanent space to live. Although this act might also be motivated by a desire to own a hiding place (as nobody knows her whereabouts), buying the apartment also seems to indicate a newfound wish for stability and a desire to move away from her family roots, both literally and figuratively. Slowly, Salander seems to be moving from a day-to-day existence governed by the immediate to one in which she is able to project herself into the future and question what she hopes to achieve in her life and how she would like to live. On buying her apartment, she thinks to herself that this is a space in which she could work, even though she has no clear idea yet of what kind of work she could do.

The Emergence of a Woman

While in Genoa, Salander also undergoes one puzzling and dramatic body modification: breast augmentation surgery. Research exploring motivations for breast augmentation surgery has identified a number of different factors.[9] One of the most important is a desire or drive for femininity, as larger breasts are thought of as being sexier by both men and women. Other important factors include body image dissatisfaction, internalization of the social ideal (that is the degree to which one buys into the socially promoted body ideal), and low self-esteem. Some of these motivations resonate strongly with Salander's. Femininity is an important issue with her, and on several occasions she is referred to both as childlike or doll-like and anorexic-looking. These descriptions give the impression that some might perceive her as a not-yet-fully adult woman in terms of responsibility, personal agency, and sexuality. Her appearance also lacks elements that are associated with femininity in terms of sensuality and her physical figure. Following her breast augmentation, Salander, while still very slender, no longer looks like a child. Given the dialectic relationship between her identity and her appearance, she begins to feel and act like an adult as well.

Other aspects of Salander's motivations to have breast enhancement surgery are more individual and specific to her personal concerns. As noted previously, she has a tendency to mark important events of her life on her body so as to imprint them in her narrative. This time, instead of choosing a tattoo, she has cosmetic surgery. Just as her tattoos served as indicators of past experiences, her breast augmentation surgery is probably in some way commemorating her becoming an adult. It's a rite of passage. Salander's lack of faith in herself is at the root of the painful end of her relationship with Blomkvist, whom she perceives as having abandoned her. She may be using the surgery to mark both the ending of her relationship with him—who played an essential role in validating her as a person and allowing her to exist—and her sudden independence, thanks to her new comfortable financial situation and change in status after so many years of guardianship. Interestingly from a literary standpoint, she learns of the death of her mother immediately upon her return to Sweden, reinforcing the fact that she is now an adult, but also indicating the end of a second very important relationship in her life.

---

9 A. S. Solvi, K. Foss, T. von Soest, H. E. Roald, K. C. Skolleborg, and A. Holte, "Motivational Factors and Psychological Processes in Cosmetic Breast Augmentation Surgery," *Journal of Surgical Reconstruction* 63 (2010).

Victimization is another central issue for Salander. During a childhood marked by an abusive father, internment in a psychiatric institution, and forced guardianship (which deprived her of agency and later resulted in abuse), Salander has been victimized by the male figures in her life, and perhaps symbolically by the patriarchal society she lives in. Her choice to have breast enhancement surgery and to reclaim her femininity is also a way of putting an end to this repeated victimization, as if she were deciding to be a victim no longer. Salander has become confident enough to be visibly feminine, and to assert herself as a sexual being on her own terms. She is choosing to embrace femininity rather than it being conferred upon her by others through societal and gender roles. Following her breast augmentation Salander begins to take responsibility for her life, culminating in her active participation in her trial to expose the individuals who conspired to abuse her.

It is interesting to note the shift away from body modifications in the form of tattoos and piercings to cosmetic surgery. While body modifications are more often likened to self-mutilation and involve some pain as an important aspect,[10] cosmetic surgery is typically looked upon as enhancing, rather than mutilating, one's appearance. It could therefore be considered that Salander is moving away from more hurtful practices into something that could be thought of as self-care. This operation brings Salander closer to social ideals of beauty and indicates a willingness to be more part of society. It also seems to reveal that her ambivalence regarding her sexuality and attractiveness has receded; she is now more consistent with the rest of society in how she views her body. In this way, her plastic surgery coincides with the removal of the tattoo and piercings and conveys the change in her relationship with the world and herself.

An Eloquent Silence

While Salander may lack communication skills, she is an expert at expressing meaning through her appearance, which she modifies

---

[10] A. R. Favazza, *Bodies Under Siege: Self-Mutilation and Body Modification in Culture and Psychiatry* (The John Hopkins University Press, 1996).

to suit her purpose. On a more unconscious level, however, Salander's appearance is also a mirror of her interior self, quite accurately reflecting her mood as well as less transient personal traits. As she evolves, her appearance does, too, so that it can continue to accurately express who she is. As time goes on, Salander's appearance adjustments and her psychological health seem to parallel each other as they improve: her progressive abandonment of her body modifications and provocative style are indicators of her more positive self-image. Although it takes Salander a long time to find her voice, until she does, her appearance shouts out who she is in terms of her personality, personal narrative, and even personal growth in a very effective way.

T. H. ERIC BUI, MD, PhD, is a psychiatrist, currently a research fellow in psychiatry at Massachusetts General Hospital/Harvard Medical School. He received both an MD and a PhD in Neuroscience from the University of Toulouse (France) where he also completed his research/teaching/clinical fellowship.

RACHEL RODGERS, PhD, is a clinical psychologist. After completing her PhD at the University of Toulouse (France), she was awarded a Fulbright scholarship to conduct postdoctoral research at Northeastern University, Boston.

To date, Dr. Bui and Dr. Rodgers have authored a number of scientific articles focusing on body modifications and other related fields of psychopathology and have presented their work at a number of international conferences.

What is it about Lisbeth Salander that gets under our skin? Misty Hook suggests that the answer lies in Lisbeth's defiance of what we understand to be the normal behavior for a person of her gender. Our culturally imposed beliefs about men and women are deeply entrenched, and in order to be considered "normal," we are expected to limit our behaviors to fit within expectations for our gender. Here, Hook classifies Lisbeth as a "gender outlaw," and explains what exactly that means to those who love her—and those who love to hate her.

LISBETH SALANDER AS A GENDER OUTLAW

MISTY K. HOOK

When I used to teach Gender Issues, I'd begin the semester by asking students what our lives would be like without gender. I've never had a class that wasn't stumped by this question, because the answer is so overwhelming. Gender is everywhere; it's foundational. Gender dictates what we call people—pronouns, our given names, how we refer to others, and even insults—what we wear, how we speak, what careers are considered appropriate, the sports we play, the toys and games we enjoy, how we choose our leaders, what we value, the food we eat, how we play and compete, and even where we go (e.g., the "ladies room"). Even more seriously, gender tells us when we can do things (like differing times for field use in women and men's athletics), if we can belong to certain clubs (for example, "gentlemen's clubs" or the Augusta National Golf Club where women are not welcomed), whether we can work certain jobs (like construction for men or Hooters server for women), and even if we get discounts ("Ladies Night"). But most of all, gender dictates how we act. Contrary to popular belief, though, these behaviors aren't biological imperatives. Many people want to believe that women are biologically destined to act one way while men are genetically "preprogrammed" to act another way. Perhaps it would be easier if this were the case, but it isn't.

I want to clarify that sex is not the same thing as gender. A lot of people confuse the terms and use them interchangeably, but that is inaccurate. Sex is a biological term describing the physical body while gender is the way a society believes people of a certain sex should behave—the guidelines and expectations members of a society internalize and use to govern our (and others') behavior *based on* our physical bodies. This is where we run into trouble: people want gender to be as clear and definable as sex, and it's not (though, as we'll see a little bit later, sex isn't exactly clear or definable either).

Just for fun, do an experiment. Ask someone you know to first list feminine characteristics and then list masculine characteristics. Most people are likely to describe women as emotional, nurturing, physically weak, verbal, soft, intuitive, cooperative, and focused on appearance (academic types might throw in relational—valuing connection with others—and passive). These same people probably will describe men as stoic, active, physically strong, analytical, hard, rational, competitive, and focused on career (the same academics would add independent and dominant).[1] Some people might go even further and say that men like sex and women don't. We've all heard people say things like, "That's just how men are," or, "What do you expect? She's a woman."

Why do people do this? Why do we rigidly lock people into one gender role or another (the either/or of femininity and masculinity) and want them to act as that category dictates they should? Wouldn't it be better for everyone if we just allowed people to behave in the manner they choose no matter what gender they happen to be? The answer, of course, is yes, but I doubt this will ever come to pass. The reasons we're unlikely to unfetter ourselves from gender expectations are long and complicated, involving social psychology and stereotyping (which includes everything from cognitive biases, social learning, social identity, realistic group conflict, and social categorization) but, in my opinion, the short answer is this: simple laziness. Human beings can frequently be lazy thinkers, especially when considering gender, a category that cuts across all others (e.g., class, race, nationality, religion, age). In some cases, human beings' tendency to take heuristics, or mental shortcuts, can help us be more efficient thinkers but, in the case of gender stereotypes, the shortcuts often have negative consequences. We all have gender schemas, which are cognitive structures that determine the way someone detects, evaluates, and organizes incoming information.[2] People who have weak gender schemas do not pay much attention to "gender" as a constructed concept and simply adjust their behavior to fit in with the

---

[1] I. K. Broverman, et al., "Sex-Role Stereotypes and Clinical Judgments of Mental Health," *Journal of Consulting and Clinical Psychology* 34 (1970). Although this study is over forty years old, sadly it is still relevant and, as such, is the gold standard in this area. Recent replications of it still show approximately the same results.

[2] S. L. Bem, "Gender Schema Theory: A Cognitive Account of Sex Typing," *Psychological Review* 88 (1981).

stereotypical gender norms and expectations of their culture. In contrast, people with strong gender schemas focus heavily on gendered information. However, while people with strong gender schemas are aware of stereotypical gender roles, that awareness does not always mean they impose "masculine traits" on men or "feminine traits" on women. Instead, their greater awareness of gender allows them to exhibit personality traits for both sexes. Thus, while many people are lazy thinkers with regard to gender, others are not.

So why do we stereotype gender? Basically, it takes way too long to get to know people on an individual basis. It's much easier to interact if you know what to expect from people ahead of time, and stereotypical gender roles help a great deal with this. Think about it. When you meet a woman, you might first ask her whether she's married or has children. When you meet a man, the topic of what he does for a living might come up first. When interacting with girls, you may find yourself giving compliments on their appearance; boys will more likely be asked about or complimented on their activities. We hate to think this is still the case after decades of struggling for parity between the sexes, but research finds there's still a large gulf between what we expect in regards to the roles of women and men.[3] Thus, even upon first meeting someone—young or old—we make assumptions about her or his interests based solely on that person's gender.

Our lazy thinking takes us even further. Not only do we know how each gender should act, but we also have cultural "scripts" that we follow in social situations.[4] A script is a mental representation, or idea, of a sequence of events, and gender is a driving force in most scripts. We have them for everything from initial meetings and dating to sex and marriage. For example, imagine that you are at a dance club. (Of course, dance clubs differ a great deal, so the following is based on one in a mainstream setting.) For such a club, you might picture lots of women

---

[3] R. S. Ostenson, "Who's In and Who's Out: The Results of Oppression," *Lectures on the Psychology of Women* (2005).

[4] P. A. Mongeau, M. C. M. Serewicz, M. L. M. Henningsen, and K. L. Davis, "Sex Differences in the Transition to a Heterosexual Romantic Relationship," in *Sex Differences and Similarities in Communication*, 2nd ed., eds, K. Dindia and D. J. Canary (2006).

dancing. Many of the men are looking at the dance floor, drinking, and scoping out the women. Once a man finds an attractive woman, he approaches her to ask whether she wants to dance with him. If she does, she will let him in closer and give an indication she's interested. Thus, the basic scripts for this social event are: (a) women are there to dance and be seen while men are there to choose their partners; (b) men initiate interactions with women and women follow their lead; and (c) couple interactions involve two people of the opposite sex. If we all follow these scripts, then everyone knows their place and independent thought isn't necessary. Once you know gender roles and learn the various scripts, you really don't have to think much about nor do you have to get to know people individually to know how to behave in relation to them. Your brain is free to think about other things.

It's only when people act in unexpected ways that we have to pay attention: we are motivated to figure them out so that we can return to our preferred thinking mode. This is exactly why the *Saturday Night Live* skit "It's Pat!" was so popular. The whole gag revolved around people trying to decide whether Pat was feminine or masculine. Pat was so androgynous—possessing equal amounts of feminine and masculine traits—that determining gender was impossible. This situation was something people could laugh at because, while androgyny can be puzzling, it is generally nonthreatening. Since androgynous people exhibit qualities of both genders, everyone can relate to at least some of their behavior. For men, androgynous people do not infringe upon their territory of masculinity (because their feminine qualities "soften" them), so they can be either ignored or treated as objects of amusement. Similarly, women do not need to be wary of androgynous people. In fact, the androgynous nature of many adolescent boy bands may be one reason young girls like them so much. They are still an acceptable focus for romantic feelings (because of their masculine characteristics) but are singing about love and emotions (familiar, safe feminine characteristics). Thus, the "natural order" of things is not challenged.

However, people who refuse to be defined by stereotypical gender roles—so-called gender outlaws—are an entirely different story.[5]

---

[5] K. Bornstein, and S. B. Bergman, eds, *Gender Outlaws: The Next Generation* (Berkeley, CA: Seal Press, 2010).

Androgynous people have a foot in both gender role categories, but gender outlaws exist mostly in one category when they should be in the other. As such, they don't just take a lot more brainwork to classify, but also point out the fallacies involved in rigid gender roles and as a result end up infuriating traditional society. Lisbeth Salander is one such gender outlaw, and her status as one is a large part of why her trilogy is so mesmerizing.

Let me go on the record now and state that Stieg Larsson was a literary genius. I'll enlarge upon this theme more throughout this essay, but for now it is sufficient to say that he wrote three books filled with the most intricate and tightly woven plots ever published and created one of the most fascinating literary heroines of all time. He accomplished this in part by making his heroine a gender outlaw. There are plenty of fictional heroines known for their brains, courage, and accomplishments. Some of my favorites include Elizabeth Bennett, Scarlett O'Hara, Anne Shirley, Jane Marple, Nancy Drew, and Hermione Granger. However, in each case, the heroine clearly identifies as feminine. This is no accident. Women who do not act feminine are treated differently than those who are. As such, the narrative would have to focus on those differing personal dynamics (otherwise, it would lose a sense of realism) and not the original story the author wanted to tell. Even Larsson made certain that his incredible cast of female supporting characters demonstrate intelligence, strength of character, and sexual agency (everyone from Miriam Wu, Erika Berger, and Monica Figuerola to Annika Giannini, Sonja Modig, and Harriet Vanger) and still endorse at least some aspects of the feminine gender role. For example, Monica Figuerola is a tall, heavily muscled and strong woman, yet still acts feminine through the way she dresses and her desire for children, which can be seen as a typically feminine desire. Lisbeth Salander seemingly does not. While Larsson's supporting female characters were important, the Millennium trilogy is Lisbeth's story.

Lisbeth does not compromise. Not only does she not look traditionally feminine, but she goes even a step further and, through her extremely short hair, multiple piercings in her eyebrows and nose, unusual tattoos, and rebellious clothing, ensures that her appearance is as unconventional as possible for a woman. It is acceptable for women to have pierced ears or piercings in strategic places (like the belly button), and tattoos of something feminine (e.g., flowers, butterflies, hearts) placed somewhere relatively unobtrusive are acceptable in general, but their appearance is supposed to be pleasing to the eye. Lisbeth takes care that her look is as off-putting as possible. Her freewheeling sexuality also sets her apart. She decides with whom, in what situation, and for what purpose she has sex and does not let the dictates of gender influence her in any way. The "traditional" cultural script regarding sexuality is that a woman is supposed to have a minimal number of partners, have sex only for loving purposes, and be the passive recipient of sexual activity. In direct contrast to this, Lisbeth has multiple partners, has sex for the physical pleasure of it, and is very active. She not only initiates sex whenever she desires it, but is willing to ask for what she wants from her partner.

It is not only Lisbeth's appearance and sexuality that makes her unconventional though; it is also her intellectual prowess in a typically male-dominated field (computer hacking no less!), lack of nurturing behavior, strength of character, lack of emotionality, and overall assertiveness that make her seem more masculine than feminine. Yet Larsson throws us a twist when he gave Lisbeth the biological trappings of a feminine woman. Through no fault of her own, Lisbeth is very skinny, short, and fine limbed with a face that could, with some makeup, look at home on a billboard. Thus, although the appearance she consciously cultivates is masculine and unconventional (read: powerful), her physical presence is more feminine and even sexy. Many, like Mikael Blomkvist, Miriam Wu, Lisbeth's island friend George Bland, and several casual pickups, are very amenable to having sex with her. Throughout the trilogy several people, including her boss Dragan Armansky, are surprised to find themselves attracted to her sexually in spite of her nonstereotypical appearance. Thus, given her feminine appearance and contrary gender role behaviors, people either have to use their brains to figure her out (which most people do not want to do) or they don't know what to do with her and, as such, fear her.

One of the more interesting things Larsson did with Lisbeth's character was show how some of the very characteristics that make her so fascinating also cause her to become a victim on a grand scale, and almost all of it has to do with her status as a gender outlaw. From a very young age, Lisbeth did what most girls never do: she persistently fought back no matter the cost. Whenever a bully picked on her, she would fight until she literally could fight no more. Then, she sought revenge (also not a stereotypical feminine trait). In fact, the event that started the whole governmental cover-up of Zalachenko's existence was Lisbeth's attempt to kill him. It was both her high level of intelligence and her need for revenge that caused her to make a Molotov cocktail to throw at her father. The massive governmental conspiracy that followed her attempt occurred because of who Zalachenko was, but it was Lisbeth's own behavior that instigated it. If she had remained quiet and acquiescent like her sister—certainly not a gender outlaw like Lisbeth—then no governmental cover-up would have been needed. During her incarceration, it was Lisbeth's refusal to be relational (i.e., to talk with her doctors and be "nice") and her persistence in the face of futility (her refusal to eat or submit to being medicated) that led to her being strapped down against her will and force-fed.

Lisbeth's rejection of the traditional dictates of her gender led to other problems once she was free of the hospital. Her lack of relational skills meant that she never got along with any of her foster families, and her need for revenge led to an arrest for assaulting a man who tried to grope her. Her high level of sexual agency led some to conclude she was a prostitute (because women are not supposed to seek out sex unless they are getting paid for it), and her unconventional appearance brought both attention and hostility. Mix in her lack of social support (something women are known for) and you can understand why Dragan Armansky worried that she was easy prey.

Her flouting of stereotypical gender role behavior continued to get her into trouble and, in *The Girl Who Played with Fire*, she set a series of events into motion that led to her being seriously injured and in legal trouble. Her unwillingness to connect with others, her persistence, and her need for revenge led Lisbeth to assault and tattoo Bjurman. This caused him to hate her and this hate compelled him to set up a meeting with another of her powerful enemies, her father. Lisbeth's intelligence and persistence brought her to Dag and Mia's house shortly before they were killed, which led to the police suspecting her of their murder. Lisbeth's altercation with the gang members ended positively for her because she refused to back down in a fight, but her injuring of the two men and stealing of the motorcycle led the police and press to further suspect her of criminal behavior. Her intelligence and vengeful nature once again got her in trouble when she went to her father's house for the showdown in which she was gravely injured and eventually charged with attempted murder. And, in the almost final blow, it was her status as a gender outlaw that made the press go wild with speculation, disdain, and calls for her head. This mattered because, as Mikael stated, her battle this time was going to be with the mass media as much as with the courts.

While the miscarriage of justice in Lisbeth's case was of epic proportions, the victimization of gender outlaws is not unusual because they seem so threatening to others. Unlike androgynous people, gender outlaws not only call for increased thought in order to understand them, but also flaunt their lack of convention and their subversion of stereotype. Lisbeth is a great example of this. Her mode of dress is designed to irritate people, and she never makes any effort to help others understand her or to reassure them about her intentions. If anything, she goes out of her way to behave in ways she knows will upset them, including being silent or impolite, disclosing very little about herself, not following basic rules, and breaking the usual conventions for body language. For Lisbeth, body language signals, like making or not making eye contact, increasing or decreasing personal space, touching or shrinking from someone's touch, and even smiling, are weapons she uses to push people away or get them to do what she wants. Women are socialized to be relational, and body language is a huge part of this. Lisbeth doesn't play by the accepted rules. Unlike most women, she rarely uses physical signals to draw people toward her or make them feel more comfortable.

Lisbeth's defiance of the traditional rules that most of us obey is tremendously scary for most people. Watching someone defy our expectations of gender roles forces us to call into question some of the foundational beliefs we share as a culture; it's kind of like having the rug pulled out from beneath you. If we cannot count on women to act feminine or men to behave in masculine ways, then what can we count on? How will we know what colors to wear, what pastimes to engage in, how to communicate or, in some cases, even how to think?

The feelings of anxiety associated with questioning cultural beliefs aren't usually acknowledged consciously, but instead manifest as a general feeling of discomfort. It is this sense that something is "off" that can, and often does, lead to the desire to classify gender outlaws as mentally ill.

As a psychologist, I obviously believe that the tenets of my discipline can and usually are used for good, but unfortunately that isn't always the case. In Western culture, when people see behavior that is confusing or (in their opinion) just plain wrong, mental illness is a great way to explain away the behavior. They don't have to understand that person's behavior because they can use the explanation that they are "crazy." Doing so simultaneously discounts the experiences of the "ill" person and keeps her or him away from the larger community. Labeling such people as crazy also allows those following the cultural script to reassure themselves that their own behavior is correct and "normal"—and discourages others who might want to deviate similarly from that norm. Thus, a label of mental illness can be used to keep people in line. When this happens, a psychiatric diagnosis often injures the "ill" person more than it helps her or him. Larsson again shows his genius by demonstrating, through Lisbeth's (inaccurate) diagnosis, just how easily psychiatry can be used to justify and even enforce the status quo. In Lisbeth's case, psychiatry was used to undermine her determination to stand up for herself (which challenged the status quo of acquiescing to power), to pathologize her choice of gendered behaviors (which challenged the status quo that women are supposed to be relational, sober, and chaste), and to subvert her charge of rape (which challenged the status quo that men's sexual desires trump women's control over their own bodies).

As Lisbeth discovered, a diagnosis of a mental disorder can lead to negative effects in relationships, jobs, access to health care, legal considerations, and even civil liberties. Her diagnosis, even though it was inaccurate and unfair, probably exacerbated her tendency to keep her distance from people (because she wouldn't want to get close enough to someone to feel that she needed to reveal her troubled history), to have poor job opportunities (because few would hire her with that kind of a background), and not to be believed by the police, the media, or the courts (because her version of reality couldn't be trusted). Conferring a diagnosis of mental illness on her even gave Teleborian and his cronies justification to lock her up and throw away the key, at least for a few years. These issues are also the reasons why people diagnosed with mental illness are at great risk of being abused.

Gender outlaws are often very familiar with the difficulties that being labeled as disordered can bring. While Lisbeth's situation was extreme, gender outlaws in our world are also sometimes diagnosed with a disorder, just because we don't know how to deal with them.[6] For example, in the current edition of the Diagnostic and Statistical Manual of Mental Disorders (DSM-IV-TR), there is a diagnosis for *gender identity disorder*—for those who feel that they are trapped in a body of the wrong sex and want to be the sex opposite to the one their body is. The same thing can happen with people who are excessively gendered (i.e., exhibiting the extremes of stereotyped gender role behavior). The description in DSM-IV-TR for *dependent personality disorder* reads like a manual of excessive feminine traits, and *narcissistic personality disorder* could be interpreted as masculinity on steroids, as it includes a lack of empathy and having a sense of entitlement. So, in reading between the lines, when people take gendered behavior to extremes or when they do not want to conform to the traditional dictates of their gender role, we like to classify them as mentally ill because we have no other explanation for it. However, what would happen if we did have another explanation? What if instead of forcing people into rigid categories, we found both a biological and anthropological basis for eradicating the social constructions that keep us bound by gender?

As it happens, we do have such an explanation. Various biologists and cultural anthropologists are challenging the idea that there are only two sexes. Biologist Anne Fausto-Sterling points out in her book

---

[6] There are several issues that are "hot-button" topics with regard to the DSM and gendered disorders. The first citation is for gender outlaws and the DSM. The second citation is for the excessively gendered.

D. Karasic, and J. Drescher, eds, *Sexual and Gender Diagnoses of the Diagnostic and Statistical Manual (DSM): A Re-Evaluation* (Birmingham, NY: The Hawthorne Press, 2005).

M. Ballou, and L. Brown, eds, *Rethinking Mental Health and Disorder: Feminist Perspectives* (New York: Guilford, 2002).

Sexing the Body: Gender Politics and the Construction of Sexuality that there is a long-shunned and largely "invisible" category of people, called the intersexed, who are born with mixed indicators of biological sex. One of the reasons that many people do not know about the intersexed is because they do not look different from people who are traditionally female or male. In fact, some intersexed people don't even discover that they are intersexed until they run into problems with fertility. According to standard medical literature, *intersex* refers to three major subgroups: *hermaphrodites*, people who have one testis and one ovary; *male pseudohermaphrodites*, people who have testes and some aspects of the female genitalia but no ovaries; and *female pseudohermaphrodites,* people who have ovaries and some aspects of the male genitalia but no testes.

Research indicates that intersexed people may comprise up to 4 percent of births, or approximately 175,000 people in the United States alone. Cultural anthropologists have provided evidence of intersexed people in Native American societies (the *berdache* of the Sioux comes to mind) and in other cultures. The Talmud and the Tosefta—Jewish books of law—list regulations for intersexed people, as do the legal traditions of Europeans in the Middle Ages. Until very recently, parents of intersexed children in modern-day society were often forced to "choose" the sex of their child, which was accomplished via surgery and/or drugs. However, some intersexed individuals protested this tradition and even established the Intersex Society of North America to help them have more of a voice. Now parents often wait to see what happens and allow the intersexed individual to decide what s/he wants to do. Given the existence of intersexed people, it seems clear that, instead of having only two sexes, we actually have five.

So what does this have to do with the character of Lisbeth Salander? Lisbeth isn't intersexed, but she forces us to consider the larger question of why, with this broader range of sexes, we confine ourselves to only two genders. Why are we so interested in limiting our range of behavior? Once again, I could launch into a long-winded explanation involving social psychology, patriarchy, and even religion but will instead limit (ha!) myself to one word: power. When we do not allow people a wide array of choices, their behavior is constricted.[7] This applies more than with sex and gender. Consider for a moment what would happen if we included intersexed people as part of the sex continuum. What gender role would they be supposed to embody? A male pseudohermaphrodite might be ambitious but is s/he also supposed to be nurturing because s/he has some female genitalia? And what about sexuality? If intersexed people were more accepted and recognized by mainstream society, then suddenly sexuality is a lot more fluid because the labels of heterosexual, homosexual, and even bisexual become irrelevant. If a hermaphrodite (who is neither male nor female) falls in love with a woman, is s/he heterosexual or homosexual? What description could we possibly give to the sexuality of a female pseudohermaphrodite who has sex with a male pseudohermaphrodite? You see the problem; the current labels and definitions don't really apply. If we do away with these restrictive labels and people are allowed to love whomever they want, then the culture's power to determine how we behave, who we have sex with and/or marry is destroyed. Kind of blows the mind, doesn't it?

Lisbeth Salander is fascinating and dangerous because she gives us a small taste of how society could be different. By dressing unconventionally and behaving how she wants, Lisbeth essentially takes back some of the power that was denied to her during her childhood. She is telling society that she will do whatever she pleases regardless of their restrictions, explicit *or* implicit. Lisbeth watched as her mother, Agneta, was forced to give up her body, her sanity, and eventually her life as the sexual victim of a psychopath—and no one cared. Lisbeth once tried to play by the rules, by talking to authority figures and asking for help, but, like her mother, it brought no rewards. Instead, she was dismissed, abused, locked up, and ignored. Had she adhered to the feminine gender role and remained passive and obedient, Lisbeth never would have gotten what she wanted nor would she have

---

[7] For more information on who benefits from the constriction of gender behaviors, read this excellent series by Marilyn French: Marilyn French, *From Eve to Dawn, a History of Women in the World*, vol. I-IV (New York: The Feminist Press at CUNY, 2008).

been treated fairly. Consequently, she refuses to be constrained by the dictates of her gender and lives life on her own terms. Her sexual agency is a natural extension of that rebelliousness.

Let's spend another few moments with Lisbeth's sexuality, and with sexuality in general. The basic cultural script for feminine sexuality used to be that women should remain virgins until they're married. After the wedding, sex becomes more of a duty to please their husband versus something they desire for themselves. Although that script has gotten more flexible in modern times, it's still the case that you will be called any number of names, from the ubiquitous *slut* and *whore* to the ever popular *bitch*, if you deviate significantly from it. In giving us many strong female characters who not only like sex but also actively and assertively seek it, Larsson challenged conventions of both belief and literature. Erika Berger, Miriam Wu, Monica Figuerola, and even Cecilia and Harriet Vanger all seek to satisfy their sexual appetites outside the structure (and commonly accepted confines) of marriage. Some even participate on the fringes of what is considered acceptable sexual behavior. Miriam is a lesbian who is into bondage, while Erika experimented with group sex and has an open relationship with her husband. And then, of course, there is Lisbeth. Although she did show that gendered expectations do affect her when she surgically increased her breast size (thereby proving that gender roles are internalized whether we like it or not), in general her sexuality is unfettered by expectation. She enjoys casual sex, sleeps with both women and men, propositions those in whom she has sexual interest, and experiments with bondage—when she trusts the person. Even more interesting, she shows more than once that the names people use to keep women in line—the aforementioned *slut, whore,* and *bitch*—hold no power over her. Several men call her these names, and they barely get a blink in response; her behavior changes not one iota. Given all this, her sexuality is as far from stereotypically feminine as possible.

In giving her sexuality free rein, Lisbeth seems to be having a lot more fun than most women who are constrained by rigid gendered expectations. As a gender outlaw, she once again shows us what is possible if we change our views of sex and gender. If the traditional labels of heterosexual and homosexual are no longer applicable, then healthy sexual behavior no longer depends upon the sex of the people having it, and maybe not even upon the type of sexual activity. Instead, it must fall under the category of mutuality. Simply put, mutuality is each partner having the same relationship to the other. Is each partner consenting to, participating in, and enjoying the interaction? If the answer is yes, then the sex is mutual and positive. However, achieving mutuality is much easier said than done because we all bring our personal baggage into our sexual interactions. Lisbeth is no exception.

From an early age, Lisbeth was exposed to the sounds and consequences of her parents' sex life, a life in which her mother was used sexually and then beaten physically by her father. Lisbeth understood that sex for her mother was a prelude to something painful and degrading. At the age of twelve, when she was in the process of becoming a sexual being (also known as adolescence), Lisbeth tried to protect her mother and was thrown into a psychiatric hospital. There she was at the mercy of another sexual sadist, Dr. Peter Teleborian, who became aroused by her physical confinement. Years later, when she was finally allowed to leave the hospital and foster care system, she endured not only the "casual" molestation that many women experience from strange men sexually harassing and groping her, but also serious sexual violence (with the two rapes from Bjurman). Lisbeth didn't have anyone to teach her about her body or about what sex could be like. When she began having sex, all she knew from firsthand experience was that it was linked to pain, humiliation, and domination. For someone who'd never had control over anything, most particularly her own body, power was a prominent issue. Thus, sex for Lisbeth had to be only about the physical pleasure and what she could control. That is why casual sex with partners she chose held such allure for her.

So how did Lisbeth find a place of mutuality in her relationships, and how did she develop a different attitude about sex and intimacy? Before we meet her in *The Girl with the Dragon Tattoo*, we learn that Lisbeth's sex life was focused solely on physical contact. Even her relationship with Miriam Wu wasn't yet one of friendship; at that time, it was still based almost entirely on sex. She seemed to enjoy the pleasure that physical proximity and sexual touching brought, but she avoided emotional intimacy like the plague. Lisbeth never allowed her physical relationships to include the qualities that are essential to emotional intimacy: love and affection, trust, personal validation, and self-disclosure. Lisbeth had never had relationships that included these components. Her mother was unable to give her the love and validation that she needed, her sister gave her nothing, her father was a psychopath, her foster families were insufficient, and Lisbeth viewed all health care professionals with suspicion. The closest she ever came to any kind of emotional intimacy was with Holger Palmgren, her initial legal guardian. Holger gave Lisbeth validation and as much affection as he could (while still being appropriate as her advocate) and, while that relationship did blossom into a kind of friendship, it still was a relationship that was forced upon Lisbeth by the courts. As such, it could never amount to anything mutual. This is why her relationship with Mikael was so important and scary for her; it changed everything.

From the beginning, Lisbeth's relationship with Mikael was different. He knew some valuable information about her but, unlike others, he didn't use his knowledge to hurt her or influence her behavior. Instead, he validated her abilities and offered Lisbeth his own brand of spontaneous and gentle affection. Mikael's ability to make Lisbeth laugh and even touch her was so unusual that even her boss, Dragan Armansky, was struck by the difference in her interactions with Mikael. What Dragan was seeing, what he was so jealous of, was the beginning of Lisbeth's education in emotional intimacy. As she continued working with Mikael, she discovered that she liked being around him because he didn't react badly to her abilities or to her behavior. She realized that he trusted her, so she began to trust him. She told him more about herself than she had with anyone else and even bragged to him that she was one of the best hackers around. Her relationship with Mikael was different in another way as well. She became his friend before they became lovers. Consequently, unlike her previous physical encounters, Mikael was someone she knew and had some emotional attachment to before they shared physical pleasure. In short, Lisbeth finally experienced emotional intimacy. What she discovered about emotional intimacy, though, the thing that threw her most for a loop, was that emotional intimacy is wonderful but still has one drawback: it leaves you vulnerable. When Lisbeth realized that she loved Mikael, the door was open for her to get hurt and she walked right through it.

However, despite the huge emotional blow dealt by what she interpreted as Mikael's rejection of her, Lisbeth's relationship with him helped her grow. Before Mikael, she might not have spent as much time and effort with a recuperating Holger Palmgren. She probably would not have been as gentle with and protective of George Bland, the teenage boy she met on Grenada. She most likely wouldn't have made the effort to go see and connect with Miriam Wu after Miriam was attacked. She might not have been able to trust Annika Giannini enough to allow her to help Lisbeth win in court, and she almost certainly would not have thought to offer Erika Berger her assistance in finding her stalker. Lisbeth went from not caring about anyone who could love her back to slowly learning how to participate in relationships that were solid, reciprocal, and had the potential to be warm, loving, and mutual. That is the power of emotional intimacy. It draws you in, and once you're there, no matter how painful it gets, you want to stay.

In his incredible trilogy, Stieg Larsson gave us the story of a gender outlaw who was beginning to learn how to love and be loved. Along the way, he showed us how detrimental rigid gender roles can be in people's lives and gave us a taste of how different society could be if only we all were freer to be who we truly are. We got a wonderful group of nonstereotypical women who were not as constrained by gender as most. As for his male characters, the ones who were most despicable were quite cleverly provided with a counterpart. For every man who exhibited the extremes of gendered behavior, we got a man for whom gender is just an aspect of his behavior—a man who is flexible and accepting. For every Zalachenko (who personified the extremes of masculinity, an individual with Narcissistic Personality Disorder if I ever saw one!), we got a Mikael Blomkvist. Mikael eschews many traditional masculine behaviors (he isn't competitive, cold, or dominating) and he tends to be attracted to women who are strong, assertive, and interesting. For every Nils Bjurman, we got a Holger Palmgren. For every Peter Teleborian, we got an Anders Jonasson. For every Ronald Niedermann, we got a Paolo Roberto. For every Martin Vanger, we got a Henrik Vanger. My guess is that Larsson was planning something similar for Lisbeth. Although we will never know, I suspect that Camilla Salander, her twin and mirror image, would exhibit extreme femininity to counter Lisbeth's outlaw status and that his next book would have visited that controversy between the two girls. However, wherever he was intending to go with future stories, we have something fantastic that Larsson gave us in the fiction of the Millennium trilogy: a guide to a more accepting future in our real world. If we pay attention and try to reshape our gendered culture into something less confining, then maybe one day my students will be able to tell me what a world without gender would look like.

MISTY K. HOOK, PhD, has had a lifelong interest in gender issues and psychology and was thrilled to find that she could parlay that interest into paying work. Consequently, after getting her doctorate in counseling psychology, Dr. Hook spent five years as an assistant professor of psychology teaching classes on gender and family issues. She is now a licensed psychologist in private practice where she deals a lot with gender issues in both her writing and counseling. She hopes that her work will nudge people toward a genderless and more equitable society.

At crucial points in Lisbeth Salander's life, she's refused to speak because she has suffered unbearable trauma at the hands of those meant to protect her: speaking out, she's learned, causes her more harm than good. But to those who don't know her life story, it seems like her muteness is a sign of obstinacy, defiance, or even stupidity. We readers get to see the method behind her supposed madness and the reasons for her behavior, but for people like Lisbeth in the real world, there is no shortcut to understanding what is happening in their heads. David Anderegg delves deeper into the reasons for silence in psychotherapy patients, how their treaters can surmount the silence, and what Lisbeth might be saying when she chooses to say nothing at all.

WHAT TO SAY
WHEN
THE PATIENT
DOESN'T
TALK

LISBETH SALANDER
AND THE PROBLEM OF SILENCE

DAVID ANDEREGG

P sychotherapy, when it first began in Sigmund Freud's day, was almost immediately labeled "the talking cure." According to some historians of psychoanalysis, the talking cure was discovered almost by chance during the treatment of the famous patient "Anna O.," who suffered from hysteria. She talked to Freud's partner Josef Breuer incessantly and, in so doing, seemed to relieve herself of her neurotic symptoms, including coughing, squinting, occasional paralyses, visual problems, numbness in her arms, and an inability to speak in her native German (although she could speak perfectly well in English). She did not require the application of hypnosis that had, up until that moment, been the treatment of choice for the removal of hysterical symptoms. Anna O. talked and talked and talked; and then she got better. It was this fateful encounter that led Freud to suggest the method of free association: the patient was not hypnotized but was instead instructed to lie down upon the couch and say "whatever came to mind." From that moment on, psychotherapy became the standard treatment for hysteria and, shortly thereafter, a host of other psychoneurotic illnesses for which there had previously been no effective treatment.

But there's just one little problem: What do we do when the patient doesn't talk? Not only can she not participate in the "talking cure," but we don't even know what's wrong. We can't cure without talking. Indeed, we can't even diagnose the problem. Unlike other branches of medicine, psychiatry is at a distinct disadvantage when it comes to diagnosis because diagnoses are almost always "clinical," or based upon the evaluator's opinion of patient-reported complaints, rather than "objective." Objective tests are almost completely absent in psychiatry; we cannot draw blood or take an X-ray to confirm a diagnosis. Despite the wonders of modern neuroscience, with PET scans and fMRIs yielding all those exquisitely colored images of the brain, we still need a patient to talk to reveal what is wrong. Since psychiatrists are often tasked with dealing with distortions of reality—excesses of anxiety, disturbances of mood or thinking—we have to hear the patient's self-reported version of reality in order to understand what is going on.

This is the position the unfortunate Dr Peter Teleborian finds himself in when dealing with the adolescent Lisbeth Salander. Of course, Teleborian is not necessarily interested in curing his patient; he is interested in controlling her. He is interested in gathering evidence of her insanity so that she can be hospitalized, placed under guardianship, and thereby controlled into an indefinite future. But the crazy *pas de deux* between Lisbeth and Teleborian has a ring of truth for all mental health professionals who have worked with oppositional patients who are children or adolescents. Even those of us who are not agents of a corrupt state secret service (and child pornography addicts to boot!) can recognize ourselves in the maddening silent dialogue between these two powerful characters. When our patients don't talk, we can't do our jobs. And when we can't do our jobs, we get frustrated. And when we get frustrated, we make mistakes, both intentional and unintentional. And when we make such mistakes, it is always the patient who suffers.

Like Lisbeth Salander, the nontalking patient is almost always in therapy against her will—whether because she's a minor or because she is under a court order. Indeed, it would make no sense for an adult to enter psychotherapy, make the time to go to the appointment, pay the fee, and then not talk. Even crazy people are not that crazy. Occasionally, adult voluntary patients who have been talking in psychotherapy will stop, and this presents treatment difficulties. British psychoanalysts D. W. Winnicott and Nina Coltart have provided some fascinating examples of how to respond to sudden or prolonged silences in adult treatment.[1] But the majority of nontalking patients are not voluntary patients. They are usually children or ado-

---

[1] Coltart reported on a patient who did not speak to her at all for a period of several weeks. Then, "I simply and suddenly became furious for his prolonged lethal attack on me and on the analysis. I wasn't going to stand it for a second longer, I shouted, without the remotest idea at that moment of what alternative I was proposing! This outburst of mine changed the course of the analysis," Her report is found in Nina Coltart, *Slouching Toward Bethlehem* (New York: The Guilford Press, 1992). Also see D. W Winnicott, *Holding and Interpretation: Fragment of an Analysis* (New York: Grove Press, 1987).

lescents, brought to a doctor because they are driving someone in their family crazy. Occasionally they are psychotic people whose silence is alarming for other reasons, but they, too, are usually nonvoluntary patients. So the backdrop for the nontalking patient is usually one of felt coercion right from the outset, an issue forgotten by too many well-meaning child therapists who forget that children almost never choose to come to therapy.

When a patient doesn't talk in psychotherapy, we therapists can use our previous experience to make guesses about why he or she is silent. Indeed, some patients come to treatment because of a failure to talk in contexts outside the therapist's office: the diagnosis of "selective mutism" is given to children who can talk in some places but will not talk in others. Usually these children will talk at home or to some family members, but they will refuse or are unable to talk at school, and their progress in school suffers as a result. But whether the failure to talk is global, so to speak, or localized to our office, we always start with the same guesses.

Fear

Many patients, both children and adults, do not talk because they are afraid. Children who live with unpredictable adults sometimes also live with the paralyzing fear of saying the wrong thing, the thing that will turn the barely controlled parent into a raging lunatic or a depressed zombie. This is relatively rare; most abusive adults are depressingly predictable, and their children quickly learn how not to say "the wrong thing." But for a few, "the wrong thing" is never predictable, and so the best policy is silence. And children who are moving into a new environment, like a first year in school or group care, sometimes overgeneralize and apply the coping-at-home rules to the new situation. We can guess, and we can carefully assess the home situation as best we can, to see if fear is the primary problem when confronting a silent child. Of course, hectoring them to try to get them to talk will not work because the more unsafe they feel, the less likely they are to talk.

Another form of fear is the fear of revealing something dangerous. We know that abused children are sometimes explicitly enjoined not to speak about what goes on at home. There are the few cases of child abuse in which children are threatened with further harm: "If you tell anyone what I have been doing to you, I'll kill you," or, "If you tell, I'll do this to your baby sister." But there are more general cases when children know how crazy their home is, and they intuit that the helpful professional sitting across the table might be a little too zealous. Talking about what goes on at home might endanger the only home they have ever known. In my own work as a child therapist, I have encountered more than one intractably silent child who correctly intuited that if she revealed how crazy her parents were, she might be taken out of their home.

A ten-year-old patient of mine, whom I shall call Agnes, did not speak for several months in psychotherapy. I know her mother had been depressed at times, but her mother avoided me as much as possible: a babysitter dropped her off and picked her up, and I sometimes went for several weeks without talking to her mother. Agnes, a smart little girl, was so silent and inactive that she was failing to engage in any schooling and she had no friends of any kind. She did not talk to me, and I waited as best I could, trying desperately to find something she would talk about. Sometimes I would read to her, or invite her to play a board game, which she always refused. Eventually we found something to do, an activity that involved destroying or at least defacing various toys and objects in my office. After that she did start talking, probably because I stopped suggesting she do so. I also demonstrated, by tolerating her aggression, that perhaps I could be trusted. But when she did start talking, she said too much: she revealed how often she and her sister went unfed; how the house was filled with animal feces; how she had to get to school on her own because her mother did not emerge from the bedroom for days at a time. Child welfare laws being what they are, I had to report her family to the child abuse prevention authorities. The family was thrown into even more chaos, and Agnes refused to come to see me at all. Years later, when I saw her on the street, she refused to acknowledge my existence.

Psychosis

Sometimes patients cannot talk because they cannot think normally. One relatively well-described psychotic symptom, called "thought blocking," occurs when the patient loses his or her thoughts midsentence. It's not that the person's mind wanders or gets distracted; rather the thought seems to disappear. According to psychoanalytic theory, this symptom causes the entire apparatus of conscious thought to deep-freeze, usually as a result of psychotic-level anxiety. This is also a result of fear, but fear of a different order. For many psychotic people, thoughts are not recognized as thoughts—that is, as bloodless representations of reality—but are experienced as reality itself. Thought blocking is then a response to such a terrifying state of affairs; it is as if a patient is saying, "My thoughts are so real that they are not even thoughts; therefore, it is best not to have any." Since these patients lose their thoughts, they certainly can't talk. They literally have nothing to say.

A psychotic patient of mine in his early twenties, whom I will call Robert, was just such a man. He was in a long-term hospital setting and had been for several months. While he regularly attended his therapy sessions, he never spoke a word. He was taking lots of antipsychotic medication but, contrary to marketing propaganda, this kind of medication does not work for everyone. Finally, I decided that all my prodding was making him even more anxious and making me feel even more hopeless. In an effort to move him in some direction, I suggested we go for walks. He consented, and these long walks provided both a change of scenery and the opportunity for some less-fraught interaction. I could say, "Oh, look at that beautiful car," or, "Oh, look, there's a bluebird," and he would respond with real interest and an occasional comment of his own. I thought this was progress. I was a junior therapist at the time, and shortly after I encountered a senior therapist whose opinion I respected and who, in a public meeting, insisted I was failing to notice that Robert's silence had to do with unexpressed rage: rage against me, against the therapeutic process, and against reality itself. In other words, I was supposed to tell Robert that I knew his failure to speak was because of anger so overwhelming he could not even think it. I followed my orders, and Robert promptly went to bed for the next several months. I regretted my having been coerced into making an error with Robert. If he was, as I now suspect, already terrified about the power of his thoughts, my interpretations must have magnified that terror. Dealing with a silent patient requires time and patience, as we shall see, and bullying almost never works (except when one is lucky, like Nina Coltart; see footnote 1).

Anger

The senior therapist in the previous example was not wrong about Robert's anger; he was just wrong about how to treat him. Anger is the most common reason for patients' silence in psychotherapy. It is most often a form of protest, the equivalent of a hunger strike. The fact that anger is self-defeating is not the point. Anger defeats the therapist, the only adult in the room, and by defeating the therapist, the angry child feels as if he or she is defeating the entire world of adults. In therapy, the child's resistance to cooperate can at times be explicit and profound.

An example of this kind of protest in contemporary practice can be found in the psychotherapy of children of divorcing parents. Divorce is common now, and enlightened parents have often read somewhere (or heard in their mandatory divorce education classes required by the court system) that children tend to blame themselves for a divorce. Many such parents, therefore, bring their children to a psychotherapist when the divorce has been announced, even before the child has any of the typical symptoms of adjustment difficulties, like sleep disorders, school failures, or defiance. The child is dragged to the therapist's office and told, "This is a talk doctor . . . If you talk to him, he will help you feel better about our divorce." For a child who is very angry about a parental divorce, this is a ludicrous proposition. She is in full protest mode, and all she wants is for her parents to listen to how much she does not want this divorce to happen. In this context, talking to the therapist is sold to the child as the equivalent of taking some kind of amnesia-inducing drug. This doctor has the power, when you talk to him, of taking away your feelings. He will make you forget that you are angry. In effect, 73 he will compel you to give consent to the end of your world. Why would you want to talk to him?

Sometimes this is explicitly stated, sometimes not. I have certainly had children say to me, "Why should I talk to you? I've said what it is I have to say; I don't want this divorce to happen. What else is there to say?" The experienced child therapist sometimes has to privately acknowledge the truth of these sentiments while also voicing to the child that the divorce is a done deal, one that *not* talking about is not going to undo. It's a tricky moral position, and often a depressing one, to work with a child who is absolutely right when he says, "My parents are choosing their own needs over my needs," or, "The adult world is not going to listen to me, to conform to what I need, so why should I waste my breath?"

An adult patient or therapist can sometimes remember his own adolescence as a useful path out of this sad morass. In my own history as a high school malcontent, I was referred to a therapy group along with several other malcontents. We met with a nice guidance counselor in an obscure corner of the school and ranted about the abuses of power to which we were subjected on a daily basis. Then we ranted at him for not listening to us because, if he were listening, he would make it change. He was a nice guy, or tried to present himself as such. If you're so nice, make it stop, we said. And of course he had no power to make anything stop; his job was to allow us to let off steam. I can see how useful it was in retrospect, but at the time I thought the whole thing was just stupid. But all of us in our little corner were garden-variety malcontents, and none of us were so committed to our rage that we stopped talking completely.

Lisbeth's Silence

Lisbeth Salander's silence is not primarily due to fear or to extreme psychopathology. Indeed, early in her life she speaks up on her mother's behalf despite her fear, but her speaking is not enough to protect her mother. And although she is presented to the world as psychotic, she is not and she knows it. She is well aware of the difference between thought and reality; indeed, her perception of reality is usually crystal clear and pitiless.

Lisbeth's silence is the silence of anger, but she is not a garden-variety malcontent. From the very first time we meet her, she is presented as a woman of extraordinary willpower; she is someone who will absolutely not back down from any position she has taken, even if it is self-defeating. Indeed, the appeal of Lisbeth as a character is largely this: anyone who has ever been an adolescent can identify with the heroic aspect of her refusal to cooperate with authorities of any kind. She is the teenager we all thought we were but, because of her great gifts, she is able actually to defeat the authorities over and over (unlike ourselves, who eventually had to capitulate).

Lisbeth's history emerges in pieces in the second volume of the Millennium series, and when it is revealed it is completely sympathetic to her point of view. She is an adolescent who has seen great, terrifying injustices—the abuse of her mother at the hands of her father—and has tried to remedy the situation. Even after "All the Evil," in which she tries to immolate her father, she still naively believes that she might see some justice.

First she had thought that everything might work out somehow. She had tried to explain her version to police officers, social workers, hospital personnel, nurses, doctors, psychiatrists, and even a pastor, who wanted her to pray with him. She had tried to explain to Teleborian. The result of her efforts was that on the night she turned thirteen, she lay strapped to the bed. (*The Girl Who Played with Fire*)

Her father's protection by the state security apparatus is a done deal. At this point, Lisbeth is still trying to be heard. Her interaction with Teleborian is what changes her mind. "The night she turned thirteen she decided never again to exchange a word with Teleborian or any other psychiatrist or shrink. That was her birthday present to herself." Later, when a friendly nurse asks Lisbeth why she refuses to talk to doctors, she says, simply, "Because they don't listen to what I say" (*The Girl Who Played with Fire*).

Lisbeth is a typical adolescent with a terrifying story. She sees no point in cooperating with a corrupt adult world in which children are abused and then ignored. But her extraordinary bad luck brings her into contact with Teleborian, a doctor who seems to view therapy as a battle of wills and who cannot stand to lose such a battle to a child. When she does not talk, he feels he is losing the battle, so he places her in solitary confinement—the equivalent of torture, as she later discovers—in an attempt to make her do so. But he cannot break her will. He is fascinated by her, apparently because of her power to resist, which makes him even more resolute in his efforts to break her spirit.

While extreme in its particulars, this power struggle is completely familiar to therapists who have had to sit with silent patients, adolescent or otherwise. What else is there for an angry, coerced child to do, once placed in a situation that demands speaking, but be silent? Children like Lisbeth correctly intuit that there is a certain type of therapist—the therapist who likes to be in control—who is driven mad by this behavior. This therapist can be a sort-of-good therapist—that is, someone who really does want to help but wants even more to succeed in curing the patient whether she wants it or not. Such therapists are good for many people, but can be led into errors by their own ambition. Or the therapist can be bad, like Teleborian, wanting only to control and harm for his own sociopathic reasons. But whether sort-of-good or just plain evil, therapists who are vulnerable to power struggles will be drawn into them with silent children, and will almost inevitably succumb to errors in judgment, or worse. Whether the child is initially frightened, psychotic, or just really, really angry, when an encounter turns into a power struggle, there is nothing a therapist can do to win.

Except wait. Sitting patiently, wanting nothing . . . just waiting for the patient to come around. It's not rocket science; it just takes enormous discipline. It also helps to have a good theory to use as a guide. Psychodynamic therapy, with its emphasis on a value-neutral therapist who is not hungry for an outcome other than helping the patient develop insight, is a useful and comforting theory that highlights the benefit of patience. It is not for nothing that several psychoanalytic therapists practice Buddhist meditation, trying to achieve a state "beyond memory and beyond desire" while they sit with their patients.[2] If one really does not want anything from the patient, she will know it and will be able to feel comfortable, maybe even safe, in that not-desired space.

I have been known to do all sorts of things to make this situation clear to silent patients. I once spent several weeks' worth of sessions reading the newspaper while a surly adolescent boy sat in his chair in the corner of my office. "I guess you don't want to talk, but I get bored doing nothing," I would say, "so I'm going to read the paper. If you have something to say, let me know." I have even been known to quote one of Winnicott's famous lines: "I don't really have anything to say right now except I thought you might need to hear my voice so you know you have not killed me off with your silence." I once spent several months playing absolutely wordless chess with a young man—and this one a voluntary patient—who had no words to speak to me.

And, speaking of chess, readers of the Millennium series may have noticed a pattern in Lisbeth's relationships with her friends. When under the guardianship of Palmgren, she played chess with him, usually silently. What she likes about Palmgren is that he is quiet, and patient, and does not seem to want anything from her. This holds true for her relationship with Blomkvist, as the entire first volume of the Millennium series is an account of a relationship that develops wordlessly. They work together and talk about work, but he never asks her about herself. He does not seem to want her to be different, nor does he seem to want her to be anything other than what she is. This is what a good therapist should be. Blomkvist is truly neutral and *disinterested* about Lisbeth, and a relationship flourishes with him precisely because of his neutrality.

Of course, creating this kind of relationship requires a patient therapist. It also requires a treatment setting that allows for things to unfold in a leisurely fashion. In today's mental health world, long-term therapy is becoming increasingly rare. Psychotherapy, if paid for by third-party payers such as health insurance companies, is more often than not a focused, time-limited, and plan-driven experience. We can all be thankful that truly silent patients are still relatively rare, because

---

[2] Wilfred Bion, *Seven Servants* (New York: Jason Aronson, 1978).

this contemporary mode of treatment is not designed for them. They need time to relax, to be ignored, to be playful, to come around on their own timetable. They need to find a way to make the coercive fact of being brought to therapy into a noncoercive safe space. That takes time . . . the illusion (if not the reality) of all the time in the world. "You and I have all the time in the world . . . so let me know when you wish to speak" is what we implicitly promise to such patients. This is what Blomkvist finally does for Lisbeth, and that is why she almost learns to love him.

Of course, she does grow up in the end. The entire Zalachenko affair is made public at her trial, and the judge drops all charges against her, but not without demanding something in return. She is formally ordered to give an interview regarding what she knows of Zalachenko, and at first she refuses. But the judge says:

> "If I rescind your declaration of incompetence, that will mean you have exactly the same rights as all other citizens. It also means you have the same obligations. It is therefore your duty to . . . assist the police in the investigation of serious crimes. So I am summoning you to be investigated like any other citizen who has information that might be vital to an investigation . . . Like any other Swedish citizen, you can refuse to obey such a summons. How you act is none of my concern, but you do not have carte blanche. If you refuse to appear, then like any other adult you may be charged with obstruction of justice or perjury. There are no exceptions . . . So, what is your decision?"

> After thinking it over for a minute, Salander gave a curt nod. *OK. A little compromise.*

This judge, wise man that he is, throws her a bone: "How you act is none of my concern . . ." But she finally sees that there might be a benefit to her in talking to the authorities. The adolescent malcontents that live inside each of us might be disappointed, but the adults that we have become can recognize with some relief that, with her curt little nod, she acknowledges that she can imagine some good that *might* come of cooperating with the authorities. With that little nod, she decides to break her silence after all. Lisbeth Salander has finally grown up.

DAVID ANDEREGG, PhD, is a professor of developmental and clinical psychology at Bennington College and a psychotherapist seeing children and adults in private practice in Lenox, Massachusetts. He is the author of *Worried All the Time* (Free Press, 2003) and *Nerds: Who They Are and Why We Need More of Them* (Tarcher/Penguin, 2007). He also writes the blog "Young Americans" for PsychologyToday.com. He also serves on the Editorial Board of *Psychoanalytic Psychology*.

One striking element of Lisbeth Salander's character is her emotional isolation from others. Her apparent desire to be an emotional island means she makes a tremendous effort to prevent people from getting too close. Psychoanalyst Prudence Gourguechon sheds light on Lisbeth's difficulties in relating to others, what she's trying to protect herself from, and how Mikael Blomkvist slipped past her defenses into her heart.

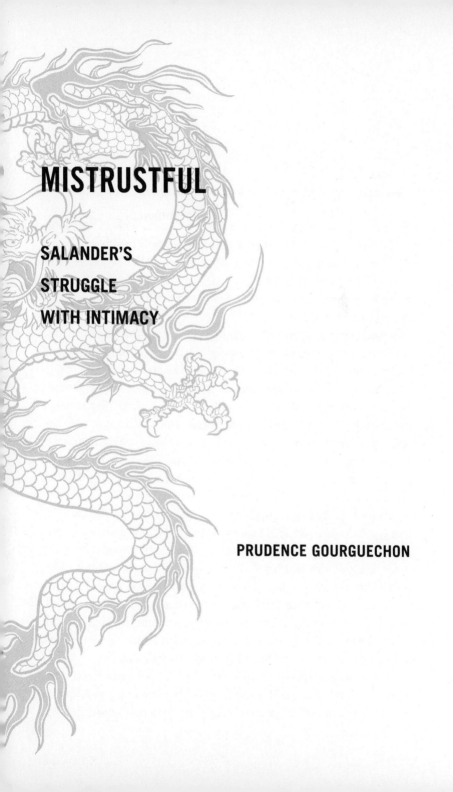

MISTRUSTFUL

**SALANDER'S
STRUGGLE
WITH INTIMACY**

PRUDENCE GOURGUECHON

An old one-liner:
Q. How do porcupines make love? A. Very carefully.

Stieg Larsson's Millennium trilogy presents us with an intriguing contradiction: Lisbeth Salander assiduously avoids emotional attachments but, seemingly paradoxically, becomes very attached to Mikael Blomkvist. Can using psychoanalytic and attachment theory help us explain this apparent conundrum and their unexpected relationship?

Salander has a number of psychological difficulties, including a fear of intimacy and of emotional vulnerability. She is both fearful of and wants to be understood. She wants to be evaluated by her true qualities, not her superficial appearance. But these are only a heightened version of dilemmas all humans face in navigating their way through relationships, both those of friendship and of love. What is wrong with Salander is not that she is abnormal or inhuman, as many characters perceive her, but that she is so deeply human. She keeps her distance because she can too easily feel penetrated, intruded upon, controlled, and violated—fears all of us grapple with to greater and lesser degrees.

There is a great deal of psychoanalytic and psychological knowledge that can help us understand Salander and the paradox she embodies regarding intimacy, and I want to give you a compact road map to the numerous theories and research findings I will be describing. We'll begin with classical psychoanalysis and its valuable concept of intrapsychic conflict. From there I will head to some diagnostic considerations, including a detailed description of the traits exhibited by a person with schizoid personality disorder (and Salander fits within those criteria). Next we'll visit attachment theory, after which I'll discuss a rich and creative body of thought in psychoanalysis known as "British Object Relations Theory." We'll examine the effects of trauma on the psyche, and then include some social factors, specifically aspects of gender politics.

Each theoretical perspective explains Salander's complex dilemma from a slightly different angle, and when we knit the threads together we will arrive at an interesting and poignant narrative that shows the full picture of an amazing young woman.

Intrapsychic Conflict—the Need-Fear Dilemma

One of the most basic and useful psychoanalytic concepts holds that human psychological life is often driven by *intrapsychic conflict*, or the *unconscious* processes that put all of us in a tangle. In other words, we are pulled emotionally one way, but pushed, by different emotions, in another. For example, pursuing a strong desire may be powerfully opposed by guilt over the desire.

In Salander's case, the core intrapsychic conflict with which she struggles swirls around the area of relationships. Like all of us, she is driven by a basic human need for closeness to avoid the pain of loneliness. This is sparely and subtly documented in *The Girl with the Dragon Tattoo*. Her need for intimacy is easily overlooked, yet there are hints such as the shocking and spontaneous hug she gives Armansky as they hammer out the details of their work relationship. And then there is the three-day vigil she maintained as Advokat Palmgren struggled for life following his stroke. Still, she is tremendously fearful of closeness, more so than the average person. She is mistrustful of other people, of their motives, their integrity, and their intentions toward her.

In the late 1960s, Burnham et al published the book *Schizophrenia and the Need-Fear Dilemma*, which identified a particular intrapsychic conflict. This conflict, known as the "need-fear dilemma," opposes an intense wish for holding, closeness, and skin-to-skin contact (the "need") with an equally intense "fear" that one will be devoured or destroyed by the person to whom one becomes close. The conflict lies below the level of conscious awareness for the person who suffers from it, but is nonetheless a powerful motivating force. Because the conflict is unconscious, it may be "acted out"—that is, put into action without thought or awareness. So someone with this conflict might fall in love extravagantly, but become easily disillusioned and angry with his or her beloved. Or he or she may simply keep their distance from people while living with a low-grade depression or using substances to numb the need side of the conflict.

The concept was originally proposed as a way to understand the inner state of seriously ill individuals—initially people with schizophrenia—and later people with severe personality disorders. In fact, the conflict and its impact may be more dramatic and visible in people with more severe emotional troubles. In my own practice I have come to believe that every one of us, emotionally healthy or more disturbed, grapples to some degree with the need-fear dilemma. We are hard-wired to affiliate with others, yet we are all prone to being deeply wary of the risks inherent in relationships: losing our autonomy, being hurt or rejected, experiencing loss, having to take another into account, or even deeper fears of dissolution. I like the phrase "need-fear dilemma" because it vividly and economically captures a painful state. Salander personifies this conflict, though she is more aware of the fear and less aware of the need.

A scene from *The Girl with the Dragon Tattoo* neatly illustrates Salander's need-fear dilemma. It is the end of the day in the cabin they are temporarily sharing in Sandhamn, and Blomkvist asks her how she became a hacker. She storms away to bed without a word. There is a suggestion that she leaves because she is humiliated by his discovery of her differentness. She knows she has always known how to hack—it was not something she learned—and she knows this is not normal. Her flight and anger are an expression of her fear that Blomkvist is getting too close. He is probing one of her secrets, and she fears he will be repulsed by her. Note that Blomkvist does not stop her from leaving the room. Larsson writes, "Irritating her yet further, he did not react when she left so abruptly." Blomkvist's neutrality and acceptance irritates her precisely because it is so sensitive and permissive. It's not the fact that Blomkvist doesn't react to her leaving or that he doesn't try to make her stay that irritates Lisbeth. It is that his failure to react demonstrates how much he understands and accepts her real self, and that is what angers her. Blomkvist's permissiveness means she can't hate him and thus keep herself distant from him. His nonjudgmental sensitivity to her need for distance paradoxically stimulates Lisbeth's desire for and ability to tolerate closeness, which in turn results in fear. But the need again resurfaces: though deeply insecure about her body and afraid of the potential for vulnerability, she decides to seduce Blomkvist (giving in to the need for closeness), wordlessly.

Schizoid Personality—A Different Approach to Being Human

Salander definitely does not have schizophrenia, though she is sometimes mislabeled with the diagnosis. But might she have features typical of a schizoid person? Although the names are similar, schizophrenia and schizoid personality are really quite different. Schizophrenia is a biological illness with distinct symptoms such as hallucinations, delusions, deterioration of self-care, and bizarre social behavior. Schizoid personality describes people who are uncomfortable around others and avoid intimacy. As with most personality types, there is a spectrum. Someone may have some schizoid traits but not a psychiatric disorder, while others may have a severe schizoid personality disorder. When I refer to "schizoid individuals" or "schizoid personality" I am referring to someone who falls anywhere along this spectrum.[1, 2]

Ideas about this diagnosis yield a rich perspective on Salander's character. In a key book on diagnosis using a psychoanalytic perspective,[3] Nancy McWilliams describes schizoid individuals as hyperreactive and easily overstimulated. They tend to be extremely sensitive to sensations (to light, sound, touch), as if they lack skin. They feel alienated because they experience things so differently from others, and therefore their perceptions and experiences are rarely validated.

---

[1] Donald L. Burnham, Arthur I. Gladstone, and Robert W. Gibson, *Schizophrenia and the Need-Fear Dilemma* (New York: International Universities Press, 1969).

[2] *Editors' Note:* In this essay, the term *schizoid personality* does not refer to a mental disorder in the Diagnostic and Statistical Manual, fourth edition (DSM-IV) unless it is followed by the word "disorder," as in *schizoid personality disorder.*

[3] N. McWilliams, *Psychoanalytic Diagnosis: Understanding Personality Structure in the Clinical Process* (New York: The Guildford Press, 1994).

According to McWilliams, schizoid individuals do not struggle overly with shame and guilt. They tend to live as outsiders, onlookers, who are separated from the world. They may be very creative, and live most vividly within an internal world of imagination. In Salander's case, the internal world in which she lives most comfortably is one based on her interfacing with the internet. There she can make anything happen, penetrate any mystery, and even make and keep virtual friends. (Internet "friends" can provide the schizoid person a midway ground between isolation and intimacy and are thus easier to make and maintain.)

McWilliams' depiction of the schizoid person's attitude toward relationships suggests that they crave closeness with others but fear destruction and engulfment. This is essentially a restatement of the need-fear dilemma. Further traits of the schizoid person, according to McWilliams,[4] include an "allergic" reaction to compliance and conformity, social awkwardness, and a disregard for social conventions (although they are not necessarily oblivious to social niceties). Often they prefer eccentricity, as this allows them to avoid closeness. We see a stunning example of this in the courtroom scenes at the end of *The Girl Who Kicked the Hornet's Nest*, when Salander wears an exaggerated costume of spiky Goth jewelry and black makeup. The eccentric, aggressive appearance communicates indifference, impenetrability, and invulnerability.

What is the genesis of a schizoid personality? Like most things in psychiatry, its final form is fed by the three streams of psychological, biological, and social forces (George Engel's classic, invaluable "biopsychosocial model"[5]). Psychoanalysts have identified several psychological factors that may contribute to the development of schizoid tendencies. Parents who perennially intrude on the child, or are excessively smothering, are one example, as are experiences of extreme neglect and loneliness. We don't have evidence of "smothering" in Lisbeth's past, but she certainly does have a history of

---

[4] N. McWilliams, *Psychoanalytic Diagnosis: Understanding Personality Structure in the Clinical Process* (New York: The Guildford Press, 1994).

[5] G. Engel, "The Clinical Application of the Biopsychosocial Model," *American Journal of Psychiatry* 137 (1980).

extreme neglect and parental failure. I don't doubt the presence of biological factors in her case, especially given the excruciating hypersensitivity that leaves Salander psychologically raw and in need of thicker than usual defensive walls. From the social angle, it is no wonder Salander avoids people. She has been subject to torture, rape, misunderstanding, neglect, betrayal, loss, confinement, and violence, all at the hands of those who should protect her. She has had not one but many psychopaths controlling her destiny throughout her short life. Her mother appears to have been warm and well intended (judging from Salander's affection for her), but inadequate and unable to protect her daughter from a violent gangster father or from a government that put a higher priority on protecting him than on the fate of a young mother and her children. Children so betrayed by adults can have a hard time feeling anything but grave mistrust for others in later life.

Salander is quite preoccupied with the issue of her secrets, both not having them known and the implications of having them discovered. Being "opaque" to others would be comforting to a schizoid person. One of Salander's moments of greatest emotionality comes when Blomkvist observes that she has a photographic memory. Seemingly a benign discovery, Blomkvist's awareness of her secret is deeply disturbing to Salander, not because of the particular content of his discovery, but because knowing one of her secrets lets him too far inside her perimeter.

Attachment Theory—When Getting Close Goes Wrong

Attachment theory is a thriving area of psychological research founded on psychoanalytic concepts developed by John Bowlby, Mary Ainsworth, and others beginning in the 1960s. The term *attachment* describes the process by which an infant bonds with his or her caretakers and vice versa. *Attachment theory* explores what goes right or wrong with this process, and what the lifelong impact of patterns of early attachment may be.

Attachment theorists have delineated four characteristic types of attachment behavior or style. One of the four types of attachment style is the "dismissing category."[6] Individuals with the dismissing type of attachment tend to be schizoid, obsessive, detached, and unemotional. They have great difficulty forming intimate connections later in life. Attachment researchers Sidney Blatt and Kenneth Levy write that these individuals "find it terribly difficult to acknowledge the importance of either early or current attachments."[7] This poignant description is extremely apt for Salander. She is frustrated with herself for failing to remember to be a friend, for failing to say good-bye to Armansky when she left Stockholm, and for leaving George Bland on Grenada without an explanation or farewell. We could almost say that she *fails to remember that she is connected* to people, and has to work consciously to overcome the instinctive tendency to behave as if she is not.

It seems obvious that a person with a dismissive style of attachment learns the behavior because of a desire to be defensive and self-protective—it's the same story as the need-fear dilemma or the understanding of the schizoid personality. All three of these perspectives help describe the isolated, frightened, needful person who prizes detachment, eschews emotion, and struggles forever with intimate relationships—in short, our Salander. She fits all these categorical descriptions exquisitely.

British Object Relations Theory—Understanding Solitude and Intrusion

There is, however, another body of thought I find especially useful and fascinating in looking at Salander. "British Object Relations Theory" is a branch of psychoanalytic theory originally associated with the English psychoanalysts Ronald Fairbairn, Harry Guntrip,

---

[6] M. Main, "The Organized Categories of Infant, Child and Adult Attachment: Flexible vs. Inflexible Attention Under Attachment-Related Stress," *Journal of the American Psychoanalytic Association* 48 (2000).

[7] S. Blatt, and K. Levy, "Attachment Theory, Psychoanalysis, Personality Development and Psychopathology," *Psychoanalytic Inquiry* 23 (2003).

and Donald Winnicott. These thinkers found that Freud's drive theory, which explained peoples' problems and motivation in terms of sexual and aggressive drives, was too limiting. Instead, they developed a new, powerful, and influential body of thought focusing on the impact of early and later human relationships. They felt that people were motivated primarily by a need for relatedness and a need to protect themselves from its inevitable dangers, and they wrote about patients who had particular difficulty in this area. All of this should sound like a familiar refrain by now. However, the British object relations theorists captured some additional nuances of this struggle that are extremely important in rounding out our story.

Psychoanalyst Guntrip could be talking about Salander when he writes in "The Schizoid Compromise and Psychotherapeutic Stalemate":

> A patient is ill because for some reason, he was not treated as a person in his own right during his childhood. He feels an urgent necessity to defend his own independence and freedom of self-determination as a person; and he feels this all the more, the less of a person deep down he feels to be.[8]

The facts we know about Salander's childhood suggest that her personhood was consistently ignored even before the incarceration, at which time it was obliterated. Certainly her monstrous father saw no one as a person, and her overwhelmed, abused mother undoubtedly lacked the resources to attend to and reinforce her strange little girl's personhood.

Guntrip describes a patient of his as having "a most unyielding need to keep herself going without any help, and [she] found it exceptionally hard to put any real trust in me." Couldn't this be Blomkvist expressing his frustration with Salander?

Elsewhere in that same article, Guntrip describes this type of patient with the following evocative language:

---

[8] H. Guntrip, "The Schizoid Compromise and Psychotherapeutic Stalemate," *British Journal of Medical Psychology* 35 (1962).

They maintain a kind of brinksmanship, or half in half out relationship to things in real life. They do not properly belong to anything. It is amazing how far systematic noncommittal can be carried in relationships with friends, organizations, jobs, houses or what not, so that the patient is forever on the move.[9]

All these traits—not belonging, decidedly noncommittal, always on the move—are powerfully present in Salander. There are many examples in Salander's story that demonstrate these traits, such as her refusal to stick to a regular work schedule and office routine, her multiple hidden apartments, and her sudden removals (e.g. to Granada).

British pediatrician and psychoanalyst D.W. Winnicott, an extremely creative thinker, had a particularly intriguing idea. Winnicott believed that every human being had a core or "true" self that *required* some degree of isolation to maintain its organization and authenticity. In a way, this idea flips the schizoid concept on its head. To feel sane and good and together, *every* person needs to be able to be, essentially, left alone some of the time. Winnicott believed this applies to being left alone when with others as well. An image that captures the pleasure and necessity of "being alone with others" is a father sitting in an armchair reading a newspaper with his daughter at his feet drawing a picture. Another would be a couple, on Sunday morning, reading the *New York Times* in companionable silence. In these vignettes, you don't have to choose between being alone and being with others. Having such opportunities to be alone with others provides an opportunity for growth and restoration; Winnicott says this allows a sense of "going on being" that is essential to psychic equilibrium. Intrusion and "impingement" from others interfere with this state of necessary isolation and prevents healthy development.

The concept of impingement is worth spending a moment on. Winnicott has in mind a situation where a baby is enjoying a few moments of solitary time, or simply "being," and the mother interrupts or bothers the baby because of her own needs or lack of attunement. She encroaches on the baby's peace of mind, causing tension, distraction, and disorganization. We can see how an infant with the

[9] Ibid.

biological trait of extreme hypersensitivity, as I propose Salander has, would be especially disrupted by impingement and seek ways to avoid it, including isolating herself. (We don't know for sure that Salander was hypersensitive as an infant, but it is reasonable to suppose she was based on the behavioral and cognitive eccentricities she exhibits as an adult.)

To a degree that is quite remarkable, Blomkvist does not intentionally intrude on Salander. This is one of the major reasons she can tolerate a relationship with him. Her friends Armansky, Miriam Wu, and Holgren also all treat her need for distance with respect, and try their best not to "impinge" on her. They seem to recognize that she has a greater than normal need to be left alone.

Trauma—The Psychic Toll

With Salander's substantial history of trauma she could not help but have troubles with intimacy. The symptoms of posttraumatic stress disorder (PTSD) include neuropsychiatric ones such as flashbacks, numbing, nightmares, and depression. But this doesn't really tell us about the internal psychological experience of a traumatized person. What are the effects of trauma on the psyche and the soul?

Loss of trust is a core issue in PTSD, and this relates to the essence of trauma. An experience is traumatic when it exceeds the ordinary bounds of any normal person's ability to cope. Essentially, the traumatized person has been profoundly let down by the world and things have happened that are not supposed to happen, ever. The capacity for trust is often further damaged when parents, caretakers, leaders, and authorities fail to provide protection from the trauma. Consequently, the traumatized person feels there is no one they can count on to protect them from the unthinkable. The sense that there is a meaningful moral order in the world is forever damaged. Such lack of protection and the disorganizing cognitive, moral, and emotional toll of trauma can have varied effects. For some survivors of ongoing trauma, the experience and its effects initiate a life of self-destruction that includes substance abuse, abusive relationships, and other troubling behavior. Other survivors, especially those blessed with extremely high intelligence like

Salander, will find ways to build constructive lives (though these are usually constricted), but they will still be damaged in terms of their sense of safety in human relationships. For Salander, the use of her extraordinary intellect and problem-solving ability became a powerful survival mechanism, countering the helplessness and powerlessness that trauma induces. Think about Salander's obsessive studying of math proofs in *The Girl Who Played with Fire*. For her, this activity would be calming, organizing, and reassuring, because the certainty embedded in math proofs is the opposite of an unpredictable and uncontrollable universe.

Mikael Blomkvist—Why Does Salander Make an Exception for Him?

So far, we have explored a range of ways to understand Salander's avoidance of close relationships: the need-fear dilemma, the fundamentals of the psychology of a schizoid personality, attachment theory, contributions from British object relations, and the psychology of trauma. This combined body of theory can now stand as a foundation as we attempt to understand the other side of the question: Why does she make an exception and allow herself to become intimate with Blomkvist? How does she allow herself to get so close to him, and even, to her horror, fall in love? And what is the source of her anguish when she ends the relationship at the end of *The Girl with the Dragon Tattoo*?

In many ways, Blomkvist also fits the picture of a schizoid personality; he, too, avoids too much closeness and erects thick walls around himself. As his sister says at the end of *The Girl Who Kicked The Hornet's Nest*, "My brother is completely irresponsible when it comes to relationships. He screws his way through life and doesn't seem to grasp how much it can hurt those women who think of him as more than an affair." The key point in this characterization is the phrase "he doesn't seem to realize." It's not unlike Salander's "forgetting" to pay attention to her friends. He is "polyamorous," which in Blomkvist's case also means he doesn't get too close to or dependent on any one person. He rarely sees his daughter and, though fond of her, when he is not with her he seems almost to forget she exists. His longest and most cherished relationship is with a woman married to another man. He often lives deeply inside himself, profoundly engaged with crafting stories he feels passionately about. He craves solitude. Blomkvist's favorite place is his spartan cabin at Sandhamn. There is little of the world there, in the wilderness, to intrude on his solitude or interrupt his inner thoughts. And Lisbeth can stay there with him in either wordless comfort or intense collaboration.

Blomkvist's schizoid personality is a major factor in Salander's ability to get close to him. They are of like minds, and the similarities in their personalities are mutually protective. Two porcupines understand the prickliness of one another; they don't suddenly run to embrace each other but instead know to warily approach their compatriot. So it is not surprising that one schizoid person could find comfort and companionship with another. Both will be careful to avoid intrusion and excessive neediness. Both will spend much time inside themselves, and would find it a great relief not to have to explain this or to be met with a partner's demands for attention. They can achieve a uniquely comforting state of being "alone together." It is precisely because Blomkvist keeps his distance and respects her remoteness that he is able to get into her heart.

Salander is surprised that Blomkvist possesses the ability to penetrate her defenses and to get her to talk about personal matters and private feelings.

> She talked about herself in a way that she would never, even under threat of death, have imagined doing with any other person. It frightened her and made her feel naked and vulnerable to his will. At the same time . . . she felt that she had never before in her life had such a trust in another human being. (*The Girl with the Dragon Tattoo*)

This leads eventually to what she calls a "terrifying realization" that she is in love for the first time in her life.

I think Blomkvist may well love Lisbeth as much as she loves him and has even more trouble recognizing it. He always uses the safer word "like" in place of "love" to describe his feelings, but his emotions seem to go beyond that. A poignant scene in the end of *The Girl Who Kicked the Hornet's Nest* has Blomkvist in Salander's enormous, empty new apartment. "He felt as if someone were squeezing his heart. He felt that he had to find Salander and hold her close. She would probably bite him if he tried." Like her, he rarely gains awareness of his loving feelings. As strange as Salander is, or perhaps because she is so strange, he can be "alone with her together" as described above, and not have to actively guard himself against intrusion and impingement. Simply put, she won't ask too much of him.

So the first factor that allows Salander to get so close to Blomkvist is his own schizoid-like personality, which naturally comes with a great respect for the boundaries of others. The second factor that allows Salander to make an exception to her mistrustful and isolationist tendencies is Blomkvist's ideological stance toward women. Blomkvist is that rare creature: a true male feminist. After Lisbeth has abruptly and (to him inexplicably) cut off their relationship at the end of the first novel, we learn something more about Blomkvist's somewhat unusual attitude toward women.

His attitude had always been that if a woman clearly indicated she did not want anything more to do with him, he would go on his way. Not respecting such a message would, in his eyes, show a lack of respect for her. Blomkvist's behavioral code toward women is nuanced and delicate. He accepts their sexual interest but almost never initiates sex. He is absolutely respectful in all relationship matters, except fidelity. And even then he is very frank about his intentions and never pretends to be a one-woman man.

Not only does "no mean no" when it comes to sexual encounters but, according to Blomkvist's code, he makes sure that "yes doesn't mean no" as well. He never sulks if a woman withdraws from or rejects a sexual relationship, instead seeing this as her absolute right. Right after Salander meets him in *The Girl with the Dragon Tattoo*, she is astonished to observe that "she had not felt an iota of threat or any sort of hostility from his side."

Public writings about Stieg Larsson suggest that he was, like his protagonist Blomkvist, a male feminist. Biographical information also suggests that he lived his life in a way that exemplified his beliefs, and his novels make his ideology known. He cast Blomkvist's sister Annika as a prominent advocate for women, describing how "[Blomkvist's] little sister began to appear in newspapers as representing battered or threatened women, and on panel discussions on TV as a feminist and women's rights advocate" (*The Girl with the Dragon Tattoo*). And lest we be in doubt about his views, Larsson provided statistics about violence against women at the beginning of each part of *The Girl with the Dragon Tattoo* and mini-historical essays about women warriors at the beginning of the various parts of *The Girl Who Kicked the Hornet's Nest*. Throughout the series we are introduced to no fewer than five women warriors, each of a different type; Salander herself, a true Amazon who fearlessly battles demons from hell; Erika Berger, a corporate type who nonetheless is dedicated to her cause of telling the truth; Harriet Vanger, who murders her abusive father; Annika Giannini, the unassuming but triumphant advocate; and the murdered Mia Johansson, who had researched the exploitation of women in the sex trade. All of this strongly indicates that Larsson admired women warriors and saw them as underappreciated, and that he also deeply deplored violence against women. It seems likely he constructed his hero/alter ego Blomkvist as holding the same views.

A small but interesting male feminist, or "pro-feminist," movement has been active since the 1990s. The belief system within this movement includes the idea that men continue to receive unwarranted power and privilege in society compared to women, and that this male privilege is related to sexual violence against women. Male feminists believe that the current cultural model of masculinity is oppressive to women and constricting for men. They oppose violence against women, sexism, and pornography and support women's reproductive rights and equality in work. They feel that aggressive hypermasculine behavior is actually due to male insecurity.[10]

Blomkvist is a perfect example of the male feminist. He likes strong women, even women warriors, never wishes to dominate them, and fights against men who are violent toward them. He is

---

[10] A website that provides a summary of the views of male feminists is www. pro-feminism.co.tv.

very careful never to take advantage of male privilege, such as when a young intern's crush makes him intensely uncomfortable rather than excited in *The Girl Who Played with Fire*. He is extraordinaryily respectful of women in sexual matters, even if he is lacking somewhat in empathy.

Salander knows several kind and nonthreatening men—Armansky, Plague, and George Bland to name three—but because of her past abuse and exploitation, her internal, psychological world is full of men who hate women. She accepts no excuse for violence directed at women because of this, and becomes angry at any suggestion that insanity, childhood trauma, or some cause other than simple hatred of women be invoked as an explanation of a man's hateful behavior.

Blomkvist's innate sexual politics make him relatively safe, trustworthy, and unthreatening—almost uniquely so. This helps make it possible for Salander to make an exception for him and allow him to become a friend, confidante, and sexual partner, and to earn greater intimacy with her than almost anyone else in her life. Here, gender politics and psychology intersect. Blomkvist's silence, acceptance, and lack of aggression are the direct opposite of Salander's abusive, violent, aggressive father. In psychoanalytic terms, Blomkvist is the "good father" she never had. He's protective of women, respectful of them, and not frightening. Salander dares to edge close.

The answer to the question of why Salander makes an exception and allows herself to get close to Blomkvist is thus multidetermined. We know that her innate temperament, her trauma history, and the foundation of her personality—based on damaging early relationships and early attachment failures—have created a fiercely independent, remote young woman who defensively keeps a great distance from people and prefers to live socially in a virtual world. Like others with a schizoid personality she is eccentric, unemotional, and cannot or will not follow society's conventions. She has a great need for quiet, solitude, and time to think, and needs not to be intruded upon. She comes across a man, Mikael Blomkvist, who is so similarly constructed that, to her shock, she is capable of a much closer connection to him. He is rather schizoid himself, liking solitude and silence and keeping a good distance from people. He is unusually sensitive to gender politics, particularly avoiding any hint of manipulating or dominating women. He is not threatened by an aggressive and powerful woman. She feels safe with him and is concerned about him—the combination is an entirely new experience for her.

So why does Salander fall apart and shut Blomkvist out completely at the end of *The Girl with the Dragon Tattoo*? She is on her way to do the incredible—declare her love for him—but she sees him in an intimate conversation with Erika Berger and is convinced that they are about to go to his apartment to have sex. Certainly this would be a hurtful and frightening situation for anyone, but Salander's reaction is extreme, almost violent. She won't return his calls and emails and eventually leaves the country. The severity of her reaction can be understood psychoanalytically as a defense mechanism at work. Discovering that she was in love with Blomkvist was so terrifying and shattering that she used the sighting of him and Berger as an excuse to suddenly shift directions and run away. At this point in her psychological development, she ultimately could not handle the threat that closeness—and the implied potential for loss or betrayal—meant for her.

All fans of the trilogy mourn the premature death of Stieg Larsson. We have become so attached to Salander and Blomkvist that the loss of their future is painful. We will never know what would have happened between them. However, based on their psychology, it is possible to venture a guess about the path their relationship would have taken had Larsson lived to extend the series. I predict that Salander and Blomkvist would have gotten back together and might have even forged a permanent relationship. They are extremely well suited to each other—better even than it might appear on the surface. They share a dedication to personal intellectual and creative activity, a preference for solitude and privacy, and a tendency toward interpersonal distance. They share an aversion to intrusion and impingement. Neither seems drawn to parenthood. They might, just might, be able to find with each other the elusive and precious balance point where need is tempered and fear reassured, making it possible to achieve a tentative, careful intimacy.

The last lines in *The Girl Who Kicked the Hornet's Nest* directly address Salander's increasing ability to risk an intimate, interdependent relationship. "It was troubling," she thinks, "that one of the few people she trusted was a man she spent so much time avoiding." After some hesitation, "she opened the door wide and let him into her life again." Surely this is a sign of her emotional growth, the open door a metaphor for her newfound willingness to open up her *self* and let him inside.

PRUDENCE GOURGUECHON, MD, is the past president of the American Psychoanalytic Association. She is nationally known as a commentator who uses psychoanalytic concepts to explain a wide range of phenomena in politics, popular culture, and news events, as well as television, books, and movies. She has been quoted in the *New Yorker*, the *New York Times*, the *Wall Street Journal*, CNN, the *Chicago Tribune*, and other major media. Dr. Gourguechon has a practice in consultation to business, political campaigns, and marketing/advertising, as well as a clinical practice in psychiatry and psychoanalysis in Chicago. She blogs at the websites for the Huffington Post and *Psychology Today*.

PART 2

THE GIRL
WITH
THE TORNADO
INSIDE

Stieg Larsson uses fiction to plumb the depths of the real world—the one we live in. Indeed, his incisive look at the wretched treatment of women in Sweden blew the cover off of the idyllic image many of us have of Scandinavian society as progressive and open-minded. If you thought this element of the book was fiction, it's not. Wind Goodfriend explores the psychology of *män som hatar kvinnor* ("men who hate women," the original Swedish title of *The Girl with the Dragon Tattoo*) and how they are too often encountered in modern society in general. As Goodfriend reveals, sexism can take a number of forms, and it plays a pivotal role in shaping not just the Millennium trilogy, but also the character of Lisbeth Salander.

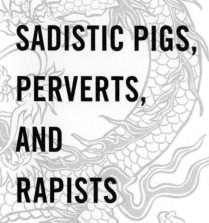

SADISTIC PIGS, PERVERTS, AND RAPISTS

SEXISM IN SWEDEN

WIND GOODFRIEND

The world is full of bad people in various forms: sadists, murderers, pedophiles, sex traffickers, and rapists top many people's lists for the worst criminals against humanity. While these crimes can be found in every country around the world, some cultures have more than their fair share of perpetrators. If one examines the psychology behind the actions of the people on this list, a common theme emerges: sexism. Sexism is not just a theme in these crimes; it's also one of the most pervasive themes in the Millennium series. Lisbeth Salander, the trilogy's main character, has been surrounded and suffocated by sexism for her entire life.

Sexism in Sweden

Most readers of this essay are familiar with sexism in the United States, but the Millennium trilogy isn't set in the US or written by a US citizen; it's set in Sweden, and was written by a Swedish author. In 2010, Amnesty International and the European Union produced a report, called "Case Closed," identifying troubling statistics about sexual crimes in several European countries.[1] The very first lines of this report state, "Sexual violence against women and girls is a worldwide phenomenon. There are no countries where women live free of the threat of such violence and no class or group of women is exempt from its destructive effects." According to "Case Closed," Sweden is the rape capital of Europe; there are forty-six reports of rape for every 100,000 Swedish citizens. This is twice the rate in the United Kingdom, and four times the rate of Germany and France. The report also notes that it's likely that only about 5 to 10 percent of rapes are actually reported to any kind of authority, such as the

[1] Amnesty International, "Case Closed: Rape and Human Rights in the Nordic Countries (Summary Report)," (London, England: Amnesty International Publications).

police. Of these, only a small fraction will actually be pursued in a court of law.

What accounts for these sickening numbers? "Case Closed" suggests that they are due to a deeply ingrained foundation of sexism in Sweden, what the report calls "discriminatory attitudes about male and female sexuality." Female victims of rape in Sweden (and, unfortunately, in the US and probably most of the world) are often made out to be the ones at fault, perpetuating what psychologists refer to as "rape myths." According to the report, these women are stereotyped as unemployed, uneducated, and/or alcoholic.

Throughout the Millennium trilogy, Lisbeth Salander is labeled as all of these, most often by the men who hate and abuse her. These men see her as unemployed (although they assume she sometimes works as a prostitute for extra cash). They see her as an addict, someone who got hooked on drugs and alcohol at an early age as a sign of self-destruction (one of the pieces of "evidence" used in Dr. Teleborian's report on her mental health). They repeatedly label her as unintelligent—or, in their words, "retarded." Clearly, sexism permeates Salander's world.

Sexism is a topic of increasing importance in psychological literature, and many scholars have discussed the way different forms of sexism have become clear over time. Perhaps the most basic form of sexism is what has been labeled "Old-Fashioned Sexism" by psychologist Janet Swim. In a 1995 article, Swim and some of her colleagues detailed that Old-Fashioned Sexism is the blatant sexism of previous generations, in which people believe in traditional gender roles (such as the man should be the breadwinner while the woman cooks and takes care of children), different treatment of men and women (such as men should make higher salaries), and have gender stereotypes (such as men are simply more intelligent).[2] While this form of sexism certainly still exists, Swim points out that, in modern times, forms of sexism may be less straightforward and more varied.

For instance, many people today exhibit what Swim calls "Modern Sexism." This form is more subtle, and fits in nicely with the trend

---

[2] J. K. Swim, K. J. Aikin, W. S. Hall, and B. A. Hunter, "Sexism and Racism: Old-Fashioned and Modern Prejudices," *Journal of Personality and Social Psychology* 68 (2005).

of being "politically correct." Modern Sexists deny overt statements that men are more intelligent, or that women are better at nurturing. Instead, they argue that sexism is no longer a problem in today's world, and that women have the exact same opportunities as men. They therefore bristle at programs such as Affirmative Action and dispute that groups supporting women's rights are still needed.

More recently, two other psychologists, Susan Fiske and Peter Glick, have suggested two additional forms of current-day sexism. The first is perhaps the most clandestine and, therefore, sneakily damaging. "Benevolent Sexism," as they call it, is the notion that women are, in fact, more pure and moral than men. They are delicate princesses who deserve to be treated as such; they should be adored and adorned. On the surface, Benevolent Sexism seems to idealize and compliment women; what's wrong with thinking that women are superior? The problem with this form of sexism is that it only allows women to be "superior" in limited, stereotypical ways, such as being "pretty" and "soft." It suggests that women are actually weak creatures who need protection, and they certainly aren't suited for any type of leadership role.

It's hard to see examples of Old-Fashioned, Modern, or Benevolent Sexism in Lisbeth Salander's world. However, there is one type of sexism left to be discussed, and this final type is, unfortunately, ubiquitous in her life. This final form, "Hostile Sexism," was also suggested by Susan Fiske and Peter Glick. Individuals who endorse Hostile Sexism believe that women are trying to take control and that they'll do whatever it takes to accomplish this task. Women are all radical feminists who want to crush men and take over the world, often by using a teasing form of sexuality. When women complain about sexism, they are simply making up complaints about nothing as a way of gaining power. Women, Hostile Sexists believe, are whores.

Hostile Sexism is the most dangerous form, because it leads to violence. When men believe that women are out to take over, they will be on the defensive whenever they interact with women. Some will go as far as to do everything in their power to "reestablish" dominance and power, from beating their wives, girlfriends, or female strangers, to raping, or ultimately, to murder.

To make Hostile Sexism extremely clear, consider the scale used to measure this psychological construct. Published by Glick and Fiske in 1996, the questionnaire includes several beliefs inherent to the concept of Hostile Sexism. When people take the survey, they read each sentence and indicate how much they agree or disagree, using a scale like this:

0	1	2	3	4	5
Disagree Strongly	Disagree Somewhat	Disagree Slightly	Agree Slightly	Agree Somewhat	Agree Strongly

Here are the eleven statements used in Fiske and Glick's questionnaire measuring sexism:

1. Many women are actually seeking special favors, such as hiring policies that favor them over men, under the guise of asking for "equality."
2. Most women interpret innocent remarks or acts as being sexist.
3. Women are too easily offended.
4. Feminists are seeking for women to have more power than men.
5. Most women fail to appreciate fully all that men do for them.
6. Women seek to gain power by getting control over men.
7. Women exaggerate the problems they have at work.
8. Once a woman gets a man to fully commit to her, she usually tries to put him on a tight leash.
9. When women lose to men in a fair competition, they typically complain about being discriminated against.
10. Many women get a kick out of teasing men by seeming sexually available and then refusing male advances.
11. Feminists are making unreasonable demands of men.[3]

---

[3] P. Glick, and S. T. Fiske, "The Ambivalent Sexism Inventory: Differentiating Hostile and Benevolent Sexism," *Journal of Personality and Social Psychology* 70 (1996).

Lisbeth Salander's world has been full of men with extremely high amounts of Hostile Sexism, starting from the day she was born. Three men have been especially important to her personality, decisions, and fate. While not all of them have committed crimes directly against her, their sexist actions have all shaped her life.

Advokat Nils Bjurman

The first man we encounter in the Millennium trilogy who exemplifies Hostile Sexism is Salander's legal guardian, Nils Bjurman. It's not until *The Girl Who Kicked the Hornet's Nest* that we learn how early Bjurman became involved in Salander's life, starting all the way back when she was twelve and he helped conspire to lock her in a children's psychiatric hospital. But we see their adult relationship begin to unfold in *The Girl with the Dragon Tattoo* when he takes over as her legal custodian and must actually meet Salander in person to discuss her finances.

At their third meeting, Salander realizes how much of a Hostile Sexist Bjurman might be. Although he's supposed to be asking about her job, finances, and professional life, he quickly turns the conversation into one about her personal sexual life. When she initially refuses to answer his questions, she sees that his conclusion is that she is, indeed, mentally retarded—a label supporting her weaknesses and therefore supporting her inability to be an independent, mature adult. Understanding the volatile power dynamics of the situation in which she is trapped, she answers his inappropriate questions, including whether she enjoys anal sex and what kind of sexual positions she prefers.

Bjurman asks these questions to confirm that she is, as he believes, a "whore" whom he can use to his own liking. Specifically, his liking includes dominating her and violently raping and strangling her, almost to the point of death. His sadistic pleasure in overcoming her is clear. Bjurman's role as her legal guardian surely adds to the enjoyment he receives; several psychological studies have shown that men who rape and sexually harass combine sexual excitement and power.

Being dominant over another human being is sexually exciting for extreme Hostile Sexists, and Bjurman's thought process after the forced oral sex shows classic signs of Hostile Sexism. In *The Girl with the Dragon Tattoo*, he notes to himself, "She was going to have to be kept in check. She had to understand who was in charge." And later, he makes a promise: "You're going to wind up eating this, you fucking cunt. Sooner or later I'm going to crush you."

Salander's response to his first crime—demanding a blow job in his office in exchange for access to her own money—is to acquiesce. Always expecting men to treat her badly, she often waits to decide how to react after fully assessing the impact of every situation. Bjurman's behavior does not surprise her. "By the time she was eighteen," we learn in *The Girl with the Dragon Tattoo*, "Salander did not know a single girl who at some point had not been forced to perform some sort of sexual act against her will." Based on the crime statistics from the European Union on Sweden, this may be close to the truth. Hostile Sexism is so pervasive in Salander's life that she has come to believe that it's simply how the entire world is structured. She trusts no one—especially men—because she has repeatedly been the victim of Hostile Sexism in its worst forms. "In [Lisbeth's] world, this was the natural order of things. As a girl she was legal prey . . . There was no point whimpering about it. On the other hand, there was no question of Advokat Bjurman going unpunished" (*The Girl with the Dragon Tattoo*).

Although Salander has accepted the existence of Hostile Sexism in her world, she has not accepted the role of victim. Although she would never consider asking anyone for help, she stands up for herself and her rights in an extremely powerful way. After Bjurman's sadistic rape, she physically forces him to accept the tattoo on his chest that labels him, so that he'll remember not to mess with her ever again. Later, when he tries to set up her murder, she again takes steps to protect herself and regain control (although, ultimately, the problem of Bjurman is eliminated by someone else). This example is a perfect way to see how Salander reacts to Hostile Sexism. She will simply not accept it. "She went around with the attitude that she would rather be beaten to death than take any shit" (*The Girl with the Dragon Tattoo*).

Martin Vanger

While Martin Vanger is really only in the periphery of Salander's world, his presence has a huge impact on her adult life and her relationship with Mikael Blomkvist. The reason Salander and Blomkvist meet is because of their mutual curiosity in solving the murder of Harriet Vanger. This case uncovers a long history of sexism, incest, and relationship abuse in the Vanger family, pivoting around Harriet's brother, Martin, and their father, Gottfried.

When Martin kidnaps and tortures Blomkvist in his secret basement dungeon, we get an insight into the mind of an extreme Hostile Sexist. Martin explains to him, "You would not be able to understand the godlike feeling of having absolute control over someone's life and death." There are certainly many people who enjoy power and even take on a god complex, such as some politicians or doctors, and believe they don't have to follow the rules of "ordinary" people. But why is Martin's life focused around the kidnapping, rape, torture, and murder of women?

Martin's father was his teacher. Gottfried taught Martin to disrespect women, to hate them and treat them as objects, and he combined these lessons with sessions of sexual abuse, forever combining Martin's hatred and sexual obsession. Both of them originally tried to enlist Harriet in their personal cult of sex and sadism, but she fought back. This, of course, was disappointing to them. Martin explains, "We tried . . . to talk to her. Gottfried tried to teach her. We thought that she was one of us and that she would accept her duty, but she was just an ordinary . . . *cunt*" (*The Girl with the Dragon Tattoo*). The focus here is dual. First, Martin assumes that his sister's "duty" is to be a sexual slave to her own father and brother. Second, when she refuses this role, she is labeled as a "cunt," perhaps the worst word he can think of to describe "ordinary" women who try to retain some form of self-respect and power. These are clearly keystones of Hostile Sexism, and these attitudes at least contributed to his justification for the crimes he committed.

Alexander Zalachenko

While Zalachenko is the last character we meet in this list of men, he is the first and most powerful influence on Salander's life. From the very beginning, Salander's example of men was a misogynist who enjoyed beating his girlfriend every few months, just for the fun of it. It's clear that Zala has never considered any women useful, intelligent, or worthwhile. When Salander finally reunites with him as an adult, years after trying to kill him with a gasoline bomb, he reflects on their earlier life together and on his relationship with Salander's mother. He explains to Salander that her mother was a "whore" who got pregnant on purpose as a method of trapping him into the relationship. He goes on to insult Salander in a variety of sexist ways, calling her a "dyke" and suggesting that Niedermann—her own half brother—should rape her because that might do her some good.

A revealing moment between them is seen in this same conversation, after Zalachenko tells Salander that Niedermann is her half brother. Due to his status in the family, Niedermann has been taken in as a protégé, an heir to the family business of crime. Salander learns that Zala actually has several children scattered about the globe, and she asks if any of her sisters have a stake in the business. Zala is clearly startled—even shocked—by this suggestion, showing that he has never considered the very idea that one of his daughters might be able to follow in his footsteps. As all Hostile Sexists do, Zala assumes that women are basically worthless and only cause problems. The impact he has on her is undeniable, and her reaction against Zala's sexism is the catalyst for the complications that occur for the rest of her life.

Lisbeth Salander—the Most Hostile of All?

The list of other examples of male Hostile Sexists in the Millennium series is quite long. In addition to the men discussed above, we meet Erika Berger's stalker, Inspector Faste, Bjork, and Dr. Teleborian. Most of these men have shaped Salander's life and personality, either directly or from the shadows. Every description of her is a display of how she has internalized their hatred and become raw to the world. Her reaction to sexist men has been to withdraw from all social conventions and social interactions. She's covered in tattoos and piercings, and she wears clothes specifically chosen to deter people from talking to her or even making eye contact. If she avoids contact, people can't hurt her or interfere with her life. Dragan Armansky was taken aback by her upon their first meeting, and his impression was not good: "She looked as though she had just emerged from a week-long orgy with a gang of hard rockers." She's so introverted that people assume she's stupid, and repeatedly we see that she has zero trust in any other human being.

The question thus becomes: Has Salander become what she hates? Has she become a person who immediately judges others and finds them beneath her? Does she think others are simply pawns to be used to her liking? Is she a Hostile Sexist herself, but against men? In a follow-up to their 1996 paper about Hostile Sexism against women, Glick and Fiske published another article[4] in which they discussed just such a reciprocal attitude: Hostile Sexism against men. While most psychological researchers study traditional sexism (that is, sexism that hurts women), it is certainly the case that women might hold Hostile Sexist beliefs against men that are just as damaging as their counterparts against women.

Using the same zero to five scale from earlier in this essay, people who complete the questionnaire measuring Hostile Sexism against men state their level of agreement with these sentences:

1. A man who is sexually attracted to a woman typically has no morals about doing whatever it takes to get her in bed.
2. When men act to "help" women, they are often trying to prove they are better than women.
3. Men would be lost in this world if women weren't there to guide them.
4. Men act like babies when they are sick.

---

[4] P. Glick, and S. T. Fiske, "The Ambivalence Toward Men Inventory: Differentiating Hostile and Benevolent Beliefs About Men," *Psychology of Women Quarterly* 23 (1996).

5. Men will always fight to have greater control in society than women.
6. Even men who claim to be sensitive to women's rights really want a traditional relationship at home, with the woman performing most of the housekeeping and child care.
7. Men usually try to dominate conversations when talking to women.
8. Most men pay lip service to equality for women, but can't handle having a woman as an equal.
9. When it comes down to it, most men are really like children.
10. Most men sexually harass women, even if only in subtle ways, once they are in a position of power over them.

Would Salander put a five next to most of these items, indicating "Strongly Agree"? It seems fairly likely, given her character. It's clear that many of her decisions are based simply on making the point that she does not trust anyone, especially men. She assumes that all men are going to abuse her in some way.

When Salander does research on Wennerström in *The Girl with the Dragon Tattoo*, she learns that he got a young girl pregnant and forced her to have an abortion. Her reaction to this is simple: "One more man who hates women." Later, in *The Girl Who Played with Fire,* she confronts a man named Sandström who enjoys raping prostitutes and then photographing them. Her statement is clear: "I don't understand why men always have to document their perversions." This mind-set informs us about two fundamentals of her thought process. First, she groups *all* men together with this statement, indicating that she believes all men are the same. Second, not only are all men the same, but they are all perverted in some way and enjoy looking at the documentation to prove it. In this same encounter, she calls Sandström a "sadistic pig, pervert, and rapist." This is apparently her definition of most men, and indeed it is practically a mantra for Salander. Even when she first met Advokat Palmgren, who later became a great friend and legal savior in some ways, she assumed that he was some kind of twisted pedophile who wanted to see her naked and abuse her.

Salander's assumptions that men are all alike, that they are all untrustworthy sexual demons looking for an opportunity to abuse 113 her, is unquestionably Hostile Sexism. She commits crimes related to Hostile Sexism as well, forcing Bjurman to accept her tattoo, blackmailing people, hacking into their personal affairs, and even planning to murder them if necessary. So: Is Salander just as bad as all the men in her life?

While Salander is definitely guilty of being a Hostile Sexist, the answer must be no. There are two saving graces that make Salander different from the other Hostile Sexist characters in her life. First, she only resorts to acting against men (or women, for that matter) when she must do so in self-defense. Salander's primary reaction is to leave people alone and hope they do the same. She is relatively antisocial, and is never proactive in seeking ways to hurt other people. This is a major difference from the men outlined above, who purposely seek out victims for their crimes and truly enjoy abusing them.

Second, while Salander might initially assume that all men are untrustworthy, perverted idiots, she does actually give them a chance to prove her wrong. For example, she waits patiently for Advokat Palmgren to molest her, and when he doesn't, she begins to trust him. She assumes that Dragan Armansky is going to be a terrible boss, but eventually he trusts her enough to give her bigger assignments, and she rewards this trust with a hesitant friendship. Most importantly, she allows Mikael Blomkvist to enter her life as a trusted friend and lover. Originally on guard against him and what he might do to interfere with her life, Salander realizes that he is magnanimous and—even more importantly to her—that he is respectful of her choices.

Salander falls for Blomkvist because he does not meet her expectations. We see her own surprise about this situation as she considers what role he'll have for her. After their relationship begins to develop in *The Girl with the Dragon Tattoo,* she thinks to herself, "She had been sharing a house with him for a week, and he had not once flirted with her. He had worked with her, asked her opinion . . . and acknowledged that she was right when she corrected him. Dammit, he had treated her like a human being."

Although Salander is surprised about this turn of events (which again underscores her sexist assumptions), she is open to the possibility of individual differences in the world of men. She is willing to consider each man as an independent entity, and she is willing to respect (and perhaps even love) a man who respects and loves her in return. This essential trait in her personality is what allows Salander to step away from the lineup of other Hostile Sexists and become a sympathetic and relatable person. This ability for her to love another person is what makes us able to love her. Salander becomes the hero of the story because we can all empathize with the damaging effects of being a lifelong victim of personal atrocity. It's understandable that she has no trust in men because the vast majority of men have been abusive and sadistic. In fact, her very ability to realize that all men are *not* alike is remarkable, considering her uniquely shattered childhood and her continuing abuse as an adult. Her resilience when surrounded by Hostile Sexism is what makes us cheer her on, and hope for a better future.

WIND GOODFRIEND, PhD, is an associate professor of psychology at Buena Vista University. She earned her PhD in social psychology in 2004 from Purdue University. In her final year of graduate school, Dr. Goodfriend received both the "Outstanding Teacher of the Year Award" and the "Outstanding Graduate Student of the Year Award" for her research. She was named Faculty Member of the Year at Buena Vista University in 2008 and again in 2011. In addition to her work as a university professor, Dr. Goodfriend is the Principal Investigator for the Institute for the Prevention of Relationship Violence.

iven Lisbeth Salander's father and half brother's tendencies toward violence and her own violent streak, fans of the Millennium trilogy may well wonder whether Lisbeth's propensity both metaphorically and literally to shoot first and ask questions later is as much a matter of her genes as her upbringing. Joshua Gowin explores the psychology of violence and the extent to which nature and nurture each play a role.

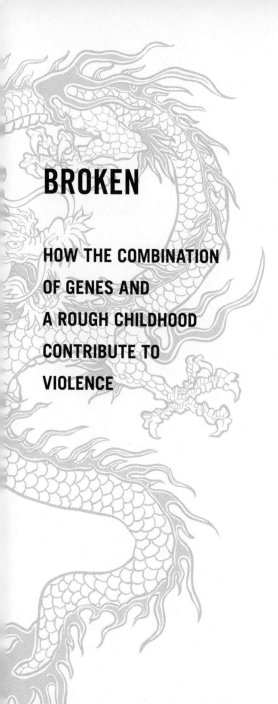

BROKEN

HOW THE COMBINATION OF GENES AND A ROUGH CHILDHOOD CONTRIBUTE TO VIOLENCE

JOSHUA GOWIN

Violence in the Blood

Most women have a few standard deflections to cut the conversation short when they receive unwanted attention from a male suitor at a bar. They may mention that they have a boyfriend, or perhaps they'll employ a friend to come to their rescue. After an evening of come-ons from Chris MacAllen at a hotel bar in Grenada, Lisbeth Salander pushes her pursuer into a swimming pool. A few weeks earlier, when she's had enough of a local's antics at a bar in Saint Lucia, she knocks him over the head with a brick, pays her tab, and then skips town. Clearly, Salander is not most women. She's not like most anyone.

You might expect that kind of violence from a sociopath—someone without regard for the suffering of others—such as Alexander Zalachenko, Lisbeth's father, or Ronald Niedermann, her half brother. Zalachenko regularly beat Lisbeth's mother, Agneta, while Lisbeth was growing up. When Lisbeth was twelve, he beat Agneta so brutally that she became permanently brain damaged. When asked about his actions, he justifies his violence by saying that Agneta was "a whore." He offers no other explanation and never indicates that she provoked him in any way.

Niedermann shows a similar callousness. He commits nearly all of the murders in the second and third installments of the Millennium trilogy. In addition to the planned murder of Nils Bjurman, Niedermann impulsively decides to knock off Dag Svensson and Mia Johansson when he finds out they're investigating Zalachenko and threatening to expose the family crime operation. He abducts and nearly kills a dental hygienist so that he can steal her car as he flees the scene of the double murder of two police officers. He also takes the life of the treasurer of the motorcycle gang he does business with, Svalvsjo MC, as he robs their entire bankroll. Never does he seem angry with any of his victims. Like his father, Niedermann murders to clear a pathway to his goal the same way someone might move a shopping cart from behind their car before backing out of a parking space. Violence is his primary tool for getting what he wants.

For many, the thought of meeting a group of people at a country farm and assaulting each other with handguns, an ax, and a Taser might imply some sort of covert warfare or a gang fight. For Zalachenko and his offspring, it's a family reunion. Lisbeth arrives at the farm outside Gosseberga intending to kill her father, and Niedermann welcomes her with a few blows from his fist. Zalachenko shoots his daughter three times and tells Niedermann to bury her body, not realizing that she's still alive. Both Lisbeth and Zalachenko leave the farm in critical condition, headed for the hospital, while Niedermann flees the police. Clearly, Zalachenko and his children share a penchant for violence. The question is why.

Zalachenko did not play much of a parental role in either Lisbeth's or Niedermann's life. Lisbeth hardly saw him aside from the occasions he dropped by to sleep with and abuse her mother. Niedermann was the result of a brief affair Zalachenko had in Germany, and he did not get to know his father until adulthood, when they both ended up in Sweden. If Zalachenko didn't raise his children to be violent, does that mean that Salander and Niedermann inherited his aggressive temperament? Traits like eye color and blood type are determined by our genetic material, our DNA—so what about tendency to violence? Do children learn to be violent, or is that risk present from birth?

A common way to test the degree to which a trait is determined by our genes is to see how likely twins are to share it. Identical twins share 100 percent of their DNA, whereas fraternal twins only share, on average, 50 percent, just like all siblings do. If studies show that identical twins share a trait more often than fraternal twins, scientists conclude that the trait is heritable. And the *more often* identical twins share a trait compared to fraternal twins, the greater the role genetics play in determining the presence of that trait.

The largest and most comprehensive study of the genetics of violence looked at all twins born in Denmark between 1881 and 1910 and noted how many crimes they had committed.[1] If violence resulted

---

[1] Gottesman Cloninger, "Genetic and Environmental Factors in Antisocial Behavior Disorders," *The Causes of Crime: New Biological Approaches*, eds. Mednick, Moffitt, and Stark (New York: Cambridge University Press, 1987).

solely from our genes, then nearly all identical twins of violent criminals would have committed violent crimes, too. Instead, the study found that the actual rate was 77 percent for identical twins, and only 52 percent for fraternal twins. From this, we can conclude that genes do not completely account for violence, but because identical twins had a higher rate of correspondence than fraternal twins we can see that they certainly play a role. Identical twins share a much larger proportion of aggression and violence than fraternal twins, showing that, although genes do not completely account for violence, they certainly play a role. Having Zalachenko for a father surely increased Lisbeth's and Niedermann's risk for exhibiting violent behavior.

Yet Lisbeth's fraternal twin sister, Camilla, does not get into nearly as much trouble as Lisbeth. In school she gets along with her peers and gets good grades. Aside from giving Lisbeth a black eye during an argument when they were eighteen, Camilla does not get into physical fights and keeps her legal record clean. She's just as much Zalachenko's daughter as Lisbeth, but her genes do not set her down the same troubled path. To fully understand the differences between Lisbeth and Camilla, we must look beyond their DNA.

It Starts in the Home

Propensity to violence is certainly not a clear-cut case of genetic predetermination. In the age-old nature versus nurture debate, we've seen that both factors play an important role in who we become. The environment in which you're raised greatly contributes to where you'll end up as an adult. Toddlers can learn to speak any language they're exposed to without developing an accent, even if none of their ancestors speak it. The food you eat and the amount of exercise you undertake affects your risk for developing diabetes, no matter what genes you have. Similarly, the treatment you receive growing up shapes your behavior, and children exposed to physical abuse often become more aggressive adults.[2] Lisbeth's childhood experiences, then, provide clues to her adult personality.

---

2 C. S. Widom, "The Cycle of Violence," *Science* 244 (1989).

Without question, child abuse can cause lasting psychological harm. Children who are physically or sexually abused go on to develop disorders such as depression, anxiety, schizophrenia, and drug addiction at twice the rate of children who aren't abused. The earlier mistreatment begins, the more severe the risk becomes.[3] One of the dismaying outcomes of abuse is the prospect that these children will grow up to become the next generation of criminals, abusing their own children and creating a cycle of violence.

Just how much, and why, child abuse and neglect contribute to criminal behavior has remained a sought-after research question for over fifty years. Although abused children are almost twice as likely to become violent compared to nonabused peers, the majority of abused children do not become violent.[4] Further, the type of mistreatment affects the likelihood that an abused child will become a violent adult. In a broad study of the effects of child abuse on adult criminal behavior, psychologist Cathy Spatz Widom followed up on 656 court cases of child abuse filed between 1967 and 1971 in which a criminal charge was filed against an adult. She then found 908 individuals born in the same county during the same years who had no record of abuse so she could compare the adult criminal records of the two groups. Among children who had a record of physical abuse, 15 percent were later arrested for a violent crime, a little over twice the 7 percent rate of children who had no record of physical abuse. Not far behind, 12 percent of children who experienced neglect—whether they weren't provided for or were exposed to dangerous living conditions—had a violent criminal record.

Although Zalachenko did not physically harm Lisbeth or Camilla, her fraternal twin sister, his extreme inattention to them could consti-tute neglect, particularly when we consider that his continued abuse of Agneta inflicted mental injury on the girls—at least Lisbeth. Although Agneta hid her daughters away in another room and told them not to worry when Zalachenko came, the girls must have had some idea of

---

[3] D. O. Lewis, "Development of the Symptom of Violence," *Child and Adolescent Psychiatry*, 3rd ed., ed. Lewis (Philadelphia: Lippincott Williams & Wilkins, 2002).

[4] C. S. Widom, "The Cycle of Violence."

what was happening. The two girls heard blows coming from the other room, saw bruises and marks on their mother, and surely guessed what had caused them. Witnessing their mother's battering infused a sense of danger into their home, yet nothing was done to stop it, meeting the criteria for neglect. Additionally, Agneta did not talk about the abuse with Lisbeth or Camilla, adding to the girls' confusion about and discomfort with the cruelty. According to Widom's research, neglect trails only physical abuse in putting children at risk to become violent as adults.

Abuse from peers can harm, as well. Bullying often damages self-esteem, creates emotional problems, and can lead to troubled behavior. What's more, unchecked bullying creates a threatening environment in which children cannot feel safe because they're constantly being pushed around. When adults don't intervene, their neglect compounds the problem.

Lisbeth faced bullies from the time she started school. Despite the tormenting from her peers, we don't hear of any teachers intervening to help her. Worse still, whenever Lisbeth tried to defend herself, she was reprimanded or disciplined. The teachers in her school permitted a hostile environment and then punished her for trying to put an end to it. When Lisbeth is accused of murdering Dag and Mia, one of Lisbeth's former teachers even tells journalists that she thought Lisbeth was odd as a child, underscoring the idea that adults did not accept her or play an appropriate role as her protectors. Rejection, from teachers and students alike, hurts.

Lisbeth's situation got worse when she was forcibly committed to St. Stefan's Psychiatric Clinic for Children under Peter Teleborian's care. Not only did Teleborian fail to help Lisbeth, he also physically abused her. Her doctor, charged by the state to care for Lisbeth and keep her best interests in mind, strapped her to a bed and left her restrained for over half of the two years she spent at the clinic. When Lisbeth tried to stop taking the medication he prescribed because it caused nausea and left her in a mental haze, Teleborian ordered the nurses to force-feed her. Following her mistreatment by Teleborian, Lisbeth learned not to cooperate with doctors and to distrust all authority figures. Abuse lastingly altered her behavior.

Still, just as giving a person a gun does not mean they'll fire it, experiencing abuse does not guarantee that someone will break the law. Widom found that 85 percent of abused children didn't commit violent crimes. The children who experienced abuse and went on to become criminals may have had some preexisting vulnerability that surfaced following the mistreatment. Would those maltreated children who became violent have turned out differently if they had experienced more love?

Adoption studies provide a way to address this question, to look at the interaction between nature and nurture. Psychiatrist Remi Cadoret followed a group of adopted children whose biological parents either had a history of antisocial behavior—such as stealing, violence, and breaking laws—or no such history. Some of the adoptive families provided a better home than others, so Cadoret then looked at any indication that the upbringing might have been troubled, like marital problems, alcoholism, or depression in the adoptive parents. The kids who had an antisocial biological parent and a rough childhood committed the most crimes. The adoptees with an antisocial biological parent that grew up in a safe home with love and support were much less likely to commit crimes or violence. So, children of antisocial parents can develop into kind adults if given love, support, and nurturing.

Now consider Lisbeth's half brother. Ronald Niedermann had some of the same genes, but a different upbringing. His role models growing up were neo-Nazis. As an adult, his father groomed him for the family crime business. He learned to use violence as a negotiating tactic, and often extracted information from his associates by means of torture, for example by cutting off their limbs with a chainsaw. In him, we have an example of a child with a family history of aggression who fell in with criminals. As far as we know, he never has a mentor that treats him with compassion and steers him toward virtue, and the result is unsurprising; Niedermann is ruthless.

Aggression and Violence: Complex Behaviors

Beyond the mixture of nature and nurture, a person's likelihood to become violent is affected by the situations he or she encounters. Context matters. Anyone is capable of becoming aggressive; the question is when, why, and how.

Before a person can become violent, that person must have the appropriate opportunity. If sufficiently provoked, even a mild-mannered person might lash out. For instance, in *The Girl Who Kicked the Hornet's Nest,* no one suspected Peter Fredriksson of stalking and harassing Erika Berger because he seemed gentle and had no apparent reason to harm her. When he was caught trespassing at her home, he eventually confessed that he felt slighted by her in high school and wanted revenge. Fredriksson resented Berger for years, but it wasn't until she became his boss and failed to recognize him from high school that he finally took action. However, some people, through a combination of nature and nurture, will strike with much less prodding. In school, Lisbeth would fight anyone who teased her. With her short fuse (possibly inherited) combined with the stress of a home fraught with violence, Lisbeth often used aggression to deal with her social problems.

Equally important to a person's likelihood of resorting to aggression is how he or she expresses it. Aggression is defined as any behavior that intends to harm another individual, so although many actions fall into that category, not all of them are violent. Passive aggression, irksome as it can be, generally does not cause physical harm. Rather, it may take the form of backbiting, gossip, or failure to comply with requests. For example, Anders Holm, an editor at Svenska Morgon-Posten (SMP), expressed his frustration with Berger when she became his boss by ignoring her requests and refusing to cooperate with her. He purposefully caused her harm, and the stress he created helped cement her decision to quit SMP and return to Millennium. Fredriksson, on the other hand, took a more direct approach. He sent Berger threats and vandalized her house, both instances of active aggression. When she stepped on the glass he broke in her living room, she sliced her foot and had to go to the hospital—an instance of physical harm. Subsequently, she had a personal bodyguard from a detective agency stay with her in her house until they caught Fredriksson. Both active and passive forms of aggression caused Berger stress and harm, but only one required police assistance to resolve.

Beyond how we express aggression, active or passive, the motive for the behavior weighs heavily on our judgment of it. We want to know the reasons behind aggression: Why did the person do what they did? Psychological research traditionally divides aggression into two categories, reactive and proactive. Proactive aggression often has a goal; it can be used as a tool to get something out of someone, like money, information, or perhaps even a thrill. But proactive aggression carries inherent risks. By striking others, you risk them striking back. Reactive aggression occurs in response to a threat, real or perceived, and usually involves intense emotions like anger, fear, or jealousy. Although Zalachenko spent years abusing Agneta with impunity, when Lisbeth was old enough to defend her mother she burned him so badly that his body was permanently scarred and he was forced to amputate his left foot. Watching her mother suffer needlessly upset her, so she retaliated.

Of all the proactive aggression in *The Girl with the Dragon Tattoo,* the most egregious may have been Nils Bjurman's rape of Lisbeth and his attempt to abuse his position of authority. To satisfy his power fetish, Bjurman takes advantage of her, thinking that he can get away with it because her record indicates she has psychiatric disorders and a low IQ. He underestimated Lisbeth; not only did she use his second rape as a weapon against him by secretly recording the encounter for later use as blackmail, but she also got revenge. She expected him to coerce her into oral sex again, but he got carried away with physical violence and nearly suffocated her to death. When she returned to his apartment, she not only played the video of the rape back to him, but she also sodomized him with a sex toy and tattooed his stomach, branding him as a rapist for the rest of his life. Comparing Bjurman's act to Lisbeth's illustrates the difference between proactive and reactive aggression. Bjurman proactively attacked Lisbeth to satisfy a sadistic fantasy, whereas Lisbeth, enraged by his violence and abuse, reactively struck back as an act of revenge and also to protect herself from Bjurman in the future. He would have no further opportunities to violate her. The aggressive behavior is almost identical: Bjurman and Lisbeth raped and humiliated each other. Yet, noting whether each was proactive or reactive, we see the difference between the two. Bjurman incites loathing, but Lisbeth, acting out of self-defense, embodies empowerment and vindication.

Under Control

Aggression is one of those important behaviors so essential to survival that every known creature makes use of it. Hens who don't protect their eggs lose them to foxes, slugs that don't guard their dinner lose it to more enterprising creatures, and penguins that don't use their razor-sharp beaks may become seal chow.

Such an important but risky behavior as aggression must be tightly regulated. Your brain evaluates the risks and the rewards and hopefully makes the right decision on when to fight and when to look on peacefully. It stands to reason, then, that the brain should have fine-tuned mechanisms designed to help you quickly decide what action to take. In the brain's most stripped-down state, there are two basic functions, similar to a car, for controlling aggression. First, there must be something to propel you forward—the drive. Second, there must be something to slow you down again—the brake. The brain has some regions that motivate behavior and prompt you to take action, and it also has regions that slow you down again and force you to think twice before doing something you may later regret. It makes as little sense to have a car that's always going ninety miles per hour as it does to have a person swinging fists at anything he or she sees; both car and person will eventually screech to a halt and the result won't be pretty.

The aggressive drive comes mostly from the visceral and emotional brain regions, such as those responsible for frustration, anger, and fear. These negative emotions arise to alert you about some discomfort, such as when a car cuts you off in traffic, forcing you to stop suddenly. The emotion rivets your attention to the source of your discomfort, the driver in front of you, and triggers an action to remedy it. Anger often leads to aggressive behavior, such as honking or giving the driver the finger. In short, the brain responds to experiences that disturb your emotional balance by motivating you to take corrective actions, some of them aggressive, just as your leg kicks after a doctor taps your knee. Hardwired and instinctive, aggression can occur reflexively unless a more levelheaded impulse intervenes. That's why we teach children to count to ten when they're angry; their initial reaction might get them in trouble. Aggression aims to remove the source of your discomfort or prevent it from bothering you again.

Lisbeth's emotions of anger and disgust motivate her attacks on both her father and Bjurman. She initially stabbed Zalachenko to get him to stop beating her mother, and when he finally returned she burned him so badly that he never touched Agneta again. (Sadly, the damage was already done, because Agneta spent the rest of her life in a nursing home.) Lisbeth's torture of Bjurman secures her financial freedom and ensures that he will never again have a position of power over her. Bjurman's biggest mistake was pissing Lisbeth off.

The brain's brake system comprises the rational regions responsible for planning, decision making, and judgment. These regions underlie a gambler's assessment of a wager: weighing outcomes and making the choice that will maximize his gains. The brake system couples closely with the emotional regions of the brain. In the same way that emotions like anger urge us to act, the brake system floods us with anxiety, slowing us down. Anxiety reminds us how high the stakes are before we do something we might later regret.

When your brain's aggression system works properly, you take action only when necessary and your actions are appropriate to the situation. When Mikael Blomkvist encounters Niedermann on a highway outside Gosseberga, he points a Colt 1911 Government at him and tells him to lie down on the ground. He then binds Niedermann's hands, ties him to a road sign, and drives off. Blomkvist threatens Niedermann's life and leaves him stranded on a highway, but only because he recognizes the danger Niedermann poses. His actions serve to take him out of jeopardy and are hardly inappropriate in the situation. The next time a car stops for Niedermann on the side of the road, Niedermann kills both passengers and steals the car. His use of aggression is both excessive and inappropriate, and his pattern of violent behavior eventually costs him his life when he's caught by the gang of bikers he mistreated.

What could go wrong with this system in the brain to create a violent killer like Niedermann? Or a hostile misfit like Salander? The simplest explanation is that the drive could be on close to full throttle, the brakes could be faulty, or some combination of the two.

Dangerous Minds

As long as we've had the tools to study the brain, neuroscientists have been investigating where the breakdown might occur that prevents restraint and leads to violence. A pioneer of the study of the brain's role in behavior, Swiss physiologist Walter Rudolf Hess developed a technique that involved drilling a small hole in the head of an anesthetized cat to insert an electrode into a region of the brain. When the cat woke up, Hess could stimulate parts of the brain to observe its behavioral effect. Stimulating some areas caused the cat to sniff, pant, or eat. Hess noticed that electrically stimulating certain areas of the hypothalamus, a region of the mid-brain closely connected to the body's hormonal system, seemed to increase the aggressive drive; the cat would growl, hiss, and strike at anything that approached it. When the stimulation stopped, the cat would stop the aggressive behavior and might curl up and go to sleep.

In a later experiment, Hess surgically removed a small portion of the hypothalamus surrounding the region where he had stimulated the aggressive drive. When the cat awoke, it arched its back, folded its ears back, and its hair stood on end. With this brain region removed, the cat hissed and displayed the same hostile behavior as when Hess stimulated the drive with an electrode. This area served as the brakes, and removing it caused the cat to be in a constant rage. Hess went on to win the Nobel Prize in Medicine for his work exploring the function of the hypothalamus.

While the human brain has many structural and functional differences compared to that of the cat, much of the general organization remains the same. Our brain regulates behavior using complementary drive and brake systems as well, but humans have advanced regions for planning, critical thinking, and decision making, notably the prefrontal cortex, or PFC. The PFC lies just behind the forehead and helps regulate aggression by controlling our impulses; it helps balance out the drive. If the PFC controls aggression, it should work soundly in nonviolent people, but not as well in violent criminals.

Positron emission tomography, or PET imaging, measures mental activity visually by tracking the metabolism of sugar, the brain's energy source. When you feel a pinch on your thigh, the part of the brain that records the sensations of the thigh will start to fire. Blood will flow to that region to provide energy for the firing, and if you take a PET scan at that time the region corresponding to your thigh lights up. Psychologist Adrian Raine used PET imaging to study the brains of forty-one people convicted of murder and forty-one comparison volunteers as they completed a mental performance task. He hoped to demonstrate a difference in the way murderers process information, and indeed the murderers' brains did function differently during the task. The criminals either had less activity in the PFC, a braking region, or more activity in the emotional brain regions responsible for the drive. The balance between the drive and the brakes was out of whack.

Zalachenko's frequent bar fights may have reflected an overactive drive or faulty brakes in his PFC. According to Gunnar Bjork, an old work associate, Zalachenko went out many evenings looking to get into a fight. Even when going about his business during the day, the slightest provocation could lead him to attack someone. Similarly, professional boxer Paolo Roberto discovered Lisbeth's wrath in the boxing ring after he teased her. Once he triggered her drive, she became a five-foot fighting fury that even a world-class boxer had to protect himself from.

Niedermann's impulsive aggression could stem from a bad braking system. Unlike his father, he doesn't initiate crime, but rather follows his father's orders to murder Bjurman and kidnap Miriam. However, any threat to his mission causes him to become violent, such as when he learns that Dag and Mia were investigating Zalachenko. He does not give any indication that he considers the consequences of his actions and, unlike most people, Niedermann does not even fear physical punishment—such as being punched by champion boxer Roberto—because he possesses a genetic disorder that prevents him from feeling pain. Like the murderers in the brain imaging study, he has no brakes.

Although the interplay between regions provides a large-scale demonstration of the brain's balancing act, many more subtle mechanisms participate in regulating our behavior. For example, neurotransmitters, the chemical messengers that allow brain cells to communicate, affect our mood and behavior. Serotonin serves as the brain's brake fluid, spilling out when the drive gets too high and creating a pressure to slow down. The brains of individuals with low serotonin levels shift toward rapid, impulsive decisions even in the face of great risk. Depressed patients with low serotonin levels, for example, commit suicide more frequently than patients with higher serotonin levels because they have less inhibition when pulling a trigger or swallowing a toxic pill. Neurotransmitter levels can vary depending on lifestyle, diet, experiences, and, of course, genetics.

In 1978, a woman in the Netherlands went to a geneticist to seek help. Her family had been plagued by outbursts of aggression and violence from a few of the men across several generations. One of the men in the family raped his sister; he was placed in a mental institution where he later attacked the warden with a pitchfork. Another male forced his sister to undress while threatening her with a knife, while two others were arsonists. At that point, nine of her male relatives exhibited violent behavior, and she wondered if their DNA might play a role. The geneticist, Han Brunner, found that the affected males all had a rare genetic mutation that disabled a brain enzyme called monoamine oxidase A, or MAOA. Like colorblindness, the gene for MAOA lies on the X chromosome, explaining why only males in the family had the trait. Females have two X chromosomes—whereas males only have one—so even if a female inherits a faulty gene on one X chromosome, the other can compensate and she won't exhibit the trait (that female will *carry* the trait, however, and have a 50/50 chance of passing it on to a son). Lacking MAOA disposed these males to excessive rage, suggesting that MAOA might be critical for controlling aggression.

MAOA works by breaking down a class of neurotransmitter called monoamines—which include norepinephrine, dopamine, and serotonin—disabling them. When neurotransmitters spill out between nerve cells to communicate, they have to be cleared away again so that the next signal can be sent. Without enzymes and other means to remove neurotransmitters, the brain would feel a constant influx of signals, like a ringing in your ears that won't go away. The explosive behavior from some of the males in the Dutch family may have resulted from an incessantly high drive.

The mutation discovered by Brunner is extremely rare, but there are two distinct types of MAOA in the population, a fast one that breaks down neurotransmitters quickly and a slow one that allows neurotransmitters to remain active for longer. The type that you inherit could explain some individual differences in aggression. Another detail from the Dutch family might provide another clue as to how MAOA relates to aggression: a number of the violent flare-ups occurred following a stressful event. The two arsonists set fires following a death in the family. Low MAOA might interact with stress to produce explosive behavior.

Zalachenko's most violent outbursts occur following stressful situations, suggesting he may have had the slow version of MAOA. When the Russian government threatened to terminate his job overseas, he killed the messenger that brought him the news and he fled to Sweden. His worst beating of Agneta came after Lisbeth stabbed him.

Similarly, Niedermann lost his composure under pressure. Although he made a career using violence as a threat, he always managed to control himself enough so that he wouldn't attract the attention of the authorities. Being tough was his job, after all, and getting caught would have ended his career. When he finally risks being exposed, his violence escalates to an extreme and he murders police officers and even his cronies in the motorcycle gang in a calamitous fit. He may have inherited the slow MAOA from Zalachenko, short-circuiting his ability to calm his violent urges during crunch time.

Alive and Well

Lisbeth's lineage was not the only troubled one in the Millennium trilogy. The Vangers had a host of hateful relatives who had engaged in cruel activity over the years, including involvement with the Nazi party and years-long feuds with each other, not to mention the combined serial-killing by Gottfried and Martin Vanger. Like Lisbeth, Gottfried and Martin had violent streaks that appear to be caused by both nature and nurture. Gottfried was browbeaten with Nazi ideology by his father and then indoctrinated his son Martin into the same sadistic rituals. The Vangers may have possessed violent genes, but their brutal, pitiless upbringing helped bring their violent traits to the surface.

As noted earlier, though maltreatment increases the risk of violence, most maltreated children do not become violent. When Harriet Vanger fled Hedeby, she left behind Gottfried's violent legacy and found a new home and people who expressed love and affection. She went on to have a family of her own, free from the cruelty she grew up with.

As Blomkvist pieces together the Vanger's history in *The Girl with the Dragon Tattoo*, he says, "Talk about a dysfunctional family. Martin really didn't have a chance. He was there at the murder of Lea in Uddevalla in 1962. He was fourteen, for God's sake. His father raped him. Martin called it 'his duty.' The sexual assaults must have gone on for a long time. He was raised by his father."

"Bullshit," Salander says. "So you're assuming that Martin had no will of his own and that people become whatever they're brought up to be. Gottfried isn't the only kid who was ever mistreated. That doesn't give him the right to murder women. He made that choice himself. And the same is true of Martin."

Lisbeth believes in responsibility—that an individual has control over their actions and must accept the consequences. In many ways, she embodies the 85 percent of abused children who turn out well, the ones who give us hope.

Following Lisbeth's release from St. Stephen's and a few failed foster families, her court-assigned guardian, Holger Palmgren, cares for her, trusts her, and treats her with respect. He helps Lisbeth find a job and, importantly, he cultivates her self-control, reminding her to think about consequences before she acts. He trains her ability to slow down her impulses, to use the brakes. In a number of places in the Millennium trilogy, Lisbeth overcomes her violent urges in situations where she might have lashed out as a child. By following Palmgren's advice, she's able to pause before acting when provoked. Even when she has Niedermann nailed to the floor in a warehouse, where she could have personally taken revenge on the blond giant for putting Miriam and Paolo in the hospital, Salander chooses to leave the violence to the Svalvsjo MC. She uses the brakes.

The Lisbeth we meet at the beginning of *The Girl with the Dragon Tattoo* keeps people in her life at an emotional distance, sometimes painfully so. Even after Blomkvist becomes close enough to Lisbeth to discuss the abusive childhood of Martin, Harriet, and Gottfried, he doesn't learn that she had a troubled upbringing of her own. He also does not know that Lisbeth's hostility will lead her to avoid him for the next two years because she is afraid he will hurt her. In her eyes, few people give her a reason to be trusted.

Through the next years, Blomkvist helps Lisbeth overcome her family and legal problems, but he always keeps her secrets to himself. When she is finally declared competent by the state and given her freedom, Blomkvist comes knocking at her door, armed with bagels and espresso. She realizes that the choice to let him in—as well as to choose aggressive solutions or to seek another path—is hers.

After two years of avoiding Blomkvist, Lisbeth opens the door and lets him in. Lisbeth, like many other abused children, coped with her experiences and emerged in one piece, unbroken.

JOSHUA GOWIN has been writing about aggression since 2007 when a violent tragedy—the murder of a student by a family member—struck the community at the University of Texas Health Science Center at Houston (UT Health) where Josh was studying. He earned a Master's degree in 2009 for his work exploring the potential of a migraine medication, Zomig®, to block alcohol-induced aggressive behavior. The same year, he interned at *Psychology Today*, where he currently writes a blog about neuroscience titled "You, Illuminated." He is currently finishing his PhD at UT Health, studying how the cycle of violence may be caused by disruptions in the body's stress system as a result of child abuse.

L arsson probes the human psyche and rakes up some truly despicable characters from the murky depths—characters who are even more despicable for the way they are able to hide their true faces. Some of these characters are psychopaths—people who callously and repeatedly use other people for their own ends. Not all psychopaths, though, are easy to spot or in jail; some are successful "snakes in suits" (or jeans or skirts), hidden in plain sight. Here, Stephanie Mullins-Sweatt and Melissa Burkley explore the nature of psychopaths—and whether the Millennium trilogy characters with whom Lisbeth Salander grapples might meet the criteria for psychopathy.

MEN WHO HATE WOMEN BUT HIDE IT WELL

SUCCESSFUL PSYCHOPATHY IN THE MILLENNIUM TRILOGY

STEPHANIE N. MULLINS-SWEATT AND
MELISSA BURKLEY

Although the most memorable character from the Millennium trilogy is a woman, the series is really more about men. Bad men. "Men who hate women," as the original Swedish title for *The Girl with the Dragon Tattoo* suggests. So what is it about these men that readers find so engrossing? Unlike the majority of bad guys in film and literature, the villains in the Millennium trilogy are not one-dimensional. Many of the male characters are corrupt, sadistic, and psychopathic, and yet they are also highly successful businessmen and prominent politicians. In this way they don't fit the typical stereotype of a psychopath and that is what makes them so interesting, and also so terrifying. Larsson's characters force the reader to abandon their preconceived notions about what it means to be a psychopath and, in doing so, provides a glimpse of the evil that hides just below the surface of everyday people. By examining the psychopathic tendencies of the series' characters, we may better understand why we find these terrifying people so mesmerizing—at least when safely trapped on the pages of a book or the frames of a film.

What Is a Psychopath?

In order to explore whether any of the characters in the Millennium trilogy are actually psychopaths, we first need to analyze exactly what the word means—in common usage, and in psychology. What comes to mind when you hear the word "psychopath"? If you are like most people, you probably think of bloodthirsty maniacs like characters from *American Psycho* or *The Texas Chainsaw Massacre*. But how well do these media depictions represent the real world? The scientific research conducted on psychopathy suggests that this image of the uncontrollable, homicidal psychopath may be quite misleading.

According to psychologists, *psychopathy* is a personality disorder defined by distinct traits and behaviors. Robert Hare, a leading expert on psychopathy, describes such individuals as "social predators who charm, manipulate, and ruthlessly plow their way through life . . . Completely lacking in conscience and feeling for others, they selfishly take what they want and do as they please, violating social norms and expectations without the slightest sense of guilt or regret."[1] Like the media, psychology has also had a long-standing fascination with psychopaths. It was over 200 years ago that the psychiatrist Philippe Pinel first identified psychopathy, labeling the disorder "insanity without delirium." Over a century later, American psychiatrist Hervey Cleckley provided the first scientific-based description of psychopathy in his 1941 book, *The Mask of Sanity*. He identified a list of traits that psychopaths typically display, including superficial charm, unreliability, lack of remorse and shame, poor judgment, lack of major affective reactions, and failure to learn from experience. He characterized these individuals as "emotionally empty."

The Successful Psychopath

When asked to imagine a psychopath, most people think of serial killers like Jeffrey Dahmer and Charles Manson. Both are examples of men whose bloodlust was so strong it overwhelmed their concern for self-preservation and eventually led to their capture. However, this is not the most common psychopath.

While it is true that serial killers may possess psychopathic qualities, it is certainly not the case that all psychopaths are violent or that all violent people are psychopaths. In fact, criminal behavior is itself considered by many experts to be ancillary to the concept of psychopathy. There are anecdotal references in the psychological literature to psychopathic lawyers, professors, businessmen, and politicians who either have not committed crimes that would warrant an arrest or have successfully avoided being investigated, let alone arrested and convicted.

Such examples represent what psychologists refer to as "successful psychopaths." A *successful psychopath* is defined as a person

---

[1] R. D. Hare, *Without Conscience: The Disturbing World of the Psychopaths Among Us* (New York: Guilford Press, 2003).

who has the fundamental traits of psychopathy (like callousness, lack of empathy, and remorseless exploitation) but who, rather than being incarcerated, largely succeeds in his/her exploitation. As the title of Cleckley's book suggested, psychopaths can wear a "mask of sanity." On the outside, they may appear normal and engaging, even charismatic. But this mask conceals significant mental illness. Such individuals either commit acts that are considered immoral but not necessarily illegal or, in many instances, commit illegal crimes but are able to control their behavior enough to avoid being caught. Contrary to the image of a raging homicidal maniac, successful psychopaths may be calm, controlled, and highly successful in their careers. What is concerning is that successful psychopaths are hard to spot because they may appear charming and can manipulate others' opinions.

Stop for a minute and think about this definition: someone who is charming, manipulative, and ruthless. Odds are you know or have been acquainted with someone who comes close to this description, and yet that person likely is not a violent criminal or serving a jail sentence. In fact, research suggests that approximately one in twenty-five people (4 percent of the population) meet the criteria for psychopathy. This means that the majority of psychopaths are not locked up behind bars; they are walking among us. They may be our boss, our lawyer, or even our spouse. And odds are that they look like a model citizen on the outside: charismatic, successful, and accomplished in their career. In fact, many of these psychopathic traits (e.g., competitive, manipulative, ruthless) might be valuable assets within certain professions, such as law, politics, or business.

In books like *The Sociopath Next Door*, *Snakes in Suits*, and *Without Conscience*, experts provide chilling accounts of successful psychopaths living and working among us. These men and women are charming predators who abuse the trust of their colleagues, friends, and significant others, manipulate their bosses, and create chaos around them. However, there have been few empirical studies of these "successful psychopaths." There have been a number of studies examining psychopathic traits in college or community samples, but none purport to study individuals who are actually successful in their endeavors.

This lack of empirical work means that little is known about successful psychopaths. Unsuccessful psychopaths are more commonly studied, mostly because they are incarcerated and thus are easier to identify and access. But successful psychopaths are harder to study. People who are truly psychopathic and enjoy flourishing careers are unlikely to volunteer for psychological research. They work hard to cover their psychopathic tendencies and benefit from their true nature being hidden. Even if a psychologist was able to find a successful psychopath, it is likely that this person would either not be especially forthcoming or would refuse to participate in such research altogether. Because researchers cannot rely on volunteers for studies on successful psychopathy, they are forced to use other means.

So how are we to know what makes a successful psychopath different than an unsuccessful psychopath? Recently, one of the present authors (Mullins-Sweatt) and her collaborators set out to answer this question. To deal with the problem of recruitment, they relied on the idea that, although a successful psychopath may not be willing to participate in their study, it is quite possible that individuals who had close interaction with him/her would be able to provide useful information regarding the personality profile of this individual. The researchers surveyed people within professions likely to come in contact with psychopaths (both successful and unsuccessful), including forensic psychologists, attorneys who specialized in criminal law, and clinical psychology professors. Participants were asked if they had ever known anyone personally who they would characterize as a "successful psychopath" and, if so, to describe these persons in terms of traits commonly associated with psychopathy and the personality traits of the Five Factor Model (FFM).

The FFM is one of the most popular models of general personality functioning. According to this approach, the five domains of personality are extroversion versus introversion, agreeableness versus antagonism, conscientiousness versus undependability, neuroticism (or emotional instability) versus emotional stability, and being open versus being closed to new experiences. Each of the five broad domains also has six more specific facets. Previous research indicates that the unsuccessful or "prototypic" psychopath tends to be low in agreeableness—traits like distrust, manipulativeness, arrogance, oppositionality, and callousness—and low in conscientiousness— which includes such traits as disobliged, giving up easily, and being rash. However, Mullins-Sweatt and her colleagues hypothesized that successful psychopaths, while also rating low on agreeableness, would instead be rated as high in conscientiousness (i.e., competence, achievement striving, discipline, and deliberation). This allows the successful psychopath to have the discipline necessary to keep their dangerous impulses in check.

The results were as expected; successful psychopaths personally known by the forensic psychologists, attorneys, and professors were characterized as being high in such psychopathic traits as callousness, dishonesty, exploitativeness, and remorselessness, but they were also high in competence, achievement-striving, and self-discipline. Interestingly, this research method was able to identify individuals who were not only successful, but also held positions of high esteem and functioned quite well in society. For example, participants described successful psychopaths who were tenured faculty members, college deans, university presidents, police detectives, mayors, attorneys, physicians, and directors of medical centers.

These findings were consistent with a research study looking at the FFM description of Ted Bundy, a notorious serial rapist and murderer who successfully evaded the police for many years. Psychologists in the study described Bundy as psychopathic, and his FFM profile matched closely in some respects to the profile of a prototypic psychopath. The most notable aspect of Bundy's FFM profile, and something he shares with all psychopaths, was the consistent low ratings on all six facets of agreeableness, including traits like mistrustfulness, manipulativeness, deceitful, arrogance, and callousness. However, what made Bundy unique from other psychopaths was that he was described as being high, rather than low, in facets of conscientiousness. It is this high conscientiousness that helps explain how Bundy was able to avoid the law for so many years and how he was able to graduate college and gain acceptance into law school. Such controlled behaviors seem to go against the stereotypic impulsiveness of the prototypic psychopath.

So while the personality profile of every psychopath is someone who is dishonest, arrogant, and exploitative, what distinguishes prototypic psychopaths from successful ones is the latter's ability to keep their behavior in check by controlling their destructive impulses and preventing detection.

Psychopaths in the Millennium Trilogy

The preceding profile of the successful psychopath provides an excellent basis for the psychological analysis of some of the most interesting and vivid characters in the Millennium trilogy. We analyze several of these key characters in the next section, using personality profiles to distinguish between the unsuccessful and successful psychopaths, starting with the character we feel is least demonstrative of successful psychopathy (Alexander Zalachenko) and working our way up to the character we feel is most demonstrative of successful psychopathy (Martin Vanger). Each character discussion begins with an analysis of their low agreeableness (or antagonism) to establish their psychopathic traits. We look at their conscientiousness next to determine whether they are successful in their psychopathic endeavors. Finally, after focusing on the men in the Millennium series, we briefly turn our attention to the heroine Lisbeth Salander, and ask the question, "Would Salander qualify as a psychopath?"

Alexander Zalachenko: The Criminal Mastermind

Alexander Zalachenko (aka Zala) is Lisbeth Salander's father and the head of a seedy criminal enterprise involved in drug trafficking and the sex trade. Although he doesn't play a major role until the second book, he is a powerfully sadistic man. In *The Girl Who Played with Fire*, we learn that Zalachenko started as a counterespionage Russian agent during the Cold War. Because of Zalachenko's political connections and the wealth of information he could provide, the Swedish government gave him asylum and the secret police (SÄPO) protected him as an invaluable informant. After settling in Sweden, Zalachenko created his own crime syndicate and, because of his status, SÄPO turned a blind eye to his criminal activities.

Zalachenko is described as "a psychopath on a grand scale" in *The Girl Who Played with Fire*. Recall that unsuccessful psychopaths are low in both agreeableness and conscientiousness, whereas successful psychopaths are low in agreeableness but high in conscientiousness. In regards to Zalachenko's level of agreeableness, there are a number of examples from the book that suggest he is low in this trait. The reader is introduced to Zalachenko when Mikael Blomkvist, reporter for the *Millennium* newspaper, is following a story about the Swedish sex trade. Throughout this investigation, Zalachenko is mentioned as a mysterious man whose very name evokes terror. He is depicted as someone who is callous and unemotional, showing no attachment to others.

Those few people who do play a role in Zala's personal life suffer as a result. Zalachenko drank heavily and savagely abused Lisbeth's mother. When Salander was twelve, Zalachenko beat her mother so badly that he caused irreparable brain damage. Salander informs the police, but Zalachenko's connections with the SÄPO protect him from being investigated. Salander then takes the law into her own hands and sets him on fire. Unfortunately for Salander, this attempt on Zalachenko's life fails and he survives. When he is later reunited with Salander in *The Girl Who Played with Fire*, he shows no emotional connection to his daughter, telling her, "You look like shit . . . like a fucking whore. But you've got my eyes." Then he threatens to have her raped by her own half brother, shoots her in the head, and leaves her to die in a shallow grave.

Clearly, Zalachenko demonstrates the lack of conscience and compassion that is critical for the identification of a psychopathic. But is he successful or unsuccessful? For that answer, we must consider the evidence regarding his level of conscientiousness. Overall, Zalachenko seems to lack the self-discipline that is distinct to successful psychopaths. Unlike some of the other bad guys in the series who hold high-profile positions, Zalachenko lives in the shadows and is forced to make his living in the criminal underground. And when it comes to his criminal activities, while he is not sloppy, he takes few precautionary steps to hide his crimes. For instance, he hid the bodies of his victims in shallow graves on his property. He also failed to control his anger and violence when dealing with Salander's mother, which led to his being set on fire, losing his leg, and eventually becoming the target of Salander's revenge. For the most part, Zalachenko is lackadaisical when it comes to his hiding his transgressions, relying instead on the SÄPO to cover his bloody tracks. But in the end, even the SÄPO tires of his antics and orders him dead.

Thus, Zalachenko appears to be low in both agreeableness and conscientiousness. He is perhaps the character in the Millennium series *least* exemplary of successful psychopathy.

Nils Bjurman: The Sadistic Guardian

Nils Bjurman is the corrupt lawyer who takes over as guardian for Lisbeth Salander when her previous guardian becomes ill. Almost immediately after taking guardianship of Salander, he manipulates and abuses her. His first step is to take control of her finances by cutting her off from her bank account and putting her on an allowance. He then bribes her to perform oral sex in exchange for the release of her own money. To a cold-hearted man like Bjurman, this bribery makes sense because, as he explains in *The Girl with the Dragon Tattoo*, "It is better than a whore. She gets paid with her own money." His violence eventually escalates and he commits an extremely brutal act when he ties Salander up and rapes her over the course of eight hours. Clearly, Bjurman meets the criteria of low agreeableness.

His level of conscientiousness is less clear. When we meet Bjurman in the first novel, he appears to be an upstanding citizen who "paid more taxes than he owed, was a member of Greenpeace and Amnesty International, and donated money to the Heart and Lung Association." We also learn in *The Girl Who Played with Fire* that Bjurman previously had completed jobs for an elite group within the Secret Police, suggesting he was a highly competent man.

However, there are cracks in his ability to control himself, especially when it comes to Salander. When Bjurman first meets Salander, as noted in the second novel, "he had not been able to resist her. The laws, the most basic moral code, and his responsibility as her guardian— none of it mattered at all." This lack of self-discipline could be seen as evidence of low conscientiousness, but later Bjurman goes on to say, "Salander was a whore at the bottom of the social scale. It was risk-free. If she dared to protest to the Guardianship Agency, no one was going to believe her word against his." This line of thinking indicates he does have the capability to weigh the risks and consequences of his actions. Further, given his occupation, wealth, and that he appears to have a "spotless" reputation—Salander is unable to find any dirt on him using her typical methods—we can postulate that he likely has at least an average level of conscientiousness.

But Bjurman underestimates Salander and, as a result, his crimes are caught on tape. Salander uses the DVD recording of the rape to blackmail him, disrupting the balance of power that he had established early in their relationship. However, his response to Salander's blackmail demonstrates he does have the capacity for systematic and deliberate planfulness. Not wanting to get his hands dirty, Bjurman does not immediately act on his impulse and attack Salander himself. Instead he attempts to have her killed by seeking out someone who despises her as much as he does (i.e., Zalachenko). But here, too, he fails to fully understand the risks involved in the decision and, as a result, he is killed by the very people he hired to assassinate Salander.

Thus, Bjurman appears to be low in agreeableness but has an average level of conscientiousness. Although he has a good job, he is not as successful as other sadistic characters in the series. He also made several risky decisions that, in the end, led to his death and Salander's eventual exoneration. As a result, we believe Bjurman would be classified as a moderately successful psychopath.

Hans-Erik Wennerström: The Corrupt Businessman

The first book in the Millennium trilogy begins with the court case against Mikael Blomkvist, who is being sued for the libel and defamation of Hans-Erik Wennerström, a wealthy financier. Blomkvist, an investigative journalist and co-owner of *Millennium* magazine, claimed that Wennerström had used state funds intended for industrial investment for arms deals. Wennerström serves as a symbol of financial corruption that, in *The Girl Who Played with Fire*, is linked to "the heart of the international Mafia, including everything from illegal arms dealing and money laundering for South American drug cartels to prostitution in New York, and even indirectly for child sex trade in Mexico."

Wennerström is described throughout the book as "boastful," "an arrogant bastard," a "crook," and a "gangster." Furthermore, his actions demonstrate he is a ruthless CEO willing to use illegal and even violent means to build and protect his wealth. Blomkvist was threatened by Wennerström during his investigation, physically attacked, and duped into publishing a story that was a fake. However, we discover by the end of the first book the extent of Wennerström's actual crimes—"devoting himself to fraud that was so extensive it was no longer merely criminal—it was business"—and that his company "was like a clearing house" for the illegal weapons trade, money laundering for suspect enterprises in Colombia, and extremely unorthodox businesses in Russia.

It therefore is clear that Wennerström's character displays low agreeableness. He fails to experience shame or remorse for his heinous acts and instead appears to gain a sense of satisfaction from them. For example, Blomkvist discovered that Wennerström had impregnated a twenty-two-year-old waitress and, when she wanted compensation, his attorney had someone attempt to persuade her to have an abortion. When she resisted, she was held underwater in a bath until she agreed to leave Wennerström alone. "She had an abortion and Wennerström was pleased" (*The Girl with the Dragon Tattoo*). Such behaviors would be classified as facets of antagonism, as Wennerström was arrogant, manipulative, deceitful, and callous.

However, it is also clear that Wennerström displays a high level of conscientiousness. He was quite successful in his endeavors, as he avoided the detection of former employers, the government, and the police. His cleverness and ambition provided the fuel for the creation and management of a number of sham companies and bank accounts. To be this successful, Wennerström had to possess high levels of diligence, organization, and self-discipline.

In sum, Wennerström's behaviors exemplify a man who is low in agreeableness but high in conscientiousness. We therefore would categorize him as a successful psychopath.

Martin Vanger: The Serial-Killing CEO

Martin Vanger is perhaps the most talented chameleon in the Millennium trilogy. The reader first meets Martin in *The Girl with the Dragon Tattoo*, when Mikael Blomkvist is hired by Martin's uncle, Henrik Vanger, the former CEO of the Vanger Corporation. Henrik asks Blomkvist to investigate the disappearance of Henrik's niece, Harriet, an event that occurred forty years earlier. Blomkvist agrees to help and moves to the Vanger estate where he is introduced to Martin Vanger, the current CEO of the Vanger Corporation.

Throughout much of *The Girl with the Dragon Tattoo*, Martin appears pleasant, polite, and helpful. His great-uncle, Henrik, described him as a good man, willing to do the right thing, which was "a rare exception in the Vanger family." Blomkvist even notes that Martin "seems like a sympathetic person." Martin's uncle further described him as a weak, introverted, and melancholic child. He noted that he "had some troubled years in his teens, but straightened himself out at university." Another relative later indicated, "Martin has turned out to be a really fine person. If you had asked me thirty-five years ago, I would have said that he was the one in the family who needed psychiatric care . . . For many years Martin was so quiet and introverted that he was effectively antisocial *[sic]*."

Despite outward appearances, Martin has a very dark side. For decades, Martin successfully hid his extracurricular activities of kidnapping, raping, and murdering women. And the apple didn't fall far from the tree; Martin's father, Gottfried, ritualistically murdered at least eight women when Martin was a child. Like Martin, Gottfried appeared to be a good citizen and was charming and eloquent. He had a prominent position in the Vanger Corporation and was considered a rising star by the age of twenty-five. Within a few years, however, Gottfried's performance declined. He drank heavily and was absent from work for long periods of time. When he would return to work, it was to travel around the country. It was on these trips where he would find women to kill. When Martin Vanger was fourteen years old, his father took him along to observe the rape and murder of a young woman. Two years later, Martin assisted his father with another murder. Following Gottfried's death, Martin continued to stalk, torture, and murder young women. This pattern of sadistic violence provides indisputable evidence that Martin (like his father, Gottfried) is very low in agreeableness.

However, Martin was "more cunning" and "shrewder" than his father, meaning his level of conscientiousness was much higher. Each time Gottfried killed someone, it led to a police investigation where he may have been caught or the crimes may have been connected to one another. Martin, on the other hand, was very careful about selecting his victims. Martin's victims—immigrants, prostitutes, social outcasts, drug addicts—were vulnerable women unlikely to be reported missing. This is what makes Martin different from his father and some of the other sadists in the book series, like Bjurman. Whereas Bjurman rapes the woman he is most interested in (Salander), Martin controls his urges and purposely stalks women who are least likely to get him caught. Martin's cautious behavior allows him to successfully keep his "mask of sanity" in place.

Martin even spoke directly to his own high level of conscientiousness in *The Girl with the Dragon Tattoo* when he reported that the kidnappings were "not done on impulse—those kinds of kidnappers invariably get caught. It's a science with thousands of details that I have to weigh. I have to identify my prey, map out her life, who is she, where does she come from, how can I make contact with her, what do I have to do to be alone with my prey without revealing my name or having it turn up in any future police investigation?" Martin was so organized and systematic, and the killings occurred so discreetly, thanks to him dumping the bodies at sea, that no one was even aware that a serial killer was at work.

Interestingly, Martin isn't even driven to kill; he is only driven to rape. But he realizes that leaving his victims alive puts him at risk, so he turns to murder. As Martin states when confronted by Blomkvist at the end of *The Girl with the Dragon Tattoo*, "I'm more of a serial rapist than a serial murderer . . . most of all, I'm a serial kidnapper. The killing is a natural consequence—so to speak—because I have to hide my crime."

Thus, of all of the characters in the Millennium series, Martin Vanger provides the best example of successful psychopathy. He also serves as an important reminder to the reader that, if we focus too much on the brutal crazed killer that we so often see in the media, we run the risk of being manipulated and swindled, or worse, by the psychopath right in front of us.

Lisbeth Salander: The Antisocial Antihero

No character in the Millennium trilogy is as fascinating or complex as the female protagonist, Lisbeth Salander. Her behavior, her lifestyle, and even her appearance has led some readers to ask, "Is Salander a psychopath?"

Many of Salander's behaviors suggest low agreeableness. For instance, Salander shows complete disregard for societal rules or norms and engages in behaviors that are both antisocial and illegal. Salander's occupation in *The Girl with the Dragon Tattoo* is that of a private investigator, and one reason why she is so skilled at this position is because she is a genius computer hacker. She also engages in a number of other significant crimes, including tax evasion, identity theft, fraud, and stealing approximately three billion kronor ($75 million) from Wennerström. In addition to her criminal activities, Salander is also quite violent. Throughout her childhood, Salander was in trouble for hitting classmates who teased her and, when she was twelve years old, she attempted to kill her father by throwing a firebomb in his car. Salander "never forgot an injustice, and by nature she was anything but forgiving" (*The Girl with the Dragon Tattoo*). Finally, Salander is distrustful of everyone and is noncompliant, displaying a complete lack of regard for authority like the police and government.

And just like the successful psychopaths she goes up against in the series, Salander is clever and conscientious. The trilogy is replete with examples of the patience and planning she uses to exact revenge against the men that have harmed her. For instance, when Bjurman first assaulted her in his office, Salander considered taking the letter opener from his desk and attacking him. Instead, she chooses to do nothing, thinking "impulsive actions led to trouble, and trouble could have unpleasant consequences. She never did anything without first weighing the consequences"(*The Girl with the Dragon Tattoo*). Following her rape, Salander spent time planning ways to kill Bjurman. She methodically decided against guns, knives, bombs, and poisons before deciding it might be to her benefit to keep him alive to grant her independence. These are the behaviors of someone with a high degree of discipline and self-control.

With her proclivity for extreme violence and seeming lack of remorse, it is easy to see why people might consider Salander a successful psychopath. Ultimately, however, we do not feel this is an accurate label for her. Although Salander is antagonistic and violent, she doesn't appear to lack a conscience, which is the hallmark trait of a psychopath. While she may not always follow society's rules, she does have her own set of moral principles that abide by a code of right and wrong. Most notably, she only attacks men who have ruthlessly hurt her or other vulnerable women. Of people like Martin and Gottfried Vanger, she says, "If I had to decide, men like that would be exterminated, every last one" (*The Girl with the Dragon Tattoo*). Salander's moral code leaves no room for compromise. When a man hurts a woman, she believes he deserves to die or be punished so that he can't repeat his crimes (e.g., the tattoo she puts on Bjurman). In this way, she poses an ethical dilemma for the readers. But whatever we think of her moral code, we feel compelled to admire her desire to protect those vulnerable to exploitation.

Her role as an avenger also demonstrates another important aspect of her personality: she seems to care for people other than herself. In general, psychopaths lack emotional connections with others and simply see the people around them as pawns. While difficult to see through her antagonistic exterior, it seems that Salander experiences concern for others, especially for women in her country who are exploited and abused.

For these reasons, Lisbeth Salander would not meet the criteria of a psychopath. And in this way, her character reveals the complexity involved with the scientific analysis of psychopaths. Just because someone is a psychopath, like Wennerström, doesn't mean he or she is a murderer, and just because someone is a murderer (or attempts murder), like Salander, doesn't mean he or she is a psychopath.

STEPHANIE N. MULLINS-SWEATT, PhD (University of Kentucky), is an assistant professor of clinical psychology at Oklahoma State University. Her research uses general personality models to conceptualize personality pathology, bridging the basic science of general personality research to the clinical understanding of personality disorders. Her research on successful psychopathy has been featured on *BBC Today*.

MELISSA BURKLEY, PhD (The University of North Carolina Chapel Hill), is an assistant professor of social psychology at Oklahoma State University. Her research focuses on stereotypes and prejudice. Her research has been featured on *Oprah Radio* and in *Cosmopolitan, Marie Claire, Men's Health,* and several other outlets. She also writes a blog for *Psychology Today* entitled "The Social Thinker."

E ven before her time at St. Stefan's, Lisbeth Salander was a troubled youth—for what appears, to even amateur analysis, to be good reason. But was Larsson accurate in his depiction of Lisbeth's response to the traumatic events of her childhood? Based on decades of work with troubled youth and survivors of trauma, Hans Steiner tackles this question while also taking on the tough task of diagnosing Lisbeth Salander. Does she have posttraumatic stress disorder? A dissociative disorder? Any disorder at all?

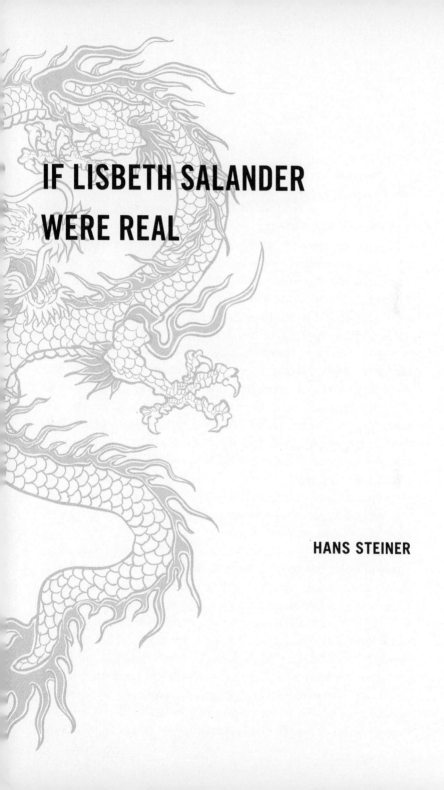

IF LISBETH SALANDER
WERE REAL

HANS STEINER

F ew characters in recent fiction have captured the imaginations of so many in so short a time as Lisbeth Salander, one of the two protagonists of the Millennium trilogy by Stieg Larsson. A quick web search of her name turns up 1,410,000 results in 0.11 seconds. Comments range from adolescent idolatry to serious and protracted discussions as to whether Lisbeth in fact is a real person. The rapid production of three Swedish films summarizing the three volumes and their current American remake also supports this contention, which raises the question: What it is about a gun-slinging, boxing, chain-smoking, bisexual, seemingly fearless Gothic princess whose range of emotions is severely constricted that touches the hearts, desires, and imagination of so many? This effect is even more surprising if one considers that the books tend to be dark in their mood and describe a series of events that are clearly outside the range of normative human experience. They are usually of a violent, deeply perturbing nature, and many of these unsettling events are even perpetrated by Lisbeth herself. What is it about a vengeful, tattooed, multiply pierced, diminutive, boyish-in-build character—who is sometimes suspected of suffering from Asperger's syndrome and is described as paranoid schizophrenic—that elicits our sympathy, interest, and even passion?

There are many possible answers to this question. The most interesting ones for our purpose lie in the deeper psychology and psychiatry of the character, which will be laid out in some detail in the main body of this essay. But another comment might be helpful as well, connecting Lisbeth's story to one of the oldest Nordic myths, which provides the narrative scaffold for this trilogy. It is the story of Brynhildr and Sigurdr, straight from the oldest Norse epic, the *Edda*. The story has been told many times in different forms throughout the Nordic and Germanic countries over the centuries, the latest and perhaps even best known permutation being Richard Wagner's *The Ring of the Nibelungs*. The Edda is essentially a story of a rebellious, powerful virgin warrior woman (Brynhildr) who stands up against a conspiracy of elders and more powerful gods to protect an innocent, gallant, idealistic, but vulnerable hero (Sigurdr). You almost can hear "The Ride of the Valkyries" play in volume one of the Millennium series as Lisbeth rides her own racing motorbike in pursuit of her torturers; and again in volume two, riding the Harley of a biker she has just incapacitated. Mikael Blomkvist is her Sigurdr although, for complex reasons to be laid out below, she has a highly ambivalent attachment to and admiration for him. I am suggesting that, at least in part, the attraction of her character to so many is related to this ancient script, one whose popularity never waned in the centuries the story has been told (the poisonous appropriation of the myth by the Nazis notwithstanding).

To get to the heart of the matter, I don't think there are many readers or admirers of Lisbeth who think she has paranoid schizophrenia, as her psychiatrist Teleborian contends throughout the volumes (in most detail during Lisbeth's trial for murder in volume three). He does so to neutralize her upon the request from the Swedish authorities involved in the conspiracy around Lisbeth's violent father, Zalachenko. Her father's violent acts were ignored and hushed up by the authorities in order to preserve Zalachenko's deep knowledge of the Soviet Secret Service for counterespionage purposes benefitting the Swedish government. Teleborian himself probably does not believe that Lisbeth is a paranoid schizophrenic, nor does Ekstrom, the prosecuting attorney in volume three. Both men are acting as pawns for the secret subgroup of governmental espionage agents. Yes, Lisbeth does think people are after her and are threatening her life, a symptom often found in paranoid schizophrenia. But, as is evident throughout the trilogy and especially in volumes two and three, all that is for very good reasons. Her beliefs are hardly false or bizarre in character, as they often would be with someone who has paranoid schizophrenia ("Martians are here to take me away," for example). Some comments by readers on the internet muse as to whether Lisbeth suffers from Asperger's syndrome, a disorder that presents as a combination of impaired social behaviors and a pervasive oddity of emotional responses, especially to stressful events in the context of normal or even superior intelligence. Hans Asperger—the physician who first identified the constellation of symptoms that bear his name—was in fact my pediatrics professor when I studied medicine at the University of Vienna in the 1960s. He introduced us to many patients he called "autistic psychopaths" (*autistic* because of their odd social interactions and insensitivity to subtle social cues, and *psychopath* because he meant to indicate that their problems represented significant pathology of the psyche[1]). The term Asperger's syndrome was not coined until much later, in recognition of his contributions to modern psychiatry.[2] I can say with some confidence that Lisbeth, as she is described throughout the trilogy, does not resemble these patients, many of whom I have personally examined during my training and in the forty years of practice afterwards.[3]

But I have in fact met several Lisbeths in my long career as a forensic psychiatrist in juvenile justice settings in Austria and America and, by extension, in the many collaborative studies I have performed in Germany, Russia, The Netherlands, and Belgium.[4] The cluster of symptoms Lisbeth exhibits is all too common in youths who have grown up in abusive families and environments devoid of support and structure, and with uncertain access to medical and mental health clinics and practitioners.

Her story is unfortunately also quite typical in the sense that, for a variety of reasons, it often happens that authorities do not act to protect these youths, even after appropriate reports have been filed by teachers, doctors, or nurses. Social services visit, but once they find out that the perpetrator is a professional of some repute and standing in the community, they back off and do not protect children. This is doubly true when assaults are committed by a father who is a police officer,

---

[1] The definition of psychopath has changed since.

[2] D. R. Walker, A. Thompson, L. Zwaigenbaum, et al., "Specifying PDD-NOS: A Comparison of PDD-NOS, Asperger Syndrome and Autism," *Journal of the American Academy of Child and Adolescent Psychiatry* 43 (2004).

[3] *Editors' Note*: For additional opinions on whether Lisbeth Salander has Asperger's, see essays in this volume by Bernadette Schell and Robin Rosenberg

[4] H. Steiner, et al., "Psychopathology, Trauma and Delinquency: Subtypes of Aggression and Their Relevance For Understanding Young Offenders," *Child and Adolescent Psychiatry and Mental Health . . .*011).

a prison guard, a professor at Stanford University, or a politician, to name some professions. I have had adolescent patients who killed their fathers who were ministers, prison guards, and professors at the most reputable universities in the country because they saw no other way out of their dilemma. Calling Child Protective Services not only did not protect them from sexual and physical assaults, but in fact put them at higher risk for harm as the perpetrator intensified his attacks on the child in rage-filled vengeance. What sets Lisbeth's case apart is the link between her abuse and a pervasive and powerful systematic political/espionage conspiracy outlined in this trilogy. I have never encountered such a scenario, but it clearly is not beyond human imagination.

What precisely are the symptoms described and displayed in this story that support the contentions that Lisbeth has *posttraumatic stress disorder* and *dissociative disorder*? These are the most salient diagnoses to be given to Lisbeth based on the novel and film descriptions of her character, her behavior, her developmental information, and her history, and both are related to her extensive and intensive traumatization growing up and after her commitment to the Swedish juvenile justice system. The depiction of her symptoms is very impressive in the Swedish version of the movies, and Noomi Rapace's acting in this regard is superb. Posttraumatic stress disorder (PTSD) involves significant reexperiencing of a traumatic event and avoidance of reminders of it; dissociative disorders involve disruptions in the normally integrated functions of a person's emotions, thoughts, and identity. This profile of likely diagnoses is extremely prevalent in juvenile delinquents.[5] The first criterion for PTSD is that the patient has experienced an event that has a potentially traumatic impact. There is overwhelming evidence that this is the case for Lisbeth: she was put in restraints as a teenager for 381 days while on a psychiatric unit; she witnessed her father brutalizing her mother on repeated occasions, ultimately resulting in her mother being brain damaged; she is forced to perform fellatio on her guardian; she is raped by the guardian while shackled to a bed; she is shot by her father and buried

---

[5] H. Steiner, et al., "Psychopathology, Trauma and Delinquency: Subtypes of Aggression and Their Relevance for Understanding Young Offenders," *Child and Adolescent Psychiatry and Mental Health* . . .011).

alive by her half brother, etc. Any one of these events would fulfill the necessary first criterion (criterion A) for PTSD. And one suspects that the list is not complete, given the pervasive disregard her father demonstrated for Lisbeth and her mother, as shown during their encounter in volume two.

The second criterion for PTSD is the presence of various forms of reliving the traumatic events, commonly through flashbacks, dreams and nightmares, and reexperiences. Again, there are multiple examples throughout the trilogy that Lisbeth is suffering from triggered reexperiencing of past events. One of the most graphic and clear examples of a flashback is the description of her sadistic psychiatric confinement in the prologue of volume two. The repetitive nature of the description, with its stark, emotionally etched elements is typical of flashbacks in which a person relives traumatic events as if they were occurring right then and there. In addition, Lisbeth repeatedly awakens from slumber in a terrorized state, having just had a nightmare where she relives the previous sexual assaults throughout the trilogy. A good example for a triggered reliving, one that actually leads her to violence, is found in volume two when she encounters a group of four drunk men who verbally taunt her. She quickly rises to the challenge and fights with them, successfully saving herself from harm. For someone who does not have such an extensive trauma history at the hands of men, the most efficient way to cope with the situation would have been to simply ignore then men and rapidly walk away; their inebriated state hardly made them efficient pursuers. The fact that Lisbeth engages them in a fight when she is outnumbered and at some risk to come to harm links her behavior to previous traumatizations. She interprets the situation too narrowly in that she sees no alternative to fighting them, indicating a trauma-driven kindling of the threat detection system in her brain from alertness to flight to fight. This type of reaction is often found in repeatedly traumatized individuals. Fighting these drunk men is a less adaptive solution than simple flight/extrication. Another example of reexperiencing is her emotionally muted reaction to meeting Teleborian again in volume three as he attempts to gather information for his psychiatric followup report. Lisbeth recoils in stubborn silence, but she dissociates when he mentions that she bit his index finger in one of their initial encounters (beautifully acted by Noomi Rapace in the Swedish version of the film when her gaze unfocuses and she stares into the distance without any emotional expression while some images of that situation are depicted). And while in the ICU after her father attempts to murder her, she has a flood of chaotic recollections of past abuses and violations, some triggered by the smell of aftershave.

Another aspect of Lisbeth's symptoms, based on new findings in my research on PTSD, also deserves attention: the rapidity with which she translates feeling threatened to becoming aggressive. This speed is remarkable and tells us that she possesses a propensity to become enraged and ready to fight, a characteristic often found in victims of prolonged and systematic abuse.[6]

Emotionally hot aggression—that is aggressive acts that are triggered by strong and predominantly negative emotions, such as fear, anger, and irritability—is an adaptive response to overwhelming threats that cannot be avoided, and this is often the case for victims of abuse. If the very person you are dependent on for survival is also your worst attacker and tormentor, there is no escaping the attack; you must fight to save your life. When animals and humans feel there is no escape from attack, there is a shift in their response from flight to fight, the final step of activation of the fear detection system. In such cases, there is a rapid activation of aggression to actual (or perceived) threats that becomes quicker and potentially maladaptive the more often it is triggered. Impulsive, defensive, emotionally aggressive acts often result in the most dire consequences for the person fending off the perpetrator, often far worse than alternative outcomes had the reaction been more carefully and slowly considered. For example, Lisbeth shows some remarkable disregard for her own safety as she pursues the vindication of her mother and the death of her abusive father in volume two. She enters her father's house, knowing him to be armed and extremely dangerous. She also knows about her half brother's presence and the fact that he will not hesitate to carry out any harmful action against her, or anyone else for that matter. Still, she proceeds without backup and protection. Even when given an

---

[6] J. Blair, et al., "The Neuroscience of Aggression," *The Principles and Practice of Forensic Child and Adolescent Psychiatry* (2009).

opportunity to escape, she persists in her original plan to kill her father despite clear and present danger, i.e., her half brother and his large armamentarium of weapons.

Lisbeth's single-mindedness and extreme reliance on herself should come as no surprise to us given the fact that she has little trust in anyone, especially not those in authority as they have only harmed her in the past. Salander's father, guardian, and psychiatrist have tormented and betrayed her, just to name a few. However, her refusal to attend to self-preservation in the face of extreme danger is unusual and supports the notion that, once her ire is ignited, there are few things that will get her to alter her course of action, even if that means that she is potentially in harm's way. As one of the girls in my care—a girl who murdered her father during one of the times he raped her—once said to me as we discussed the shooting: "You are burning up inside, and you are going to put that bullet in the fucker's head if it's the last thing you will ever do. You just don't give a shit anymore."

The third criterion for PTSD is also clearly fulfilled: Lisbeth exhibits persistent avoidance and numbing, as evidenced in her markedly diminished interest in significant, simple everyday pursuits of happiness such as shopping, recreation, or socializing. We get a rare scene of her relaxing in a bathtub, relishing the warm water pouring over her head, in volume three. But as a rule, we are not told of or shown many such activities. Lisbeth is on a mission: to gather evidence against her tormentors and the exploiters of women, to aid those that are helpful to her in this process, and to plan and execute her revenge herself. She also exhibits, again throughout all three volumes, a profound sense of estrangement from others, even if they have been uniquely helpful to her. Her girlfriend Miriam Wu complains in volume two that Lisbeth doesn't contact her for a year and then shows up unexpectedly, immediately wanting to have sex. At the end of volume one, Salander discovers she has fallen in love with Blomkvist. She then sees him on the street with Erica Berger and, instead of confronting him or discussing the situation, she decides to shut Blomkvist out of her life completely.

The final criterion for PTSD is the presence of increased physiological arousal, and Lisbeth shows many of the symptoms of this. Her sleep is labored and fitful; she has many outbursts of anger and seems chronically irritable; she is hypervigilant at all times and rarely gets caught off-guard. This is a person that has lived with significant threats for extended periods of time and, at any given moment, she is ready to go into survival mode. She is tense like a coiled spring, ready to take action as needed, either electronically or physically. The most relaxing actions she seems capable of are the chain smoking of cigarettes or a metal-throbbing ride on a powerful motorbike. These are the only times that her otherwise ever-present frown disappears temporarily.

Although we are not told the exact duration of any of these symptoms of classic PTSD, it is fairly safe to assume that they have been tormenting Lisbeth for much longer than the one month required by diagnostic criteria. In fact, it seems that she has been suffering from these symptoms for several years. Symptoms such as these, of such duration and following such extreme stressors perpetrated by people of trust, raise an additional question. Could Lisbeth have a dissociative disorder of some kind? The evidence we have from clinical work and clinical studies is that dissociative disorder often appears after many months and years of traumatization, a kind of final stage psychopathology in victims of prolonged and profound abuse. Although dissociative disorder and chronic PTSD are thought to be distinct diagnoses, they both are thought to be part of the psychiatric trauma spectrum.

Such disorders have at their core the profound separation of emotion and thinking. These disorders can affect memory and recall, and result in prolonged alterations of consciousness (labeled fugue states) and the false beliefs that events have been experienced before (déjà vu). In their most extreme form, they can result in a complete fragmentation of character, known as multiple personality. These problems occur in patients who have been exposed to a steady accumulation of trauma, happening in a crushing sequence, with no chance for reprieve in between assaults. In the wake of significant stress, all humans are capable of dissociative responses—the separation of normally integrated thought, emotion, and action. A good example would be removing oneself from the scene of an automobile accident to find help while severely injured, yet subsequently having no recall at all for having done so. By putting on hold one's emotional reactions—which in such a situation would be complete terror—one then puts into place automatic behaviors, which allow one to extricate oneself from danger, even when incapacitated. Dissociation of thought from emotion is a highly adaptive mechanism that aids in our survival.

After Lisbeth is shot in the head by her father in volume two, she reaches up to examine her head and finds blood. She also realizes—without any further alarm—that she is touching her brain tissue exposed by the wound. She goes on autopilot and hot aggression comes to the fore: she avoids the attentions of Ronald Niedermann, her half brother, and manages to almost kill her father with an axe. She subsequently attempts to shoot Ronald and misses, but calculates enough to preserve one shot should he reappear: an example of both a dissociative response and hot aggression. All these complex lifesaving behaviors are possible because she has divorced her emotions from her actions. However, generally speaking, in dissociative states, we may be capable of performing complex actions in the service of survival and avoidance of danger, but these actions are not completely consciously steered. The evolutionary purpose of dissociation is to enable the victim to engage in survival automatisms—reflexive, instinctual behavior—in the face of extreme arousal. Dissociation usually recedes and the full impact of what has just happened hits the victim with great force. At this point, a reworking—that is a conscious reexamination and reshaping of the situation—becomes possible, and the person can begin to integrate the incomprehensible and dissociated elements of the experience, and begin healing from trauma. In cases such as Lisbeth's, where there is and has been an almost uninterrupted stream of stress and trauma, dissociation never stops and reintegration of thoughts and emotion, and therefore healing, is not possible. In such circumstances, the link between behavior, thoughts, and emotions, found in normally functioning humans, becomes ever more disrupted; emotions assume a life of their own, behavioral automatisms—such as fighting or fleeing—are incongruous with situations and life demands. The patient has lost his or her emotional compass, without which it is very difficult to navigate life. Love is danger, danger is passion, threat is challenge, etc.—and everyday events can elicit extraordinary behavior.[7]

---

7 B. Plattner, et al., "State and Trait Emotions in Delinquents Delinquent Adolescents," *Child Psychiatry and Human Development* 38 (2007).

It would appear that Lisbeth was very much exposed to such sequences, and they have resulted in a special set of symptoms: the increasing incongruence between what she feels and what she thinks. For the external observer, such symptoms make the person appear quirky and odd under the best of circumstances, and bizarre and offensive when taken to the extreme. "I am also an Alien", says Lisbeth's T-shirt in *The Girl with The Dragon Tattoo*, hinting in this way that she certainly feels estranged from herself and others, and that she knows how she affects others. And some of her reactions to events are very difficult to comprehend, as her emotional expressivity (or lack thereof) is at odds with her behavior. A good example is her coming into Mikael's room and immediately having sex with him, without much lead in of any romantic sort. She seems to respect him and to be falling in love with him but, shortly after having consumed her passion in his arms, she essentially expects him to leave the bed—not usually what one wants after a tender encounter. When he refuses to do so, she turns her back and tersely comments that she wants to sleep. We are only able to understand fully such sequences when, in the film version of *The Girl with the Dragon Tatttoo*, Lisbeth visits her mother in a nursing home and they discuss how men are problematic. Their conversation is essentially about how dangerous it is to fall in love, and therefore how such an action should be avoided. This sequence—from extreme attraction to reclusive pulling back and avoidance, along with the disavowal of the emotional significance of one's relationships—often characterizes the relationships of survivors of extreme abuse. Needless to say, such relationships are extremely taxing for any partner, and almost unavoidably lead to profound problems with intimacy and commitment. Such relationships can appear extremely exploitative in character, almost like the behavior of a psychopath who disregards the rights and feelings of others and does not experience empathy.

However, readers are reminded of Lisbeth's humanity during the extremely tender encounters she has with people whom she feels grateful toward and not threatened by. In her encounters with her mother and her first guardian, whom she lovingly feeds in his nursing home following his stroke and incapacitation, there is a warmth and humorous accommodation. Clearly, Lisbeth is capable of human succor and of aiding those in need, a trace that is completely absent from psychopathic individuals.

Another essential ingredient to Lisbeth's character is her extraordinary talent in terms of electronics, programming, and web-based activities. It is not clear how exactly she acquired all these skills, given that she spent much of her formative years in juvenile forensic/ psychiatric environments—places not traditionally thought of as hotbeds of advanced education. Chances are Lisbeth is most likely an autodidact, meaning she has acquired many of her considerable skills in computing and programming on her own initiative. The protective anonymity of the web is significant in this context. One can assume multiple identities (Wasp, for one), enter the most intimate spheres of other people's lives (the porn stash of her psychiatrist Teleborian, for instance, in volume three) without ever becoming visible, tangible, or traceable. Clearly, Lisbeth is a woman of superior natural intelligence, given the electronic feats she is capable of. The medium of the web fits her needs, and sustains her by giving her a livelihood as a researcher for Armansky's agency. It is this talent and singularity of purpose that has also led people to associate her problems with Asperger's syndrome. As I said above, though, such a diagnosis is not very likely.

Her passionate interest in these matters can be brought in line with her deep-seated desire for revenge on those who have wronged her and other women (as in the case of sex trafficking in volume one); her need for anonymous distance in order to plan her predatory attacks on her tormentors; and her desire to dissociate herself from her passions. She attempts to disown her growing attachment to Mikael; her response to his assistance is only to send a (rather terse) message via email: "thank you for being my friend." It would be very hard for her to say this while looking Mikael into the eye and touching his hand. The closest she can come to that gesture is having athletic sex after they both conquer one of the many obstacles on their pathway to justice. Her attitude of "above all, do not show you care" has served her well as she struggled to survive the many assaults on her. Falling in love, becoming dependent, and feeling vulnerable to someone are the ultimate threats to Lisbeth. She would much rather be alone, roaming the globe or in an unfurnished apartment, relying on the one person she can trust: herself. She has no use for a psychiatrist, a fact she makes amply clear in volume three when she flat out refuses to collaborate with her lawyer's request to submit to a neutral psychiatric evaluation to counterbalance Teleborian's destructive opinions. She persists in this refusal despite the risk that she will be found incompetent in court and have her personal rights removed for a long time. Rather than cooperate verbally, she instead provides evidence that completely discredits her pursuers, obtained by means of a hidden camera that recorded her victimization and humiliation. She chooses the more painful but direct and irrefutable way of proving her innocence: objective evidence of Bjurman raping her.

Ultimately, one finds oneself cheering her on in her pursuit of revenge and justice, and no doubt this sentiment also contributes significantly to the pervasive interest in this unusual character. It is extremely satisfying to see somebody so downtrodden and threatened rise to and transcend the challenges posed to her.

There are of course some details of the story that would be useful to have to satisfy my psychiatric need for completeness. For instance, it is not clear what happened to her twin sister or how Lisbeth resolves the relationship—or absence of one—with her. It is likely that there was "twinning"—the existence of a privileged relationship between the sisters—which could have been a source of strength for Lisbeth even though her sister is said to have adored their father. A clean split between the sisters is unlikely. Chances are that, in the context of the extreme domestic violence described in Lisbeth's home, Camilla herself was the target of physical, sexual, and emotional abuse. We have little information about this, though, only hints.

Other details of the story are somewhat hard to embrace and endorse completely. Teleborian is a one-dimensional, despicable evil-doer. It is hard to imagine he would have risen to such prominence in a state system like Sweden's, which ranks among the most social, best organized, and best managed in the world. The use of physical restraints in health care settings is very carefully regulated and supervised by state agencies in the United States, and no doubt in Sweden. Restraints are administered by nursing staff and floor staff. It is highly unlikely that they would have passively stood by and watched such flagrant abuse for over two years. There also must have been other doctors in the system who would cover for Teleborian at the hospital during his absences, and such temporary coverage often results in shedding light on abusive practices. The extraordinary circumstances surrounding Lisbeth's case, especially given her father's status, help justify the extreme portrayal of Teleborian. But, in all my work in juvenile justice settings over several decades, I have not encountered such predatory malice. I have encountered ineptitude, disinterest, uninvolvement, and passivity, and ultimately this story could have been told in such a context, with the advantage of added realism and plausibility.

The books, and to some extent the films, use lurid, sexually charged images somewhat gratuitously in my opinion. The violence in some of the scenes is profound. I found it very disturbing that the films in particular showed such graphic details of the axe attacks in volume two when Lisbeth battles her brother and father and is grievously wounded herself. To see the axe go into her father's head and leg did not make a point that was not made already. It is all the more surprising to have such a story and movie come from Sweden, a country that censored violence in the '60s while showing sexual content freely. This story and its films certainly are not in line with this admirable tradition.

Despite these problems, the story is well told overall. The psychology of the survivor is imparted with a great amount of insight and empathy. As well, the trilogy stimulates thought, tells a gripping, dark tale, and has a mostly satisfying ending: the evildoers get their just comeuppance. We are deprived of the moment where Lisbeth sinks into Mikael's open arms, dissolves into tears, and professes her eternal gratitude and love for him. And that is a good thing, because it would be completely out of line with her character. She is doomed to be a lonely she-wolf who will experience happiness in only the most fleeting moments—unless of course she starts psychiatric treatment now. And somehow I have a feeling that, had Stieg Larsson had the chance to write a fourth volume, he would not have taken this tale in that direction. Valkyries die alone, on the top of mountains, sur-

rounded by a ring of fire.

HANS STEINER was born in Vienna, Austria, and received his doctor medicinae universalis (MD) from the Medical Faculty of the University of Vienna, Austria, in 1972. Currently, Dr. Steiner is Professor Emeritus (Active) of psychiatry and behavioral sciences, child psychiatry, and human development at the Stanford University School of Medicine, and guest professor at Medical University of Vienna. He also is a founding member of The Pegasus Physicians at Stanford, a group of doctors who write creatively. More detailed information about Dr. Steiner can be found on his website, www.hanssteiner.com.

We like to root for the underdog. We like to see our fictional heroes redeemed and to see the truth prevail. Larsson taps into these readerly desires by positioning Lisbeth Salander as a woman who has been grievously wronged. One of the facets of her life that provokes the most outrage is the injustice she suffers in the legal system, the very institution charged with upholding the rights of individuals, protecting the innocent from harm, and serving out justice. Here, forensic psychologist Marisa Mauro gives Lisbeth what she has lacked for so long—a fair shake in the court of law. Mauro uses the evidence gleaned from the Millennium trilogy to complete the kind of evaluation of Lisbeth that an expert witness would perform and submit to the court. Her findings: fascinating.

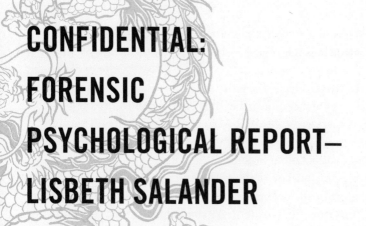

CONFIDENTIAL: FORENSIC PSYCHOLOGICAL REPORT— LISBETH SALANDER

MARISA MAURO

Courts of law oftentimes come upon questions that cannot be adequately addressed by the efforts of the legal system alone. On these occasions, the court may allow the use of experts to assist the triers of fact—the judge and jury—in understanding information or evidence that is beyond the knowledge of a reasonable person. Expert witnesses are special in that they may provide opinion in their testimony. This is in contrast to laypersons that are limited to recounting direct observations.

An expert's journey to the witness stand often begins when they are retained by the defense or prosecution for the purpose of aiding their case. Other times experts are appointed through court order or by agreement of the parties. Prior to offering expert testimony, individuals must be qualified as an expert by virtue of their knowledge, skills, experience, training, or education.

Psychologists and related professionals have become permanent fixtures within the legal system. As expert witnesses, they may be called upon to provide testimony relating to a variety of matters at the intersection of mental health and the law, including such issues as competency to stand trial, mental state at the time of the offense, treatment recommendations, and risk assessments.

All experts must take care not to become a hired gun, a hazard that may be avoided by simple adherence to professional ethics and standards. Less ethical professionals may be lured, however, by promises of compensation for testimony, favoritism, and the like. At the very least, such professionals risk losing their credibility as expert witnesses. Readers of Stieg Larsson's Millennium trilogy get up close and personal with one of these unscrupulous experts—psychiatrist Dr. Peter Teleborian. As a hired gun for the Section, a secretive unit of the Säpo tasked with protecting Zalachenko, Dr. Teleborian made a name for himself and earned favoritism from some of Sweden's most elite government officials. Throughout the three-book Millennium series, readers unravel a horror of atrocities perpetrated against heroine Lisbeth Salander, accomplished in large part due to Dr. Teleborian's unethical practice of psychiatry and his willingness to take this immoral behavior into the court of law. Dr. Teleborian essentially worked backwards in each of his dealings with Salander—formulating his professional psychiatric evaluations of her around a predetermined conclusion favorable to the Section: that she is mentally ill and must be committed to a locked psychiatric facility.

Even without Salander's cooperation (verbal and otherwise), a competent and ethical psychiatrist or psychologist could have provided the court with a more accurate assessment of risk using a variety of research-based instruments, review of the records, and information obtained through collateral contacts. (In a forensic evaluation, a collateral contact is an individual who is knowledgeable about the person being evaluated. They may support, corroborate, or add information.) A number of available psychological and risk-assessment tools provide standardized and actuarial information that aid evaluators in making a variety of structured appraisals, including those that were at issue in Salander's case.

So how might such an assessment of Salander look? Clearly we cannot ask Salander and her associates to participate in interviews and to complete questionnaires, but we can use information that could have been made available to a court-appointed forensic psychologist or psychiatrist to develop an assessment of her. The information might include police records, social welfare reports, prior psychological or psychiatric evaluations, medical records, arrest reports, and interviews. Most of these items are in fact readily available in the novels. In this essay, I've used the content of the novels to assess Salander and produce a forensic psychology report similar to the one Dr. Teleborian should have produced in *The Girl Who Kicked the Hornet's Nest*. In doing so, I have used only the information that he would have had available to him, including records from social service agencies, police reports, guardianship reports, mental health records, hospital records, and employment records. I have also used the information we learn about Salander from other characters—many of whom might have been interviewed as collateral contacts in such an evaluation—such as Miriam Wu, Mikael Blomkvist, Holger Palmgrem, and others. I have not used the omniscient point of view that the author uses in order to see inside Salander's life and mind to reveal information to the reader. Instead, I have relied on the information we are given in the text of the novels themselves.

CONFIDENTIAL FORENSIC PSYCHOLOGY REPORT— LISBETH SALANDER

EXAMINEE: Lisbeth Salander
D.O.B: 4/30/1978
DATE OF REPORT: 7/3/2011[1]
EXAMINER: Marisa Mauro, Psy.D.

REFERRAL INFORMATION:
Ms. Lisbeth Salander is a twenty-seven-year-old Caucasian female indicted on sixteen charges. Count I alleges that on or about April 6, 2005, Ms. Salander committed aggravated assault in the case of Carl-Magnus Lundin. Count II alleges that on or about April 7, 2005, Ms. Salander unlawfully threatened Karl Axel Bodin, alias Alexander Zalachenko, now deceased. Count III alleges that on or about April 7, 2005, Ms. Salander committed attempted murder in the case of Karl Axel Bodin; alias Alexander Zalachenko, now deceased. Count IV alleges that on or about April 7, 2005, Ms. Salander committed aggravated assault in the case of Karl Axel Bodin; alias Alexander Zalachenko, now deceased. Count V alleges that on or about April 6, 2005, Ms. Salander committed breaking and entering at the Stallarholmen cabin of Nils Eric Bjurman. Count VI alleges that on or about April 2, 2005, Ms. Salander committed breaking and entering at the Odeplan home of Nils Eric Bjurman. Count VII alleges that on or about April 6, 2005, Ms. Salander committed theft of a vehicle, a Harley Davidson owned by Sonny Nieminen. Counts VIII through

---

[1] Were this a real report, the date of interview would also be listed.

X allege that on or about April 7, 2005, Ms. Salander was in possession of illegal weapons including a canister of Mace, a Taser, and a Polish P-83 Wanad. Count XI alleges that on or about April 6, 2005, Ms. Salander committed theft or withholding of evidence obtained from the cabin of Nils Eric Bjurman. Counts XII through XVI allege misdemeanor charges relating to the prior XI Counts.

Salander was referred to this examiner for a forensic psychological examination by Dr. Robin Rosenberg and Shannon O'Neill, authors of *The Psychology of the Girl with the Dragon Tattoo*. Supposing this examiner were the one to which Salander was referred by her attorney, Advokat Annika Giannini, pursuant to an agreement with the District Court of Stockholm, Sweden, this evaluator would have had the following sources of information available to her:

- Indictment, *Sweden v. Lisbeth Salander*
- Police Reports
- Police Interviews of Miriam Wu, friend of Lisbeth Salander
- Juvenile Arrest Report for Lisbeth Salander
- Medical Record for Lisbeth Salander from St. Stephen's Children's Psychiatric Clinic
- Letter from Dr. Johannes Caldin, former head physician and former superior to Dr. Peter Teleborian at St. Stephen's, to Holger Palmgren, attorney and former guardian of Lisbeth Salander
- Confidential Section File for Lisbeth Salander
- Social Welfare Agency Records for Lisbeth Salander
- Collateral contact interview of Anders Jonasson, surgeon
- Collateral contact interview of Martina Karlgren, psychologist
- Collateral contact interview of Mikael Blomkvist, *Millennium* magazine
- Collateral contact interview of Dragan Armansky, Milton Security
- Collateral contact interview of Holden Palmgren, former attorney and guardian
- Collateral contact interview of Miriam Wu

- In addition, based on this information, this examiner has used her own best guess as to social history, mental status, and likely results of both a clinical interview and assessments consisting of the PCL-R, HCR-20, and the LSI-R.[2]

For the purposes of this evaluation, the contents of the above list are inferred from information available in the Millennium trilogy.

INFORMED CONSENT FOR FORENSIC PSYCHOLOGICAL EVALUATION

Prior to interview and assessment, Ms. Salander would have been informed of the evaluation's purpose and the associated limits of confidentiality and been provided with this examiner's Informed Consent for Forensic Psychological Evaluation. Specifically, she would have been told that she was being evaluated pursuant to a court order granting the defense's (or prosecution's) motion for psychological evaluation. Ms. Salander would have been informed that the outcome of the assessment, including a written report, would be provided to the court. An opportunity for questions would have been provided. It is unlikely that Salander would have asked any questions and would instead have remained selectively mute. It is also likely Ms. Salander would not have signed the Informed Consent for Forensic Psychological Evaluation, and would have been informed that the evaluation would proceed regardless, pursuant to the court order.

Given that Lisbeth Salander is a fictional character, this review obviously did not actually take place—but this essay describes the process that would have been undertaken in evaluating her.

PSYCHOSOCIAL BACKGROUND AND HISTORY

Ms. Salander could not cooperate with this evaluator to provide information regarding her psychosocial background and history, just as she likely *would* not have in the series. Therefore the information

---

2 *Editors' Note*: These three assessment tools are explained in more detail below.

provided below is based solely upon what would have existed in collateral documentation. Were this assessment to be used in a court of law, interpretative caution would therefore be advised.

Family and Social History

Available records indicate that Lisbeth Salander was born in Sweden on April 30, 1978, to Agneta Sofia Salander and Alexander Zalachenko. Her parents were never married. She was raised with her twin sister, Camilla, whose whereabouts are currently unknown. Ms. Salander's last recorded contact with her sister was at age seventeen. Their relationship was poor and sometimes turned violent. Agneta Sofia Salander is currently deceased. According to statements that Holder Palmgren and Mikael Blomkvist likely would have made in interviews, she died at age forty-six as a result of many years of chronic complications from a traumatic brain injury sustained in a 1990 assault perpetrated by Alexander Zalachenko. This information would have been collaborated in a file marked "Confidential" by the Section.

Alexander Zalachenko, also known as Karl Axel Bodin, was a victim of murder on April 12, 2005. According to statements that likely would have been made by Mr. Palmgren and Mr. Blomkvist, Mr. Zalachenko was only intermittently present throughout Ms. Salander's childhood. When in the home, he often severely abused Agneta Salander. Information that could have been obtained from the Confidential Section File on Lisbeth Salander would have indicated that, as a young girl, Ms. Salander attempted to intervene on at least two occasions in defense of her mother. During one incident, Ms. Salander stabbed her father in the shoulder. On a second occasion, Ms. Salander set her father's car on fire with him inside.

Ms. Salander is single and has never been married. There are no records to suggest that she was, at the time of the original evaluation and trial, involved in a committed relationship or has any children. Due to Ms. Salander's likely refusal to answer questions related to this assessment, her current interests, hobbies, and social activities would have been unknown, except as described by associates of hers. 175

Interviews of Miriam Wu conducted by the police likely would have suggested that Ms. Salander has previously kept some female friends and acquaintances and sometimes met a group for drinks.

Prior to her incarceration for the charges described above, Ms. Salander was a patient at Sahlgrenska Hospital in Göteborg. She was admitted on April 8, 2005, for injuries stemming from gunshot wounds to the head, hip, and shoulder and was discharged on June 5 of the same year. Ms. Salander's address of residence in Sweden would have been unknown.

Education History and School Behavior
Records from the Social Welfare Agency would have suggested that Ms. Salander completed nine years of compulsory schooling, but did not earn a certificate. As a student, Ms. Salander earned poor grades, refused to complete assignments, and often fought with other students. When provoked, the young Ms. Salander sometimes became violent.

Work History
At the time of the trial, Ms. Salander was unemployed. She previously worked as a personal investigator for Milton Security. Despite her lack of formal education, head of Milton Security Dragan Armansky likely would have described Ms. Salander as his brightest investigator and praised her intelligence. However, he also would have noted a history of frequent unexplained absences.

Drug and Alcohol Use and History
Ms. Salander's juvenile arrest report would have indicated that she was arrested on three occasions for substance related charges—twice for alcohol intoxication and once for being under the influence of narcotics. A report from the assistant head of the Social Welfare Board, compiled within one year of these arrests, would have concluded that Ms. Salander was at "grave risk of alcohol and drug abuse." Ms. Salander has no adult arrest history for drug and alcohol problems. From collateral interviews focusing on Ms. Salander's adult use of drugs and alcohol conducted with Mr. Blomkvist, Mr. Armansky, and Ms. Wu, an examiner likely would have learned that she sometimes

drank in social situations. In addition, each of the informants likely would have denied ever having any concerns regarding substance abuse for Ms. Salander.

Mental Health History
Medical records obtained from Kronoberg Prison would have indicated that Ms. Salander was, at the time of the trial, not currently under the care of any mental health professional. She was also not prescribed any psychiatric medications. Dr. Anders Jonasson, Ms. Salander's surgeon and treating physician at Sahlgrenska Hospital from April 8, 2005, to June 6, 2005, likely would have stated that at no time during her stay did Ms. Salander appear mentally ill. Psychologist Dr. Martina Karlgren likely would have confirmed Dr. Jonasson's appraisal.

Records pertaining to Ms. Salander's mental health history would have indicated that she was committed to the locked ward at St. Stefan's Psychiatric Clinic for Children in Uppsala at the age of thirteen. At that time Ms. Salander was found emotionally disturbed and a danger to herself and others. During this commitment, Ms. Salander refused to voluntarily take psychiatric medications. She was force-fed the medications mixed into her meals. Restraints were used for 381 of the 786 days of her stay. Communication, such as a letter as described in *The Girl Who Kicked the Hornet's Nest*, between Mr. Palmgren and Dr. Caldin, would have indicated that Ms. Salander's behavior was calm once the use of force-feeding and restraints ceased. At age fifteen, Ms. Salander was released following expert determination that she was no longer a danger to herself or others. Following four arrests at age seventeen (described above), Ms. Salander was ordered by the district court to submit to another psychiatric evaluation and she was once again confined to the psychiatric clinic for children. The results, which were based upon observations only by Dr. Jesper H. Löderman under the supervision of Dr. Teleborian purportedly due to lack of Ms. Salander's cooperation, lacked a definitive diagnosis, but suggested some type of emotional disturbance. Dr. Löderman recommended that the court order care for Ms. Salander in a locked psychiatric institution. The court concluded that Ms. Salander was emotionally disturbed but rejected the recommendation for involuntary psychiatric treatment in favor of guardianship.

Criminal Behavior History

Ms. Salander's criminal record would have indicated four juvenile arrests, each when she was seventeen years old. The first three arrests were substance related and are described above, including two arrests for alcohol intoxication and a third for being under the influence of narcotics. Her last arrest was for assault and battery. Charges relating to this arrest were dismissed by the prosecutor following evidence that the alleged victim had groped Ms. Salander prior to her assault and battery on his person. Additional juvenile behavioral difficulties were reported and described in Family and Educational History above. Ms. Salander has no adult arrest record.

Circumstances of the Present Offenses

Ms. Salander likely would not have provided a statement regarding her present charges to an examiner. Police reports would have indicated that Ms. Salander refused to comment in each of the seven police interviews conducted.

Behavior during Incarceration

There likely would have been no record of any institutional write-ups or disciplinary actions while Ms. Salander was in custody at Krono-berg Prison.

CLINICAL INTERVIEW DATA AND TESTING RESULTS

Current Mental Status:

Lisbeth Salander is a twenty-seven-year-old Caucasian female. At the time of an exam, hygiene likely would have been appropriate. Grooming practices would have been unconventional, including multiple piercings and tattoos and clothing that featured expletives. Ms. Salander would have appeared of slim build and petite stature. Behavior toward the examiner likely would have been indifferent and cooperation likely could not have been obtained. A total absence of speech would likely have been observed. Orientation[3] could not have been assessed. The quality of thought processes and nature of their content could not have been assessed. There would have been no evidence of response to internal cues.[4] The ability to follow directions, commands, or track verbal information[5] likely could not have been examined. Attentional abilities, short- and long-term memory, and fund of information could not have been assessed. Ms. Salander likely would have expressed a restricted range of affect and mood.[6] The presence of current suicidal or homicidal ideation, intent, or plan could not have been assessed.

Test Results and Interpretation
Hare Psychopathy Checklist–Revised: 2nd Edition (PCL-R: 2nd Edition): The PCL-R (2nd Edition) is an instrument used for the assessment of psychopathy. Psychopathy may be indicated by: the presence of impulsivity, antisocial behavior and deviance, a manipulative interpersonal style, superficial charm, shallow or labile affect, and callousness or lack of empathy. The presence of psychopathy is associated with an increased risk for violent behavior. Ratings for examinees on the PCL-R's twenty items are obtained through answers provided in a semistructured interview and review of available file and collateral information. A total score of 0 to 40 is obtained, with a score of 30 or more indicating the presence of psychopathy. Scores below 20 are not indicative of psychopathy, while scores from 20 to 30 are termed "mixed."

---

[3] Orientation refers to a function of the mind relating to understanding of the person (that is, whether the person knows his or her own name and identity), place (where he or she is), and time (the date, month, and year). Some clinicians also evaluate orientation to purpose (why the person is being interviewed).

[4] Here, internal cues refer to the presence of visual or auditory hallucinations.

[5] Here, tracking verbal information refers to the ability to understand spoken or written language.

[6] Traditionally *affect* (objective range of emotional expression) may be described using terms such as blunted, flat, restricted, shallow, inappropriate, etc. Mood (subjective emotional state) may be described as depressed, angry, anxious, etc.

Ms. Salander likely would not have cooperated with the semi-structured interview for testing with the PCL-R (2nd Edition). Ratings for each of the twenty items therefore would have been obtained solely from the review of available collateral information. As a result, caution is advised when interpreting the results. This examiner would have obtained a PCL-R total score of 14 for Ms. Salander, which is indicative of *non*psychopathy.

Level of Service Inventory Revised (LSI-R): The LSI-R is a quantitative survey of offender characteristics, history, and situations relevant for making decisions about levels of supervision[7] and treatment. The LSI-R can be used to assist the judicial system, corrections, and treatment providers with decisions relating to the allocation of resources, probation and placement, security level classifications, and treatment progress. Scores, which are associated with risk for recidivism and likelihood for misconduct, help to predict parole outcome, success in correctional halfway houses, institutional misconduct, and recidivism.

The LSI-R is composed of fifty-four items grouped into ten areas: Criminal History, Education/Employment, Financial, Family/Marital, Accommodation, Leisure/Recreation, Companions, Alcohol/Drug Problems, Emotional/Personal, and Attitudes/Orientation. Item responses are obtained through answers provided by the examinee and review of available file and collateral information. Each item is answered with either a "yes or no" or a "0 to 3" rating by the examiner. A total score is obtained from which recommendations for appropriate levels of service are provided.

Ms. Salander likely would not have cooperated with attempts to interview her for testing with the LSI-R. Ratings for each of the fifty-four items therefore would have been obtained solely from review of available

---

[7] Here, supervision refers to the level of restriction imposed upon an offender. For example, parole or probation is less supervision than jail or prison. Minimum security institutions provide less supervision than maximum security institutions.

collateral information. As a result, caution is advised when interpreting the results. On the LSI-R, this examiner believes Ms. Salander would have earned a total score of 19, which corresponds to a percentile rank of 69.7. This means that Ms. Salander's score is higher than approximately 70 percent of the female inmates in the normative group. With regards to supervision needs if granted probation, this score corresponds to the maximum level of service and higher risk for recidivism. This means that Ms. Salander may require frequent contact with her probation officer and electronic monitoring to be successful. Ms. Salander's score would have been elevated due in large part to her criminal history, including present allegations, unsteady employment, school problems, family problems, attitude, and history of mental health treatment.

Historical, Clinical, Risk Management—20 (HCR-20): The HCR-20 is a twenty-item checklist of risk factors for violent behavior. It is an approach to risk assessment that uses structured professional judgment (SPJ) to assist the examiner in making a clinical judgment about the examinee's risk for violence. The twenty items consist of ten past ("Historical") factors, five present ("Clinical") variables, and five future ("Risk Management") issues.

Ms. Salander likely would once again have been uncooperative with attempts to interview her for testing with the HCR-20. Ratings for each of the twenty items therefore would have been obtained solely from review of available collateral information. As a result, caution is advised when interpreting the results. Based upon this examiner's investigation, using the information that would have been available to the actual examiner and structured by the HCR-20, there are some violence risk factors present in Ms. Salander's case. The majority of these concerns are Historical Factors, including a definite history of previous violence, young age at first violent incident, and early childhood maladjustment and some/possible relationship instabilities, features of personality disorder, and prior problems while under supervision. Considered static in nature, these items tend to be reliable positive associations with future risk. Other risk factors include Clinical Items such as some/possible negativistic attitudes, impulsivity, and failure to respond to treatment attempts. Risk Management items, including partial noncompliance with remediation attempts and possible life stressors, are among other present concerns.

DISCUSSION OF RISK ASSESSMENT

Regardless of whether Ms. Salander were convicted of the charges described here and sentenced to prison or committed to a psychiatric facility, found not guilty and released, or given court-ordered treatment, consideration as to appropriate placement and disposition would weigh the potential risk for future violence that she might pose to the community. Whether an individual will act violently is a function of a variety of static and dynamic factors, including dispositional factors (i.e. demographics, personality), historical factors (i.e. criminal history), contextual factors (i.e. weapon availability, social support, victim availability), and clinical factors (i.e. major psychoses, substance abuse).[8] The following analysis evaluates the fictional test results for Ms. Salander, based upon factors that have some relationship to risk.

Dispositional Factors

Certain dispositional factors more associated with risk for violence recidivism include demographics such as gender (males) and age (youth), as well as certain personality disorders, such as antisocial personality disorder and psychopathy.[9] At twenty-seven years old, Ms. Salander would still be considered at an age associated with risk for violent recidivism; however, she would pose less of a risk than a younger individual since adolescents and young adults pose the greatest risk for aggressive behavior. With regard to personality pathology, Ms. Salander evidences some antisocial features, including a history of problems with the law and aggression, but does not meet diagnostic criteria for antisocial personality disorder or psychopathy.[10]

---

[8] G. B. Melton, et al., *Psychological Evaluation for the Courts: A Handbook for Mental Health Professionals and Lawyers,* 3rd ed. (New York: The Guilford Press, 2007).

[9] Melton et al.

[10] Of course readers know from the peek inside her mind and private life that Salander evidences additional antisocial traits. However, this information would

On the PCL-R, a measure that assesses psychopathy, Ms. Salander's estimated score of 16 falls well below the cutoff score of 30, meaning she does not exhibit a psychopathic interpersonal style.

Historical Factors

Historical or static factors in a person's history associated with future risk for violence include factors related to arrest history (i.e., multiple prior offenses), childhood diagnosis of conduct disorder,[11] delinquency, and early age of onset of criminality. The strongest predictor of future violence is a record of multiple prior offenses.[12] Ms. Salander has neither adult convictions nor arrest history, though she was arrested on four occasions, as a juvenile. One charge was dismissed, and her three remaining charges include two arrests for alcohol intoxication and one arrest for being under the influence of narcotics. There is no evidence to suggest that Ms. Salander was ever diagnosed with conduct disorder. She was, however, found to be emotionally disturbed as a child—a conclusion drawn based upon clinical observation alone. Conclusive evidence of childhood delinquency is, at best, minimal. Ms. Salander's juvenile arrests all occurred when she was seventeen years old. School records would have reflected some early problems with aggression, possibly at times in response to provocation. At twelve years old, the Confidential Section Report would have indicated that Ms. Salander set fire to Mr. Zalanchenko's vehicle while he was inside. Collateral interviews with Mr. Palmgren and Mr. Blomkvist likely would have suggested that Ms. Salander's behavior was in defense of her mother, a frequent victim of Mr. Zalachenko's physical abuse.

---

not be readily available to an examiner so it is disregarded here. Furthermore, it is unlikely that someone in Salander's position would have voluntarily proffered self-incriminating details suggesting additional asocial features.

[11] *Conduct disorder* is a disorder of childhood involving a repetitive and persistent pattern of behavior in which the basic rights of others or age-appropriate societal norms or rules are violated, as manifested by aggression toward people and animals, destruction of property, deceitfulness or theft, or serious violations of rules.

[12] Melton et al.

Contextual Factors

Contextual factors associated with greater risk for future violence include weapon availability, lack of social support, and victim availability.[13] With regards to weapons, there is no evidence to confirm or deny that Ms. Salander may have access to weapons in the future. The charges against Ms. Salander suggest that she had access to weapons in the past. Clinical factors associated with weapons accumulations include paranoid features and use of stimulants, and Ms. Salander possesses neither risk factor. With regard to social support, Ms. Salander would have appeared to have friendships but lacks any close familial associations. Social support networks may reduce risk for violence by increasing an individual's repertoire of coping skills and reducing emotional destabilizers.[14] Ms. Salander would have appeared to have a low risk of affecting future victims. Higher risk for future violence is associated with perpetrators who direct their aggression toward a wide range of victims.[15] The circumstances of the allegations against Ms. Salander suggest that each of the purported victims was related to the same or similar set of circumstances involving a set of connected crimes.

Clinical Factors

A final consideration is clinical factors associated with violence recidivism, including major psychoses[16] and substance abuse.[17] Current, active psychosis is modestly associated with an increased risk for violent behavior. Examples of symptoms that increase risk include delusions of persecution and thought insertion/control.[18] Substance abuse also increases one's risk for violence toward others. Ms. Salander likely

---

[13] Ibid.

[14] Ibid.

[15] Ibid.

[16] Schizophrenia and other psychotic disorders.

[17] Melton et al.

[18] The belief that thoughts can be inserted into one's mind or controlled by an external source. (B. G. Link, and A. Stueve, "Psychotic Symptoms and the Violent/Illegal Behavior of Mental Patients Compared to Community Controls," in

would not have been found to be suffering from major psychoses or substance abuse problems. In addition, there would have been no evidence to suggest that Ms. Salander had ever suffered from psychoses or any diagnosed substance abuse disorder.

DIAGNOSES

Due to Ms. Salander's likely lack of cooperation with the assessment, the diagnostic impressions would be provisional and presented to the court with caution. The diagnoses here were made based upon the likely clinical observations, collateral information, and psychological assessments completed using the aforementioned information that would have been available to an examiner at the time of the trial.

Based on these, there is no evidence from available information to suggest that Ms. Salander is suffering from a clinical disorder. That is, Ms. Salander does not appear to meet diagnostic criteria for major depressive disorder, bipolar disorder, schizophrenia, or the like. There is evidence that Ms. Salander has maladaptive antisocial personality traits, but she does not appear to meet the Diagnostic and Statistical Manual of Mental Disorders, fourth edition (DSM-IV) threshold criteria for antisocial personality disorder.[19, 20] These traits are evident in her history of unlawful behavior, impulsivity, and aggression.

Violence and Mental Disorder, eds, J. Monahan, and H. J. Steadman [University of Chicago Press, 1994.])

[19] *Antisocial personality disorder* is defined by the DSM IV-TR as a pervasive pattern of disregard and violation of the rights of others occurring since age fifteen as indicated by three of the following: 1) failure to conform to societal norms with respect to lawful behaviors; 2) deceitfulness; 3) impulsivity or failure to plan ahead; 4) irritability and aggressiveness as indicated by repeated physical fights or assaults; 5) reckless disregard for the safety of self or others; 6) consistent irresponsibility, i.e., not meeting work or financial obligations; 7) lack of remorse. The individual must also be at least eighteen years old, and had evidence of conduct disorder with onset prior to age fifteen.

[20] Psychopathy is frequently distinguished from antisocial personality disorder (APD). In the manual for the PCL-R, psychologist and PCL-R developer Robert Hare described psychopathy in three broad categories: interpersonal, affective,

CONCLUSIONS

Ms. Salander is a twenty-seven-year-old Caucasian female indicted with sixteen charges, including various misdemeanors, breaking and entering, aggravated assault, withholding evidence, unlawful threats, possession of illegal weapons, vehicle theft, and attempted murder. She was referred to this examiner by Dr. Robin Rosenberg and Shannon O'Neill pursuant to an agreement with BenBella Books for psychological evaluation.

Based upon the above analyses, it is the opinion of this evaluator that Ms. Salander should be considered a low risk for future violence to the community. It is also this evaluator's opinion that Ms. Salander is not suffering from severe psychological symptoms. Although Ms. Salander appears to have some features consistent with antisocial personality disorder—including aggression, impulsivity, and problems with the law—they do not appear to be at a level severe enough to adversely affect her well-being or the safety of others. In fact, prior to the events leading up to the charges described above, Ms. Salander's behavior seemed to be in accordance with the law and there was no evidence to suggest that aggression or impulsivity were problematic. In fact, Ms. Salander has no prior adult record.

On the basis of Ms. Salander's relatively low risk for future violence and absence of severe mental health disorder, court-ordered mental health treatment is not recommended. This includes commitment to a locked forensic psychiatric facility in the event that Ms. Salander is

---

and behavioral (lifestyle). Interpersonally, psychopaths are grandiose, egocentric, manipulative, dominant, exploitive, and cold. Affectively, they display shallow and labile emotions, have difficulty forming bonds with others, and lack empathy or remorse. Behaviorally they are impulsive, unstable, irresponsible, seek out highly stimulating activities, and often violate social norms. The DSM IV-TR diagnostic criterion for APD, in contrast, places emphasis on socially deviant behavior and criminal acts. In the criminal setting, most psychopathic offenders meet criteria for APD, but most APD offenders do not meet criteria for psychopathy. (R. D. Hare, *Hare Psychopathy Checklist-Revised (PCL-R) Technical Manual*, 2nd ed. [North Tonawanda, NY: Multi-Health Systems Inc, 2003].)

found guilty and court-ordered community mental health treatment in the event that she is found not guilty and released.

I hope that this report will be of service. Please do not hesitate to contact me with questions or for further consultation.

Marisa Mauro
Marisa Mauro, PsyD
Licensed Psychologist

MARISA MAURO, PsyD, is a psychologist in private practice in Austin, Texas. Much of her work focuses on forensic psychology. Dr. Mauro previously worked at the California Department of Corrections and Rehabilitation. Her work there was focused on violent offenders, sexual offenders, gang members, and inmates serving life sentences. Her blog, "Take All Prisoners," can be found on PsychologyToday.com. She has also taught as an adjunct professor and conducted research on personality, academic success, career success, eating disorders, and suicide.

PART 3
THE GIRL WHO COULDN'T BE STOPPED

The popularity of the Millennium trilogy is at heart about Lisbeth Salander; some readers love her, some don't, but most everyone has a strong reaction to the character and her actions. Sandra Yingling, a psychological consultant whose work has brought her in close contact with misunderstood people of many kinds, explores what it is about Lisbeth that makes her such a provocative and polarizing figure.

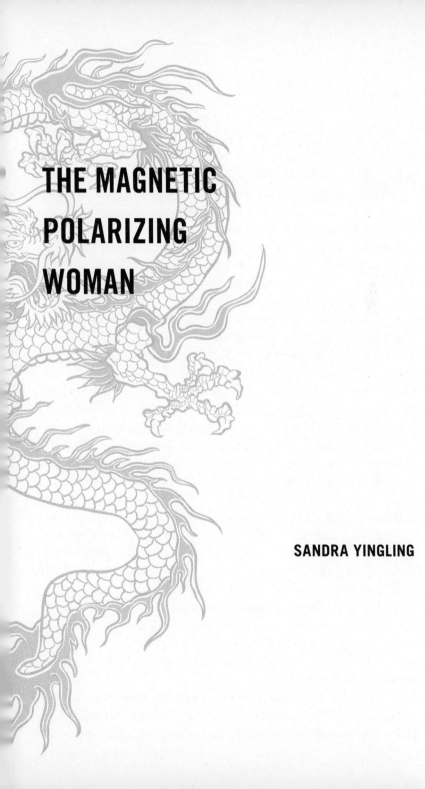

THE MAGNETIC
POLARIZING
WOMAN

SANDRA YINGLING

"**W**ho does she think she is?" This indignant question is frequently leveled at women in powerful roles in sports, the military, academia, business, or politics. Superstrong tennis star Venus Williams fought for, and won, the right for Wimbledon champions of both genders to earn the same prize money, despite a great deal of pressure from tradition-soaked tennis institutions. General Ann Dunwoody, the first American woman to become a four-star general, began her peerless military career at a time when army polls suggested that the best role for a female soldier was "cook." Dean and now Supreme Court Justice Elena Kagan, a brilliant legal scholar, endured pointless and absurd speculation about her sexuality during her Supreme Court nomination process, with journalists and pundits parsing the meaning of whether she ever sat with crossed legs. Indra Nooyi, the CEO of Pepsico and one of Forbes' "100 Most Powerful Women," insists on running her company using her own rules, even if treating employees like extended family members is frowned upon and considered a weakness in her leadership style by traditional business leaders. Hillary Clinton, currently secretary of state—but really, no description is necessary—has spent a lifetime carefully navigating toward positions of greater power while trying to avoid a recurring obstacle that threatens to sink her impressive abilities: being perceived as unlikeable. In her roles of presidential candidate or secretary of state, Clinton is described as "angry" or "shrill," while her male counterparts are characterized as "resolute" or "impassioned." In forging their unique careers, each of these women upended the status quo. And for each of these women, a chorus of voices, both male and female, has been at the ready, asking: "Who does she think she is, to have this confidence, to persist, to be successful in the face of disapproval?"

Anyone in a highly visible position can be the target of judgment and criticism, but influential women in public life are also frequently looked upon as outsiders or intruders in the historically male sphere of leadership and influence. A woman's designation of being an "other" or outsider carries with it an implication of threat that she must defuse before her actual competence is even considered. An outsider who gains power is a threat to the status quo, and to the people and institutions that define the rules and broker the power.

Harsh judgments are also reserved for women in arenas designed for rule-breaking self-expression, such as music and art: "Why does Patti Smith/Lady Gaga/Cindy Sherman have to be so grungy/dramatic/disturbing?" While many women are elevated in the entertainment arena for their beauty, women of the avant-garde drive for the kind of self-expression that rejects traditional definitions of beauty and femininity, and the very idea of "knowing one's place." Radical self-expression is designed not to please the audience, but to provoke it and perhaps encourage its audience to destroy existing boundaries and rules. Patti Smith's androgynous persona redefines attractiveness, Lady Gaga's edgy performance art costumes are not meant to appeal to men who watch cheerleaders at halftime, and Cindy Sherman's photographic lampooning of clichés about women leaves some people with the unsettling feeling that they might be the butt of her joke. Unlike women in business and politics who challenge the notion of male leadership and earn a visible but minority status, avant-garde women in the arts create their own communities and aesthetics, separate and distinct from the majority culture. This forms an openly defiant message to the keepers of the status quo.

The same question—"Who does she think she is?"—echoes for girls and women in their personal relationships as well. Women who are focused on their career goals are criticized for neglecting family caregiver roles. Women who do not embrace traditional gender roles can receive culturally sanctioned punishments ranging from being ostracized to being physically assaulted for "bringing shame" to their families. The extreme example is honor killings, in which family members decide that a woman's job or her relationship has damaged the family's reputation such that the only remedy is to put the woman to death. More familiar examples include parents who withhold financial support for education if a woman's course of study is "inappropriate," and schools that do not address bullying and teasing of girls who have interests outside the stereotyped and "popular" norm. In each case, the message is that women should conform to the expectations of others, or pay a price.

The good news is that the same women who have intense detractors also tend to have fiercely loyal defenders. People who want to see women break glass ceilings become ardent campaigners. People who find it absurd that women are measured by looks rather than ability push even harder for the promotion of women purely based on their outstanding competence. People who understand that taking risks and living on the edge can be dangerous provide unwavering, awe-struck support. People who know what it takes to put on a professional "game face" every day also want a better appreciation of the real person who emerges when it is safe for her to set the game face aside.

How can we understand why people seem driven to take intense, polar opposite positions about certain women's choices in life—their personality, their power? What makes some women so polarizing?

A polarizing person is someone whose behavior provokes others into: a) making judgments about the morality of the polarizing person's choices; b) questioning the polarizing person's right to define rules for themselves or others and c) frequently believing that the polarizing person's behaviors are intentional choices created for their effect on others.

Polarizing figures are seen, both positively and negatively, as refusing to "play the game" of conforming to others' expectations. As nonconformists, they often serve as truth-tellers despite great personal risk. (As author James Stewart recently observed, "The truth is often unwelcome."[1]) Detractors decide that the polarizing person's choices are incorrect or possibly immoral, that the polarizing person has no right to redefine rules, and that she is intentionally provoking her detractors. Meanwhile, admirers decide that the polarizing person is correct, is brave to be redefining rules, and is benefiting others through her choices.

Powerful, polarizing women often fight for the right to sit at the table, like Kagan and Clinton, and each is often the only woman at the table. Other polarizing women do not want a seat at the table.

---

[1] James B. Stewart, *Tangled Webs: How False Statements Are Undermining America: From Martha Stewart to Bernie Madoff* (New York: Penguin Press, 2011).

They may want to smash the table, or build one of their own, as artists do. Sometimes, these women purposely choose to be provocateurs, making bold statements and seeking intense reactions as an outcome. Others receive intense reactions as an unwelcome product of their personal identity or professional quest.

So which of these describes Lisbeth Salander, heroine of the Millennium trilogy and one of the most polarizing characters of our time?

Lisbeth Salander: Polarizing Woman

Lisbeth has inspired a lot of love, both from characters in her world and from readers in our world. Her persistence, feistiness, and intelligence draw admirers. However, her quirkiness, lack of emotion, and physically aggressive behavior also results in others feeling kept at a distance and uncertain of whether she is capable of a warm human relationship. Much like the successful women described above, Lisbeth makes her own rules, to the point that she sometimes has to take the law into her own hands. Her admirers see her as a heroine and her law-breaking as evidence that she is fearless and driven to right wrongs perpetrated by a corrupt system. Detractors, however, see her as a criminal and her law-breaking as evidence that she is conscienceless and antisocial. Who, they ask, does Lisbeth Salander think she is?

Who *does* Lisbeth Salander think she is? A trauma survivor who must remain vigilant toward all others. A woman who must reject any signs of femininity to ward off predators. A "freak" with analytic and technical abilities that are both a source of pride and a source of embarrassment. Most of all, a person whose secretive quest for justice frequently becomes a quest for revenge.

When other characters in the Millennium trilogy first meet Lisbeth Salander, their appraisals of her are swift, definitive, and often based on her aggressively counterculture appearance. Prospective employers look at her and think it unlikely that she has expertise and gravitas. Other women eye her with suspicion, not able to decide if she is an exploited teenaged victim or a dangerous rival. However, key characters are drawn to Lisbeth. Those characters who have the patience to see beyond Lisbeth's repelling armor of spikes 195 and studs, of tattoos and piercings, are people with both a desire to befriend Lisbeth and a willingness to tolerate her interpersonal quirks in the hope that investing in her will benefit both parties. Holger Palmgren, Dragan Armansky, and Mikael Blomkvist look beyond her unsmiling demeanor to the rare moments when a faint smirk crosses her lips, signaling a brief expression of her appreciation and trust in them. Each of these men displays self-control while quietly building rapport. Each weighs the risks of not conforming to institutional authority. And none of them are threatened by Lisbeth's single-mindedness and intelligence. These characters find her unorthodox attitude to be a worthwhile trade-off for her unique abilities. They see her as talented and intriguing, and worth the inevitable friction that she brings with her.

Characters in the Millennium trilogy are not the only ones who find Lisbeth polarizing—readers do, too. Which pole a reader gravitates toward probably says more about the reader than about the character. For example, readers who believe that rules are meant to be bent, if not broken—especially in the pursuit of justice—will side with Mikael in finding Lisbeth appealing. Readers looking for a heroine to have traditional feminine characteristics, like warmth, self-sacrifice, and even modesty, will feel thwarted. Lisbeth serves, in other words, as a projective device for readers, like a punk Rorschach test.

It is important to note, as well, that part of what is so polarizing about Lisbeth as a character is that she is female. An observation made by many controversial and powerful women is that their exact career path and public statements would not be seen as polarizing if they were men. Would Lisbeth's qualities evoke quite so strong a reaction had she instead been "The *Boy* with the Dragon Tattoo"? Would readers still be asking, "Who does he think he is?" A brilliant, monosyllabic, arrogant *male* computer hacker with little emotional expression who has a plan to put old-guard authority figures in their place is a familiar stereotype of fiction (as well as a reasonable reflection of the career profiles of successful internet moguls in real life).

To understand fully our reaction to Lisbeth, and to understand fully Lisbeth herself, we need to look deeper. We need to look past Lisbeth's behavior to what motivates that behavior. Does Lisbeth only care about herself? What motivates her to be abrupt and disrespectful—and even violent?

Understanding Motivation and Behavior

Many people behave in a way that is a near-perfect mirror of their desires. Medical students push themselves to study because they have a desire to excel. Family members meet up at holidays because of their desire to be close and share warm feelings. Campaign workers incessantly ring doorbells because they want to persuade people to vote for their candidate. But behavior does not always reveal a person's motivation. Rather, behavior sometimes reflects the roles and constraints under which a person is operating. Some medical students push themselves not because they want to do well, or want to save lives, but in order to please their parents. Some family members look forward to gatherings not to spend time with loved ones, but so they can compete for the title of best pie-maker. The goal of some campaign workers isn't based on political or philosophical beliefs, but simply to be paid for a day's work. Two people can have very different motivations for engaging in what looks like identical behavior.

When we try to judge who someone is based on his or her behavior, there is much room for interpretation, as we cannot be certain of motive. If a politician is taking time to ask his constituents about their needs, we may attribute his motivation to trying to help others; our resulting judgment is therefore positive. If we attribute a different motivation to the same behavior—perhaps he is trying to manipulate people just so he can win an election—our judgment reverses polarity and can be harshly negative. We are wired to react emotionally to intense behaviors, to determine whether we are threatened (by a "Them") or protected (by an "Us"). We are more inclined to interpret one of our own as having appropriate motivation, and to ascribe less charitable motivations to the behaviors of outsiders. This may very well be the case with Lisbeth; by being a loner she has positioned herself as an outsider to others and therefore as a threat.

A powerful framework for understanding people's key motivators was developed by psychologist David McClelland more than forty years ago.[2] This framework can help to explain Lisbeth's choices, as well as the reactions of others to her behavior. McClelland's research uncovered three main motives that everyone expresses in varying degrees: the *need for achievement*, the *need for affiliation and emotional connection with others*, and the *need for power or influence*. Everyone has all three motives; typically one of the motives is a more intense need than the other two. This becomes a person's "default" motive, the one that is clamoring to be satisfied more than the other two.

Without being aware of it, each of us tends naturally to look for ways to meet our primary motive; consciously choosing a behavior that is appropriate to one's real-world situation, even if it feels unpleasant (or contrary to our primary motive) to do so, is a mark of maturity and strategic thinking. In contrast, not being aware that motive is driving one's decisions short-circuits a person's ability to react responsibly, particularly in relation to other people and shared goals. A person with a primary motive to *achieve* may reflexively seek out opportunities to set and exceed new objectives for himself or herself—even when no one is watching and no one is rewarding the achievement—simply because it is gratifying for the person to satisfy that motive. For example, a child who invents a game—like making a certain number of baskets in practicing basketball alone—is setting and meeting or exceeding her own goals, just for fun. However, in satisfying her achievement motive by repeatedly playing this game alone, she may forget to do something required, like helping her younger brother as her mother instructed.

This sort of tunnel vision applies to any of the three motives when it serves as a person's primary motive. A person with a primary motive to *affiliate* may routinely seek out opportunities to develop or deepen friendships, even when this need is at odds with the person's responsibilities. For example, a college student may satisfy his affiliation motive by choosing to be in charge of planning parties at his dorm so he can be with his friends, though he may dimly recall that he is

---

[2] David C. McClelland, *Human Motivation* (Cambridge: Cambridge University Press, 1987).

ignoring a less enjoyable responsibility, like studying alone. A person with a primary motive to *influence* others may reflexively look for ways to persuade and have an impact on others. For example, an office worker may satisfy her influence motive by volunteering her time teaching new employees the correct office procedures because she knows she and the new employees will both benefit. However, her reflexive need to influence may interfere with her actual, less enjoyable responsibilities, like showing higher personal productivity by exceeding her prior month's sales record. She may jeopardize her job by satisfying her primary motive without thinking through the consequences.

Not all behavior is "motivated" behavior. Some behavior occurs because it is part of people's roles—it is something they would not have gravitated to if given the choice. In the work world, much of people's behavior is mandatory and defined by their role and circumstances, and so true motivated behavior is most obvious when people have free time and can choose their own activity. Satisfying one's strongest motive is energizing and satisfying and, because of this, it is likely to be repeated when the person has a choice, especially when one is "off the clock." Asking people what activity they would choose if they had free time can often reveal their primary motive. Teaching a child a new skill? Probably influence-driven. Catching up on the phone with friends and relatives? Probably affiliation-driven. Increasing running or biking distance? Probably achievement-driven.

McClelland and David Burnham noted that being aware of and managing one's own needs is a cornerstone of productivity and personal satisfaction.[3] For example, if a person with a strong need to maintain friendly connections (affiliation motive) does not have that need met at work—and further, if that need is actually interfering with work tasks—the person can answer that need and avoid the detrimental effect on his or her work by finding ways to "feed" the need outside of work. McClelland made clear that identifying and finding expression for motivational needs is the path to manageable

---

[3] David C. McClelland, and David H. Burnham, "Power Is the Great Motivator" in *Best of HBR: Motivating People* (Boston: Harvard Business School Publishing, 2003).

self-discipline. Thwarting or ignoring a motivational need leads to friction and frustration—and increases the likelihood that the need will pop up in unexpected or undesirable ways. If a person with a strong affiliation need does not have ways to feel close and connected outside of work, the need for affiliation may be expressed inappropriately at work, for example a manager treating subordinates like friends. Insisting on high standards of quality or productivity from others is difficult for a person who does not want to risk losing friendships at work. Since everyone has needs for achievement, affiliation, and influencing others, the challenge is to be mindful of these needs and find ways to express them appropriately.

Lisbeth's Motives

How are these three motives—achievement, affiliation, and influence—demonstrated in Lisbeth's behavior? Our heroine behaves like a person with an extremely high achievement drive. She is self-motivated (she prefers to define her own goals and her own rewards), compulsively driven, and holds herself to such a high standard that she exhausts herself. A typical tableau is Lisbeth hunched over her laptop, drinking coffee, her burning eyes scanning endless streams of data for evidence. She loses herself in the pursuit of information; indeed she loses any sense of time passing. Her awareness of the people around her dims. In its best form, this phenomenon is described by psychologist Mihaly Csikszentmihalyi as "flow," a highly desirable state in which deep focus creates pure immersion in the task at hand and there are no distractions to interfere with focus and creativity.[4] People are typically pleased and energized when they emerge from a state of flow and can be startled by how much they achieved as time slid by, unnoticed. In its worst form, the relentless pursuit of a goal can be the opposite of flow—compulsive and destructive behavior that is anxiety-provoking, robbing its victim of energy while never permitting satisfaction, rest, or relief. Not being able to turn off this drive can

---

[4] Mihaly Csikszentmihalyi, *Flow: The Psychology of Optimal Experience* (New York: Harper and Row, 1990).

result in burnout and alienation of others. It is often unclear which kind of relentlessness possesses Lisbeth.

Lisbeth largely behaves like a person with little need for affiliation. At first glance she appears to have no need for friends. She rarely seeks out company unless she has a specific purpose in mind. She thinks of herself as a recluse, content to spend long periods of time alone and uninterrupted, and even describes other people as irritants who disrupt how she wants to live her life. She initially reacts to others' gestures of friendship with distrust—one of her first impressions of Mikael is that he is naïve and too trusting of others and therefore fails to understand that the real world is full of predators. And, despite the fact that she is sexually active, she shrinks from physical expressions of closeness and intimacy, whether it is the comforting hug from Mikael when her mother dies or the grateful squeeze from Erika Berger in thanks for saving their magazine.

Lisbeth repeatedly tries to gain power and influence. However, Lisbeth's interest in influencing others seems primarily designed to keep them at bay, and the power she seeks is the power to make others leave her alone. When she is around other people, she compulsively collects information on them, like a solitary soldier behind enemy lines.

Much of Lisbeth's interest in understanding others is driven by self-protection. She initially sorts people into two categories: predators and prey. It is not until she has observed a person's behavior over a long period of time that she allows herself to consider a third category for them: good people who allow her to approach life on her own terms. Palmgren and Armansky are able to earn their way onto this third list by forging working relationships with her and proving repeatedly that they have control over their own motivations and goals and are willing to follow her lead.

Influence over others is a key ingredient in leadership and, while leadership is not something Lisbeth appears to have much interest in, she is willing to seize control in certain moments—such as in *The Girl with the Dragon Tattoo* when she gives expert instructions to Henrik Vanger's lawyer, Dirch Frode, to manage communication about his CEO's death. Her behavior is blunt, sure, and firm. Frode is shocked to find himself admiring her ability to take command in the emergency and then willingly follows her advice. Similarly, she begins to help Mikael once she determines that he is reliably on her side, and they both benefit from it. This influence behavior is more permission-based and nuanced; it requires her both to read Mikael's readiness to accept her help and to signal her own readiness to be influenced in return.

Influence can be expressed in one of two ways: the "win-win" version, in which one uses power and influence to benefit both another person and oneself, and the "win-lose" version, which benefits oneself at the expense of another person. A teacher bringing out a student's potential is an example of ideal influence behavior: both student and teacher "win." Criminals preying on victims is the win-lose version: criminals win at the expense of their victims. Though Lisbeth *appears* to be uninterested in influence, she repeatedly takes the law into her own hands to create moments of win-lose influence. And her work with Mikael on behalf of others can be seen as productive examples of win-win influence.

Lisbeth's Response to Others' Influence

Lisbeth often appears remote and self-contained, as if making her way through a world of obstacles rather than a world filled with people. Other people who want to make friends with her (expressing affiliation) are generally rebuffed or ignored, which in itself can create enemies. Others approach her with their own agendas—whether altruistic or selfish—and she tends to dismiss them as well, perhaps even more forcefully, because she is operating under a simple rule: no one is to be trusted. A narrow and constricted view like this comes from being traumatized at the hands of others, and can only be undone through experiencing real collaboration with others. These are the two "poles" of influence: one positive, one negative. Once Lisbeth is exposed to the positive form of influence, she can develop both ends of her polarizing persona. She is transformed, from a marginalized "Other" with a lengthy list of detractors and stalkers, to a magnetic polarizing character who also has a coterie of loyal advocates.

We can see that Lisbeth's behavior changes based on which type of influence behaviors others are displaying. McClelland's theory maintains that authority figures displaying "win-win" influence bring out more of the achievement drive in their protégées, putting wind in their sails. David Burnham's research demonstrated that positive mentors create an environment that clears the way for others to focus single-mindedly on goals with great sustained enthusiasm (stimulating achievement motive).[5] For example, Palmgren, Armansky, and Mikael all exhibit "win-win" influence behaviors toward Lisbeth that feel like natural extensions of who they are as people, not just an expression of the role they inhabit. In other words, they are in the role of boss or journalist colleague, but for these men it does not seem to be an effort to like her and to want to help her succeed. Lisbeth can sense that these men are not predators.

By contrast, others' destructive use of power and influence, particularly during her childhood, provoked Lisbeth to focus single-mindedly on the achievement of her personal goal of safety. McClelland tells us that authority figures who display "win-lose" influence behaviors may *initially* stimulate more achievement behavior in their subordinates, but this cannot be sustained, because the behaviors arise not out of shared goals, but out of fear and punishment. A "bad boss" creates compliance and even increased productivity, but not loyalty. The hidden agenda of a subordinate in this case is actually to protect oneself and then to escape. What may begin as a stimulated achievement drive to do one's best may be overridden by a stimulated need to retaliate with one's own acts of "win-lose" influence. Lisbeth was repeatedly at the mercy of authority figures, from Alexander Zalachenko to Bjurman to Peter Teleborian. Each one of these men saw that Lisbeth was a talented adversary, but no win-win was possible unless Lisbeth abandoned her principles and became a member of their corrupted group.

From these men, Lisbeth learned to turn this "win-lose" impact back on others by using violence and committing crimes herself. However, in response to people like Mikael who have a collaborative "win-win" attitude, Lisbeth is warily able to adapt and respond. She then uses her abilities in increasingly mutual ways, beginning with providing the evidence to refute libel charges faced by Mikael. Lisbeth,

---

[5] David H. Burnham, *Power Is Still The Great Motivator—With a Difference* (Burnham Rosen Group LLC, 1997).

who at first appears to have little need for other people, emerges safer and more willing to share her strength within a small circle of trusted people.

The Primary Motives of Polarizing Women

So, Lisbeth displays a behavior pattern of unwavering commitment to her personal goals (achievement), less apparent interest in warmth or affection (affiliation), and intense and varied influence behaviors. Real-life polarizing women's behavior patterns look very similar: high commitment to personal achievement goals, less apparent affection, and intense influence and impact on others that can be seen as very positive or very negative, depending on the observer's perspective.

Successful women tend to hold themselves to a high standard of achievement, but that does not mean it comes naturally or easily; they put an ongoing focus on "raising the bar" for themselves. Detractors often interpret this focus on achievement as inappropriate for women and conclude that "normal" women would want to spend more of their time creating emotional bonds with family, or being affiliative. Detractors also tend to maintain that these successful women should have less interest in being powerful and influential. They conclude that each woman is too interested in achievement and influence, and not interested enough in making friends and keeping emotional bonds from breaking.

However, highly successful women must consciously and carefully choose their public and professional behaviors, and are keenly aware that many actions and stances are simply requirements of the role that they inhabit. In order for a woman to assume a leadership role, she must consistently display both achievement and influence behaviors because they are required by the job, even if neither one is her primary motive. For example, a leader in the military must demonstrate a high degree of personal drive and accomplishment, as well as an unwavering commitment to influencing others and directing the actions of soldiers. However, achievement or influence may not in fact be a powerful woman's primary motive. Most people, upon seeing military figures on the job, could not imagine that some have affiliation as their primary motive; the individual's motives are subsumed by the behaviors necessary for the role. Such a woman, whose key source of satisfaction is through closeness with others, most likely has found ways to satisfy her affiliation motive so that it does not interfere with her work—typically through activities with family and friends.

So actual, private motives may vary greatly from one powerful woman to the next, but ideally these motives will be kept completely (and safely) to themselves. Admirers are able to imagine the effort involved in being a highly visible public figure. They are able to see the person as both human and possessing all three motives, despite the public facade. They also believe they can catch glimpses of the real, dimensional person inhabiting the role and see something of themselves in her.

This is why Lisbeth's readiness to wield influence—usually outside the confines of the law—is one of her most polarizing qualities. Detractors are certain that she does not care about others and is using power for her own gain; she seems to unleash her fury like a predator. But other readers admire her because they see another, more humane and altruistic motive beneath her apparent lack of regard: the desire to protect. The recipients of her violence are clearly labeled as predators who legal means have failed to stop. Lisbeth's reputation grows throughout the series as a criminal and an outlaw, but ultimately the reading audience understands that, although she is quite capable of wreaking havoc, she would prefer not to do so. Over time, we understand that she is not primarily driven to use her power to destroy others.

Lisbeth's True Motive

Given all this, are achievement and influence actually Lisbeth's primary motives, or are these behaviors dominant because they are necessary for her "job"? Or does her mission to understand her traumatic past fully and to make sure it stops creating horror in her adult life take precedence? Would she be engaged in fewer achievement behaviors if she had a choice? Would she be expressing more affiliation behaviors if she had a choice?

Lisbeth's history is full of not having choices. She was repeatedly on the losing side of an adult's win-lose influence behavior, beginning as an abused child in a tortuous family situation. Nils Bjurman's need for control over Lisbeth leads him to rape and torture her, proving him to be yet another person in her life whose influence behavior is of the "win-lose" variety. This type of soul-killing trauma often forces affiliation needs deep underground, but it does not get rid of them. They survive and wait for opportunities to express themselves. K. Jessica Van Vliet, who conducted research on long-term effects of experiencing trauma, noted that "individuals bounce back" from being in a state of shame following trauma by constructing a new sense of self that includes an enhanced "sense of power and control over the future."[6] This is certainly an apt description of Lisbeth's transition from childhood victim to adult avenger.

Affiliation and Emotional Armor

Lisbeth is not warm to others, but this lack of expressed warmth is likely an effect of trauma. It is unclear what Lisbeth's personality would have been like were she not traumatized by her father, and had she not ended up in Teleborian's care. Despite her apparent lack of affiliation motive, Lisbeth displays ongoing attachment through her dutiful and sorrowful visits to her mother's care facility. It was her attempt to protect her mother against a tyrant that led to Lisbeth being handed over to abusive men and repeatedly assaulted. As Lisbeth warily forms attachments as an adult, she fears that people she cares about will be harmed just through their association to her.

Lisbeth is convinced that she is unlike other people, and particularly unlike other women. Upon meeting Erika Berger, Lisbeth is struck by Berger's air of sophistication, by her professional but feminine clothing, and by her ownership of adulthood, all of which is in stark contrast to Lisbeth's view of herself as scrawny and unattractive. But Lisbeth also feels that she is unlike other people because, although she has an intellectual sense of what "normal" people are like, she is often remote from their emotional experiences and puzzled by them. She only belatedly thinks that Armansky attending her mother's

---

[6] K. Jessica Van Vliet, "Shame and Resilience in Adulthood: A Grounded Theory Study," *Journal of Counseling Psychology* 55 (2008).

funeral probably means that he has empathy for her loss. Some of this disconnect comes from her having suppressed, for many years, her own need for affiliation because it was simply too dangerous to express. Her remoteness and wariness have served to protect her in a hostile environment. Like the solitary soldier, she learned that sending up a signal flare for help is more likely to draw enemies than rescuers. She is described as learning early on that crying did not help her, the equivalent of deciding to find one's own way out of a jungle rather than signal distress.

Although in many ways Lisbeth sees herself as not like other women, she has emotional vulnerabilities that escape her awareness and then take her by surprise. By the end of *The Girl with the Dragon Tattoo*, Lisbeth is shocked by the intensity with which her affiliation motive demands expression. She first feels "strangely content" watching Mikael hunched over his computer in an exact parallel of her own moments of flow. She then realizes, as if catching up from a delay in development, that she is experiencing being in love for the first time. Her need to care for a person—and to be cared for—roars into her life, suggesting that she has only been suppressing it up until that point. The desire to be connected creates a great vulnerability; it makes sense that it would be her biggest fear.

So perhaps the armored self that Lisbeth constructed, the relentless and fearless pursuer of truth and vengeance, is the role she needed to assume in order to survive, but it does not reflect Lisbeth's original motivations. As an adult, her tentative forays into trusting other people, from Mikael to Erika Berger, seem to remind her of the need for connection and affiliation that she allowed herself to express as a child. Lisbeth remains, in part, the girl of her own past who longs to be safe and loved. But like many people who experience trauma, Lisbeth masks and protects her most vulnerable self. She builds her own do-it-yourself armor as she goes along, mimicking the win-lose world around her, but continues to watch for signs of those rare individuals who are not fooled by the offensive posture she has assumed. Her ultimate wish may lie not in the destruction of threatening madmen—a goal she can achieve—but rather in the dismantling of her elaborate combat gear, a goal she may never attain.

Polarizing and Persisting: What Else Lisbeth Has in Common with Polarizing Women

Perhaps other successful and controversial women do not have an eidetic memory, or outrageous computer hacking skills, or piercings or tattoos. But, like Lisbeth, they have provoked intense reactions in others at various points in their lives. In my management consulting work, whether the client is an executive navigating her own organizational minefields or an artist who doesn't want others to dilute his creations, a set of behaviors frequently leads to one being labeled polarizing or "difficult" including: 1) believing in something very intensely, so intensely that it doesn't matter whether others agree or not; 2) working on something with such focus that even praise feels like an interruption; 3) feeling confident in one's own expertise; 4) wanting to excel, even in an "uncool" area; 5) pushing ahead even if it means going it alone; 6) calling things the way one sees them; 7) disagreeing with someone and not compromising. It's easy to see evidence of all of these in Lisbeth.

This can be a difficult and solitary path to travel. But polarizing people draw strength from like-minded people or from their own sense of what is right. Additionally, they may feel that this path has been placed before them and they have no choice in the matter—that they must take on opposing forces—perhaps because there is no one else who can do the job. Women who choose this path may consciously do so, knowing it will be controversial and that it will brand them as different from others and perhaps isolate them. For them, attaining their goal is worth the price. Even with solid social support, love of family, and emotional resources of every stripe, the key feature of a polarizing person is autonomy. The position taken by a polarizing person is not a compromise or a consensus; it is a gesture of certainty, a reflection of one's own internal compass.

Lisbeth Salander's reaction when confronted by people at odds with her is often utter surprise at their highly emotional and highly personal reactions to her decisions. People who have a polarizing effect on others may simply forget about the people around them while they are pursuing a mesmerizing objective (for instance, satisfying the achievement motive and being in flow). Lisbeth's full-tilt intensity of focus translates to others as rudeness, or even as a threat. From this response, Lisbeth no doubt learned an important piece of camouflage: being mistaken for a person who purposely "ruffles" people is especially useful in keeping others off-balance. In motivational terms, people who are accidentally polarizing often start out self-contained—with self-defined objectives and high achievement motive—and then learn that others have intense reactions as a by-product. Polarizing people can then learn how to re-create these reactions at will, becoming provocateurs because it is effective to do so, while remaining steadfast in pursuit of their original goals and objectives. Those polarizing people who are intentionally provocative draw strength and energy from the reactions of those around them, whether positive or negative. Through her adoption of punk clothing and attitude, for example, Lisbeth is able to reposition herself, moving from victim to active creator of others' reactions. In a sense, her demeanor helps her hide her true agenda and abilities so that she is better able to act strategically.

Had Larsson continued the series, Lisbeth no doubt would have remained a polarizing person within her fictional world. Her belief that people are capable of great evil has not changed by the end of the trilogy. She would have continued to make decisions largely independently of the input of others. She has no qualms about breaking laws, defines her own rules, and has little concern for her effect on others. In building her own small group of trusted confidants, Lisbeth, like the avant-garde artist, creates a separate, autonomous community that takes down the status quo—she smashes the table rather than fight for the right to sit at it. Like the successful women who are leaders in business and politics, Lisbeth learns that achievement motive is necessary, but not sufficient on its own to create change. In addition to "doing her homework," she learns how to use win-win influence effectively so that her goals can be achieved through the concerted effort of a group, not by her alone. And because she has experienced some moments of mutuality and trust in several relationships, she may have, in the future, allowed her need for affiliation to express itself in small ways. Eventually, she may have let others, as with Mikael at the series' end, more fully into her life.

SANDRA YINGLING, PhD, derives great joy from giving advice. She learned early in life that not everyone derives great joy from receiving advice, and thus she quickly developed a remarkable degree of impulse control. She earned her doctorate in clinical psychology from New York University and was a research scientist at Columbia University's College of Physicians and Surgeons. She continues to conduct research (and offer advice) as a consultant specializing in the development of resilient leaders and their teams.

During her short lifespan, Lisbeth Salander has been bullied, cursed, taunted, harassed, molested, beaten, raped, assaulted, groped, shot, locked away, and buried alive. Yet these experiences didn't break her. How has she been able not only to survive, but thrive—not just to fight back, but become an agent for positive change in the world around her? Pamela Rutledge uses positive psychology to answer these questions (and more) as she tackles resilience: the psychological term for what has allowed Lisbeth to cope with all the adversity she has encountered and come out stronger on the other side.

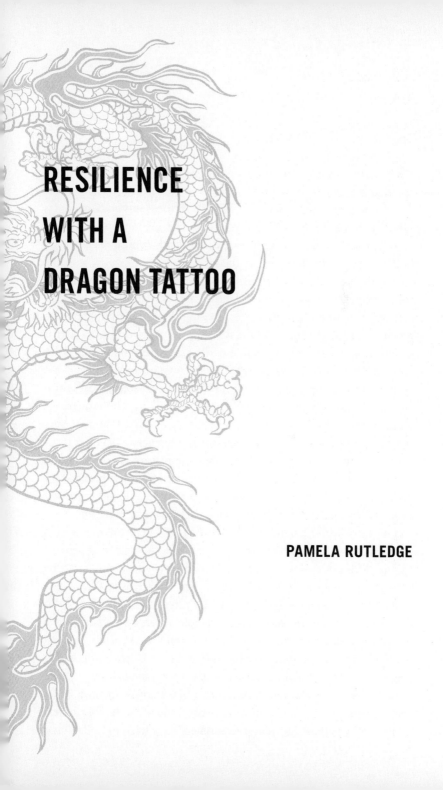

RESILIENCE
WITH A
DRAGON TATTOO

PAMELA RUTLEDGE

As soon as we step into her world, Lisbeth Salander challenges our sense of social norms, often to the point of discomfort and frustration. Her black lipstick, tattoos, and body piercings send out a clear message: "Keep your distance; visitors not welcome." Her demeanor and presentation are defiant and withdrawn, belying a bottled rage lurking just beneath the surface. Simultaneously, however, we see another Salander that intrigues us and inspires admiration. We see someone who is capable, insightful, and determined, a relentless researcher with a talent for cyber-hacking that gives her unlimited, albeit often illegal, access to the workings of the world. Salander is a character of polar contrasts that defies assessment—a sort of punk rocker meets Robin Hood—compelling because of, and in spite of, her contradictions. She provokes disapproval, but her "acting out" is also a cry for help and validation. She looks small, young, and vulnerable, while at the same time seeming road-weary and hard. Her socially inept and emotionally bereft interpersonal interactions belie her intellectual acuity for identifying intricate logic patterns and mastering technology. However, Salander's most remarkable trait is perhaps her resilience—her ability to "bounce back" after stressful and traumatic experiences, face down difficulty, and meet adversity head-on.

Like those whom Salander allows close to her—her employer Dragan Armansky, her guardian Holger Palmgren, and her friend, journalist Mikael Blomkvist—even when we feel distanced or frustrated by Salander's interpersonal inadequacies, we nonetheless admire her undaunted persistence and courage, her physical and mental skills, and her survival in the face of unspeakable adversity. As her history unfolds, it reveals a past marred by family instability, domestic violence, manipulation by a political system, and a series of abuses bordering on psychological annihilation. Her resilience is truly remarkable.

Salander's story also reminds us that, while many women who have been victims of abuse and trauma have the resilience to recover, others do not. Why is that? For years, researchers have tried to understand the psychology behind resilience, but understanding resilience has proved to be complex and elusive.

The study of resilience—what it is and how to encourage it—is part of a shift in psychology from what is known as the "medical model" of mental health, which is based on pathology, to a more positive "glass half-full," strengths-based point of view. This reorientation changes how we approach and understand behavior. Rather than seeing people as ill, where a psychologist's job is to detect and repair problems, the positive psychology approach views a psychologist's job as identifying and promoting psychological strengths and successes—such as resilience—to improve and sustain well-being.[1]

These qualities, like Salander herself, are complicated.[2] There is a forty-year history of debates about whether resilience is a trait, a process, or an outcome; a developmental path; uni- or multidimensional; time-limited; internal or external; adaptive; or optimal. There's even a debate on whether or not recovery should be included as an indicator.[3] In spite of these differences, research, particularly in

---

[1] M. E. P. Seligman, and M. Csikszentmihalyi, "Positive Psychology: An Introduction," *American Psychologist* 55 (2000).

[2] See, for example:

G. A. Bonanno, "Loss, Trauma, and Human Resilience: Have We Underestimated the Human Capacity to Thrive after Extremely Adverse Events?" *American Psychologist* 59 (2004).

C. S. Carver, "Resilience and Thriving: Issues, Models, and Linkages," in *Journal of Social Issues* 54 (1998).

A. Masten, and M. D. Reed, "Resilience in Development," in *Handbook of Positive Psychology*, eds, C. R. Snyder, and S. J. Lopez (New York: Oxford University Press, 2005).

[3] For example:

S. S. Luthar, "Resilience in Development: A Synthesis of Research Across Five Decades" in *Developmental Psychopathology: Vol. 3. Risk, Disorder, and Adaptation*, eds, D. Cicchetti and D. J. Cohen (New York: Wiley, 2006).

A. S. Masten, "Resilience Comes of Age: Reflections on the Past and Outlook for the Next Generation of Research," in *Resilience and Development: Positive Life Adaptations*, eds, M. D. Glantz, J. Johnson, and L. Huffman (New York: Plenum Press, 1999),

A. S. Masten, and J. Obradovic´, "Competence and Resilience in Development," *Annals of the New York Academy of Sciences* 1094 (2006).

neurobiology, has given scientists an increasing appreciation of resilience as an interaction of environmental, social, individual, and biological factors. Resilience, in the end, is best described as a dynamic system.[4] In other words, your ability to be resilient and overcome adversity is a product of who you are, what you know, where you are, who you're with, and how you adapt to the adversity. But the final measure of judgment rests with adaptation: whether one is able to overcome stress and trauma in a way that ultimately transforms traumatic experiences into positive growth.

In spite of appearances, Salander is just such a survivor. Therefore, we have to readjust our vision of her aberrant appearance and behavior, and ask whether her Goth[5] makeup and clothes[6], her antagonism, and her social withdrawal are coping strategies, forms of self-protection against an outside world that has proved dangerous. Are these actually manifestations of her resilience? If we take our cues from expert researcher Lisbeth Salander, and look beyond the obvious outward indicators she gives us, we can see how Salander not only survives the adversity she faces, but also thrives through a constellation of elements both innate and learned.

---

[4] See, for example:

S. C. Kobasa, S. R. Maddi, and S. Kahn, "Hardiness and Health: A Prospective Study," *Journal of Personality and Social Psychology* 42 (1982).

A. Masten, and M. G. Reed, "Resilience in Developing Systems: Progress and Promise as the Fourth Wave Rises," *Development and Psychopathology* 19 (2005).

[5] The term "Goth" refers to the Goth subculture that has roots in the British rock music scene in the 1980s. An outgrowth of the punk and post-punk styles, Goth subculture takes it cues from nineteenth-century Gothic literature. The style of dress draws mainly from variations on Victorian, punk, and deathrock (a subgenre of punk rock that emphasizes horror elements). Goth is most commonly associated with dark hair, clothes, makeup, and body piercings.

[6] *Editors' Note*: For more on this subject, see the essay on Goths in this volume by Young and McDonald-Smith.

Hardiness

Let's start with one of the most salient features of Salander's innate personality: hardiness. Psychological *hardiness*[7] is a powerful set of interrelated traits that involve a tendency to:

1. engage with or commit to a purpose—that is, to immerse oneself fully—rather than being detached or alienated (*commitment*)
2. seek ways to control or influence events rather than feel passive and powerless (*control*)
3. see adversity as a challenge rather than an insurmountable threat (*challenge*)

The combination of these traits results in a mental mind-set that predisposes one for resilience. Instead of simply giving up when faced with adversity, hardy individuals are fundamentally optimistic: to them, adversity is not only something that can be overcome, but also something that they themselves are capable of overcoming. By being resilient—by surviving and adapting in a positive way—hardiness is reinforced, thereby contributing to greater resilience. It's an upward spiral that allows an individual to frame new situations as challenges to be overcome, rather than impossible hurdles.

In Salander's case, it's hard to see any sense of optimism in her outlook, especially when she refused to eat at St. Stefan's or when she returns to visit Advokat Bjurman for the second time. She was clearly pessimistic about the behavior of the men with whom she was interacting (and her pessimism was proved correct). But the fact that she believed in her ability to take a stand and meet those challenges—by

---

[7] Psychological hardiness was first identified by Kobasa in 1979. In Kobasa's model, hardiness is viewed as an innate, individual personality trait that is a key contributor to the process of resilience. Hardiness is believed to bugger the negative effects of stress through a combination of cognitive, behavioral, and biophysical mechanisms. See: S. C. Kobasa, and M. C. Puccetti, "Personality and Social Resources in Stress Resistance," *Journal of Personality and Social Psychology* 45 (1983).

not taking the medications that dulled her thinking and by video-taping Bjurman's sexual demands—are, in fact, indicators of positive thought, as well as her efforts to seek control.

Self-Efficacy

> I haven't said a word to the bastard since the night I turned thirteen. I was strapped to the bed. It was my birthday present to myself.
>
> —Salander in *The Girl Who Kicked the Hornet's Nest*,
> speaking at her trial about her experience at St. Stefan's under
> Dr. Teleborian's care

That belief in one's own abilities is a necessary prerequisite for another facet of resilience: self-efficacy, something Lisbeth possesses in abundance. We all hold core beliefs about our own competence or capacities, and these beliefs—in addition to our belief in our ability to influence events around us—sets the stage for how we take action and actively cope with adversity.

No matter how young or overmatched she was, Salander always took action on her own behalf. Effectively abandoned by her mother and the authorities, it was left to Salander to protect herself, and she also took it upon herself to protect her family. While her choices of action may not seem appropriate by many standards, Salander did not act randomly. Instead, she always responded to perceived provocation: she hit the school bully after he punched her in the face, she assaulted the man groping her in Gamla Stan, and she attacked serial killer Martin Vanger with a golf club in order to save Blomkvist's life.

On every occasion, Salander rose to the challenge before her, believing that she could influence the outcome of the situation she was in. This, in a nutshell, is *self-efficacy*—the belief that you are capable of having an impact on your environment through your own actions. It is not a skill; it is what you believe you can do with your competence and effort. Self-efficacy is the opposite of helplessness, and the difference between persevering and giving up. While many psychologists define self-efficacy as implying positive outcomes,[8] there are times when positive outcomes are not as apparent, such as when one's actions mitigate feelings of helplessness, fear, or rage. The change effected is in the person herself, not in her external environment. Many of Salander's off-putting behaviors appear to work against her; some of them resulted in her being put in restraints or isolation, or arrested. But we might also view them as extremely effective, as they successfully assist her in achieving her main goal: to be left alone.

The early development of self-efficacy is influenced by two interacting factors: 1) a belief about how the world works (why and how things happen) and 2) a belief about your power in it (what you can make happen). Our ability to form such beliefs rests on our cognitive capacity for symbolic thought and our understanding of causality. When babies are born, they do not have a sense of self, personal agency, or cause and effect. As they mature, babies become aware that actions have reactions and physical consequences: crying makes Mom come running, a glass falling over makes water spill, or pushing a ball makes it roll. This awareness is *individual agency*—our sense of being able to take action. Individual agency on its own is unrelated to our sense of competence; it is our understanding that we are actors in the world, but does not say anything about the outcome of our actions. In contrast, self-efficacy is our belief in our own ability to plan actions successfully, predict outcomes, and effect change—either through direct experience, imitating others, or an assessment of our strengths and capabilities relative to a challenge.[9]

The development of self-efficacy ultimately rests on the responsiveness of the environment to our attempts at manipulation and control, and Salander's actions provide continual feedback that she has an impact. The results were not always desirable—such as ending up in

---

[8] A. Bandura, "Self-Efficacy Mechanism in Human Agency," *American Psychologist* 37 (1982).

A. Bandura, "Perceived Self-Efficacy in Cogntiive Development and Functioning," *Educational Psychologist* 28 (1993).

[9] A. Bandura, *Self-Efficacy: The Exercise of Control* (New York: Freeman, 1997).

the principal's office or at St. Stefan's—but they *were* triggered by her choices and actions. They provided her with proof that she could effect change. Positive feedback—"I made something happen"—reinforces our belief that we can control cause and desired effect. Psychological growth evolves as we have experiences, expanding our ability to predict and plan. Positive experiences expand our sense of competence, which in turn supports our willingness to take on greater goals and more challenges, creating, according to Fredrickson, "an upward spiral" of positive emotions.[10] In short, our successful attempts to control our environment are the most powerful way to reinforce self-efficacy further.

While in many senses Salander felt helpless as a child, unable to save her mother and unable to fight back at St. Stefan's, her self-efficacy fueled her resilience. Taking action on whatever she could impact—such as not talking to Teleborian or other psychiatrists—was a source of feedback that reinforced her sense of self-efficacy; they confirmed that her helplessness as a child was situational but not absolute. By persevering, she continued to make tiny holes in the walls of her "prison." Even seemingly negative outcomes—such as being put in bed restraints for refusing to speak to Teleborian, resisting medication, or lashing out at him—were proof that she mattered. Her resistance visibly frustrated Teleborian and impacted his reactions to her, as well as influenced the behavior of others, like the psychiatric staff who secretly brought her food. The knowledge that her behavior generated these responses, as insignificant as it might seem to us, furthered her internal resolve to keep trying. Similarly, she was even able to effect change in her circumstances during her legal helplessness as Nils Bjurman's ward, when she blackmailed him in order to regain control of her body, her finances, and her life.

On a larger scale, Lisbeth affects her world by cracking the case of Martin Vanger, thereby removing an exceptionally dangerous serial killer from society; her actions also unleash a chain of events that stop

---

[10] Barbara Fredrickson describes this as the Broaden and Build Theory. See B. L. Fredrickson, "The Broaden-and-Build Theory of Positive Emotions," *Philosophical Transactions of the Royal Society London* 359 (2004).

a sex-trafficking ring and reveal a top-secret government conspiracy. From a frustrated and abused child, the ever-resilient Salander grew to be a force for justice in the world.

Active Coping

Another part of what makes Salander resilient is the way she copes with adversity—her coping style. Coping styles are the behaviors, emotions, or thoughts that emerge in response to stressful events and determine our resultant physical and psychological functioning. These styles can be categorized as either avoidant coping or active coping (also called problem-focused coping). People like Salander—who have innate hardiness qualities and strong efficacy beliefs—do not shy away from problems; they cope by actively finding solutions. Avoidant coping seems to be the primary style of Lisbeth's twin sister, Camilla, who as a child retreated into denial about the conflicts that her father instigated and acted as if Zalachenko was a perfect father during his visits. In contrast, Lisbeth engaged in active coping with purposeful intent. Salander's actions toward her father as a child, attacking him on one occasion with a knife and on another by throwing gasoline and a match into his car, while violent and perhaps misdirected, address a problem and are goal-focused; her intent is to put an end to her father's abuse. They are not revenge, although even revenge can be viewed as an active coping style. In these cases, they are a manifestation of Salander's toughness and willingness to use whatever tools are at her disposal. Her mental strength and personality made it untenable to give up her personal power. Her coping mechanisms allowed her to retain her sense of power and emerge from a traumatic situation with her sense of self intact.

Successful active coping increases our resilience. Every time we succeed, no matter how small the victory, it contributes to that upward spiral of psychological growth and gives us more confidence in our ability to overcome adversity. In contrast, avoidant coping has been shown to contribute to slower recovery from both emotional trauma and physical illness, and is associated with greater psychological distress and depression.[11]

Finding Meaning

Believing in your own strength and power are the keys to resilience, but also important is having a sense of purpose that gives life meaning—a reason to persevere in the face of adversity beyond mere survival. Salander finds meaning in resisting and defeating oppression against women—first for herself, and then for others. She could not stand to let the "evil" win. This is what kept her psychologically intact while she was at St. Stefan's; her later actions on behalf of victims allowed her to protect others where she had failed her mother. Salander tattooed Nils Bjurman, made demands on the Vanger Corporation for retribution to the families of the women Martin Vanger had murdered, and pursued Zalachenko. All of these actions are on behalf of other victims—even those that could also be classified as acts of "revenge." (The desire for revenge, it should be noted, is not wholly destructive. It, as well as the reliving of negative emotions, can be an attempt to counteract powerlessness and function as a form of protection. On several occasions while at St. Stefan's, Salander purposefully remembered the smell of gasoline and fire from her attack on her father to remain focused and strong.)

Justice for abused and exploited women is an overarching theme in the Millennium trilogy and is reflected prominently in Salander's motivations and development. At an early age, Salander assumed responsibility for protecting her mother and, from this and subsequent abuses on her own person, internalized a strong sense of identity and

---

[11] See, for example:

S. Armeli, K. C. Gunthert, and L. H. Cohen, "Stressor Appraisals, Coping, and Post-Event Outcomes: The Dimensionality and Antecedents of Stress-Related Growth," *Journal of Social and Clinical Psychology* 20 (2001).

M. Beasley, T. Thompson, and J. Davidson, "Resilience in Response to Life Stress: The Effects of Coping Style and Cognitive Hardiness," *Personality and Individual Differences* 34 (2003).

purpose. Even after her mother's injury and, later, her death, Salander—brandishing Tasers, needles, fire, and cyber-hacking—remained intractable in situations where women were being mistreated, molested, and harmed. For Salander, there was no justifiable reason for compassion toward perpetrators against women.

Psychologist and Holocaust survivor Viktor Frankl writes about the importance of finding meaning in life, particularly in traumatic experiences.[12] Salander had experienced her own pain and devastation, and she finds meaning and purpose in using her strength to overcome and protect others from perpetrators of what she views as evil. Like Frankl, whose struggle to survive as a prisoner in a concentration camp convinced him that suffering can have a deeper existential meaning, Salander takes her experience and turns it into something positive for others. She elevates her pain and experience to a higher moral ground. Even as a lone avenger, Salander acts not only for herself but also on behalf of others.

Social Connection

It's no accident that Salander's actions on behalf of others—the broadening of her sense of meaning—increased at the same time her social connections increased and deepened. Connection is crucial to resilience. Despite the fact that Lisbeth has been betrayed many times, and profoundly, she still manages to form, maintain, and repair relationships. This is key to her survival and growth, despite the distance she enforces between herself and those who care about her. Our social attachments are the glue that anchors us in the social world. They provide a sense of strength and safety and give our life meaning, and therefore contribute strongly to our ability to be resilient. When we don't have connections—or when those social connections are negative—we not only are less able to handle difficult situations, but it increases our psychological distress and can lead to depression, increased social isolation, and antisocial or destructive behaviors.

---

[12] V. Frankl, *Man's Search for Meaning*, 2nd ed. (Boston: Beacon Press, 1985).

Early Attachments

Social connection—particularly close relationships with caring adults during childhood—is frequently identified as a key socio-environmental contributor to developing resilience because secure attachments provide the developmental anchor of emotional safety and stability.[13] Social connections lay the groundwork for secure attachments, which provide psychological security. In childhood, this allows us to explore the unknown and gain positive experiences that build our confidence to meet challenges. As adults, social connection is a psychological safety net; the knowledge that others care gives us strength. Secure attachments also create a psychological safe haven where we can be nurtured, validated, and encouraged—dusted off, patched up, and loved so that we are willing to continue to tackle new things and grow. Lack of early, secure attachment and social connections inhibit a child's development of trust and erode any sense of emotional or physical safety when interacting with the world. Consequently, lack of secure attachments can undermine the development of self-efficacy and resilience.

Early relationships for Salander were anything but supportive or safe. Teachers and other authority figures found her frustrating, uncooperative, and volatile from an early age. She was passive and bored in class and unyielding under "attack" of any kind, be it an assessment by a school psychologist or teasing by a fellow student. From within the context of her violent and unstable family life, we begin to see that Salander had no reasons to trust any authority figure—in fact, under the circumstances, we might consider it a questionable judgment if she did. Her first relationships were with a passive, helpless mother, a violent, abusive father, a sister in denial about their father's violence, and authorities who did not listen. The penalty for seeking help was incarceration in a mental hospital. Her early experiences taught her repeatedly that the only person she could trust with her safety—both physically and psychologically—was herself.

---

[13] A. Masten, "Ordinary Magic: Resilience Processes in Development," *American Psychologist* 56 (2001).

Attachment theory describes how our early relationships establish the mental models we use to organize our behavior and thoughts regarding how relationships work throughout our lives.[14] Salander's early attachment models left her untethered, with no confidence in the ability or willingness of her parents or other authorities to provide emotional or physical support or protection, from either an abusive father or school bully.

Rebuilding Attachments

The Salander we meet at the beginning of *The Girl with the Dragon Tattoo* is hostile and distant, and understandably so. But in spite of her social shortcomings and aggressive appearance, Salander has made substantial progress since St. Stefan's, due to her good fortune in having the guardianship of Advokat Holger Palmgren.

Palmgren had been Salander's trustee from the age of thirteen until she turned eighteen, but the change of his role to guardian represented a shift in the nature of their relationship and a significant turning point for Salander. Due to her multiple arrests and inability to remain in a foster home after her release from St. Stefan's, the only way to avoid institutionalization when Salander came of age was if Palmgren would agree to take on her guardianship.

> Palmgren declared that he would be happy to take on the job of serving as Fröken Salander's guardian—but on one condition "that Fröken Salander must be willing to trust me and accept me as her guardian." . . . Lisbeth Salander was somewhat bewildered by the exchange . . . until now no-one had asked for her opinion. (*The Girl with the Dragon Tattoo*)

Rebuilding and strengthening of attachment patterns, and providing a safe place to heal, are the foundations of trauma therapy with

---

[14] M. D. S. Ainsworth, "Infant-Mother Attachment," *American Psychologist* 34 (1979),

J. Bowlby, *Attachment and Loss: Vol. 1 Attachment*, 2nd ed. (New York: Basic Books, 1982).

abuse survivors.[15] Palmgren provides that type of therapeutic anchor. Theirs is the longest and most stable relationship of Salander's life, and he is the first person to treat her with respect, as if she is someone who matters. He accepted her silences without antagonism, and yet listened when she was willing to talk. He showed her that he would be consistent, supportive, and available, whatever her limitations might be. Palmgren provided some essential "reparenting" through stability, acceptance, and consistency.[16] He demonstrated a new and healthier attachment pattern that Salander could then use as a model.

Their relationship is described in *The Girl with the Dragon Tattoo* as "almost bordering on friendship," but that belies the strength of attachment that Salander felt for Palmgren and of his appreciation of her. After Salander learns that Palmgren did not die from a stroke as she had believed, she seeks him out at the rehabilitation home near Ersta. At this point he is no longer her guardian and so, in seeking him out, she has the opportunity to reestablish their relationship as equals. She is finally able to reciprocate meaningfully—an integral part of adult relationships. In a significant overture, Palmgren introduces her to hospital staff as his foster daughter, verbally validating their attachment beyond legal obligation. Salander, in turn, devotes her time and resources to his recovery with weekly visits, chess games, and funding for additional medical support to facilitate Palmgren's recovery. Palmgren ultimately recovers sufficiently to support Salander at her criminal trial, assisting Salander's attorney, Annika Giannini, and providing key evidence. Their relationship becomes increasingly mutually supportive, and it is this relationship that provides the basis for the formation of other connections—connections that

---

[15] K. J. Kinniburgh, M. Blaustein, and J. Spinazzola, "Attachment, Self-Regulation, and Competency: A Comprehensive Intervention Framework for Children with Complex Trauma," *Psychiatric Annals* 35 (2005).

B. S. N. Goff, and D. B. Smith. *Systemic Traumatic Stress* (Presentation at the AAMFT Annual Conference, Kansas State University, 2002).

[16] Reparenting is a term that originated in the transactional analysis movement, and is a therapeutic process that tries to restore emotional developmental deficits such as trust and self-acceptance. It is also used in schema therapy to reestablish healthy attachments.

created Salander's first meaningful and enduring circle of social support. Unlike earlier in her life, Salander's relationships are no longer compartmentalized and isolated; over the course of the Millennium trilogy, they become interwoven—such as when Paolo Roberto rescues Miriam Wu, or Blomkvist convinces Dr. Jonasson to give Salander her mobile Palm device—and increasingly strong.

Salander's Social Network

While Salander remains socially stilted at the end of the trilogy, each relationship we see her engage in shows a progression in her willingness to trust those willing to allow a connection to develop slowly, and by Salander's rules. Each of her primary relationships—with Palmgren, Paolo Roberto, Miriam Wu, Armansky, and Blomkvist—starts slowly but grows deeper over the course of the trilogy. When we are first introduced to Salander in *The Girl with the Dragon Tattoo*, it is through the baffled eyes of her employer Dragan Armansky at Milton Security. He notes that, "It was not Lisbeth Salander's astonishing lack of emotional involvement that most upset him. Milton's image was one of conservative stability. Salander fitted into this picture about as well as a buffalo at a boat show."

Yet Armansky also feels in that same instance that "Salander was beyond doubt the most able investigator he had met in all his years in the business." His relationship with her is professional; she is a talented, if perplexing, investigator who turns in reliably high-quality work.

However, when Salander visits Armansky unannounced after an extended absence, the nature of their exchange shows a very different understanding and indicates how much Salander has changed and allowed their relationship to grow since its inception. Armansky feels freer to express his frustration with her behavior, and Salander now cares enough to stay and listen, something that would have not happened a year earlier. She is even frightened by the potential of loss, which shows a surprising level of attachment and commitment on Salander's part, though she does not demonstrate it the way other people typically would. Salander asks if Armansky wants her to leave in *The Girl Who Played with Fire*. He replies, "'You do as you like. **227**

You always have. But if you leave now, I never want to see you again.' Salander was suddenly afraid. Someone she respected was about to reject her. She did not know what to say."

Salander's early relationships with Paolo Roberto and Miriam Wu also develop new dimensions as Salander sees proof that they are reliable sources of friendship and support. Blomkvist, too, proves that he is a reliable friend when he repeatedly recognizes Lisbeth's need for emotional distance and respects her personal boundaries. In spite of Salander's resistance, Blomkvist stands firm in his loyalty to Lisbeth during her hospitalization after being shot in the head by Zalachenko, through her arrest and incarceration, and during her trial.

Salander's virtual relationships strengthen as well. While she had enjoyed anonymous respect as the hacker "Wasp," these friendships cross into the real world when Plague and Trinity come to her aid in *The Girl Who Kicked the Hornet's Nest*. Plague even makes it clear that he's there to help her not because he expects to be paid—as he is for helping her with other hacking tasks—but because he values Salander as a friend. His loyalty surprises Salander, as she hadn't thought of their relationship in emotional terms previously.

When early attachments are missing due to neglect and/or previous trauma—as we have seen is the case with Salander—extended families and surrogate or mentoring figures can fill in the gap, contributing to the reworking of damaged internal models and advancing the development of a positive self-concept.[17] As the people in Salander's circle show their loyalty and their appreciation for her determination, resourcefulness, and intelligence—even as they better understand her shortcomings, she begins to understand that they are friends, and not just strategic contacts. As a result, she is able to move toward more reciprocal and healthy relationships, which reinforce her internal sense of resilience.

---

[17] See, for example:

A. S. Matson, and J. D. Coatsworth, "The Development of Competence in Favorable and Unfavorable Environments," *American Psychologist* 53 (1998).

J. C. Hall, "Kinship Ties: Attachment Relationships that Promote Resilience in African American Children of Alcoholics," *Advances in Social Work* 8 (2007).

Resilience as a Dynamic Process

Salander's growth in response to her increased attachments to others highlights an important quality of resilience that I haven't yet discussed in-depth: resilience as a dynamic process. An individual has the psychological and physical ability to adapt, continually interact, and evolve with experiences, both good and bad. Just as adversity can pose setbacks, positive experiences influence our trajectory, broadening our base of self-efficacy and expanding our potential for positive growth, resilience, and well-being. Figure 1 shows a conceptual map of Salander's experiences: looking at the trajectory of her resilience, we see the downward pressure of negative events and the upward pull of positive events that highlight her ability to take advantage of her strengths and meet the challenges she faces.

By the end of the trilogy, Salander has—with Blomkvist's help—emerged victorious. She has defeated the conspirators around Säpo

Figure1. Salander's Trajectory of Resilience

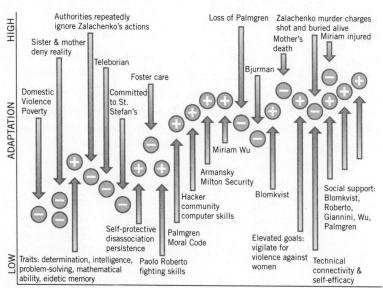

who protected Zalachenko at her expense, helped expose an underage sex trafficking ring, and exacted retribution from Ronald Neidermann and the biker gang Svavelsjö MC. She has, with help, settled the score for the abuse of herself, her mother, and many unnamed victims. But while revenge may be sweet, it is not enduring emotionally. Salander leaves Stockholm after her trial at a loss. She has to find a renewed motivation and purpose. The solution, she finds in the final book of the trilogy, is not the three months of heavy drinking she spends at Harry's Bar in Gibraltar. In a bold step, Salander flies to Paris to find Miriam Wu. This is a tribute to her personal growth and, in resilience terms, a positive outcome. The previous incarnation of Salander would have retreated to a solitary existence, remaining on the fringe of relationships and unattached to the world by emotional strings. Instead, she reaches out to reconnect with someone. Where once Salander wanted to be left alone, she has met the challenges of adversity and emerges from the gauntlet stronger and braver. Her resilience has allowed her not just to survive, but to experience personal growth that, for the first time, opens her to the possibilities of interpersonal relationships.

A Role Model for Resilience

We as readers are happy to see Lisbeth emerge victorious. We even need her to. Individual resilience to adversity is a common theme in art and literary portrayals of heroes and heroism. Salander is a hero because she overcomes the challenges she faces to achieve her goals and, like Robin Hood, her efforts are on behalf of others (although she bears the pain herself).

There's a larger message to take away from Salander's story, however. There's another way in which she is a hero, and that's in the way she models an important psychological strength for us readers. If she has the resilience to overcome against all odds, so do we.

PAMELA RUTLEDGE, PhD, is cofounder of A Think Lab and director of the Media Psychology Research Center. She is also faculty of media psychology, social media, and transmedia narrative at Fielding Graduate University, and an instructor at UCLA Extension and UC Irvine Extension. Beyond the Millennium trilogy, her passion is using cognitive and positive psychologies to understand, use, and develop media technologies for effective communication and positive impact in a transmedia world.

Lisbeth might not always get along well with others, but there is one special object she has a great relationship with: her computer. Lisbeth's technical prowess and software savvy, along with her habit of using them to gain access to places and things she shouldn't, make her a hacker. In her online universe, she is able to adopt her own identity, gain the admiration of others, seek justice, and achieve her personal ends. Also, unlike her life offline, online she's a part of a community; her hacker friends see her as one of them. Using her psychological research on hackers as a guide, Bernadette Schell compares Lisbeth to her real-life counterparts. Maybe, for as strange as she sometimes seems, Lisbeth is pretty typical—for a hacker.

LISBETH SALANDER, HACKER

BERNADETTE SCHELL

The word hacker has taken on many different meanings ranging from a person who enjoys learning the details of computer systems and how to stretch their capabilities to a malicious or inquisitive meddler who tries to discover information by poking around, possible by deceptive or illegal means.

—Steele et al, *The Hacker Dictionary*[1]

I became interested in hackers in 2000, when I was part of a university research team determined to summarize the personality and social behavioral traits of computer hackers and separate the myths from reality. Our team, consisting of two professors and two students, wanted to understand whether industry's and society's fears were reasonable in regards to the alleged toxic personality and behavioral predispositions of hackers. Could hackers cause a cyberwar or a virtual apocalypse?

Unfortunately, we discovered that answers to these intriguing questions were not easily forthcoming since there was a paucity of empirically based findings reported in the psychosocial, computer science, and business literature. Furthermore, after we set up a special website designed to have hackers respond to our survey items, we were hugely disappointed to discover that hackers did not trust us and, therefore, did not cooperate in our online study. The only way that we could crack the distrust issue was to gain the trust of a respected hacker who could help us enter the Computer Underground (a concept acknowledged by the media since 1980 to describe the virtual world of hackers). We eventually gained the trust of once-imprisoned hacker Bernie S (mainstream name Edward Cummings), who welcomed us into the hacker conference attendee community, thus assisting us in

---

[1] G. Steele, Jr., D. R. Woods, R. A. Finkel, M. R. Crispin, R. M. Stallman, and G. S. Goodfellow, *The Hacker Dictionary* (New York: Harper and Row, 1983).

bridging the research gap between myth and reality. I went on to be the Founding Dean of Business and IT at the University of Ontario Institute of Technology, one of the first Canadian universities devoted to providing undergraduate and graduate programs in IT Security (i.e., hacking with the intent of making things safer in the virtual world).

So imagine my delight and interest when a series of books appeared on the bestseller list that featured a powerful heroine who was a hacker. I was curious to see if Larsson really understood Lisbeth Salander, or if he had fallen for some of the same stereotypes that the media often present regarding hackers' thinking and behavioral patterns. What I discovered was that Lisbeth Salander's character demonstrated a sound knowledge of true hacker traits.

Hackers, Hacking, and Lisbeth Salander

Hackers are the elite corps of computer designers and programmers. They see themselves as the Harry Potters of the high-tech world. For hackers, designing software and inventing complex algorithms provides as much fun as fiddling with automobile engines can for car mechanics. Hackers have their own culture, their own language, and their own styles of dress. It is interesting to note that the word *hacker* has taken on many different meanings in the past twenty-five years. Whereas it originally referred to an inept furniture maker, the word now describes computer-savvy individuals who enjoy manipulating computer systems to stretch their capabilities and keep computer networks safe. Hackers generally come in two garden varieties: the *White Hat* hackers who use their skills to solve complex problems and to contribute positively to society, and the *Black Hat* hackers who use their tech skills for malicious ends. Black Hat hackers take revenge on people, governments, and industry, or use their skills for personal gain, often by utilizing deceptive or illegal means in their efforts to cause harm.

A slew of recent real-world hacking incidents, including attacks on Sony, Fox News, and President Obama's reelection website, as well as the *News of the World* British hacking scandal, have shone the spotlight on the growing power—and possible devastation—caused by digital warfare and Black Hat hacker exploits.[2]

We first learn of Lisbeth's hacking predispositions through Armansky at Milton Security. The company invests in cutting-edge technology and hires the best telecommunications technicians and information technology (IT) experts. Armansky observes Lisbeth for a while, noting that she likely suffers from some serious emotional problem but that there is an unusual intelligence behind her sullen façade. Though he tried giving Lisbeth complex research tasks, along with guidelines about how to proceed, she tended to listen patiently and then carry off the assignment as she saw fit—behaviors commonly noted in computer hackers. After Armansky asked Milton's technical director to give Lisbeth a basic course in IT science, the director responded that she seemed to have a better understanding of computers than most of their own IT staff.

From the many examples found in the three novels, Lisbeth exhibits more White Hat than Black Hat behaviors. She chooses to use her skills to help others (or protect herself) rather than cause harm to information or networks just for the thrill of it. However, even her White Hat hacking is technically illegal. Many hackers live in perpetual fear that they will be caught, because if convicted they will likely be imprisoned and lose access to their computers for years. If convicted of hacking in the United States, perpetrators are often charged with "intentionally causing damage without authorization to a protected computer." A first offender typically faces up to five years in jail and fines up to $250,000 per count, or twice the loss suffered by victims. The victims can also seek civil penalties. The idea of being charged and convicted for hacking haunts Salander as well:

Salander was aware that the legal description of the kind of hacking she did, both professionally and as a hobby, was "unlawful data trespassing" and could earn her two years in prison. She did not

[2] O. El Akkad, "Hacktivism 101: How Troublemakers, from the Sony Ttackers to News of the World, Carry Out Their Digital Dirty Work," *The Globe and Mail*, July 1, 2011.

want to be locked up. In her case a prison sentence would mean that her computers would be taken from her, and with them the only occupation that she was really good at. She had never told Armansky how she gathered the information they were paying her to find. (*The Girl with the Dragon Tattoo*)

"Cracking" is the term that hackers prefer to use when describing illegal trespassing for objectives involving mal-intent. Gaining unauthorized access to computer systems to make a copy-protected program run or flooding internet sites—thus denying service to legitimate users—are two cases in point. Moreover, important information can be erased or corrupted during a cracking exploit, and websites can be deliberately defaced—two more examples of causing harm to property. Unauthorized access is typically achieved by decrypting a password or bypassing a copy-protection scheme. The whole point is to gain access to a network to be able to manipulate information for some given objective. Lisbeth Salander hints at this process as she describes her means of "owning" Blomkvist's iBook in *The Girl with the Dragon Tattoo*. She notes, "Her immediate move, when she got hold of his iBook that first morning, had naturally been to transfer all the information to her own computer. That way it was OK if he dumped her from the case; she would still have access to the material."

Being discovered for hacking by those in mainstream society is perceived by hackers to be a personal flaw, especially for those who view themselves as professionals. Again, Lisbeth Salander shares this point with us in *The Girl with the Dragon Tattoo*: "With the exception of Plague and a few people on the Net who, like her, devoted themselves to hacking on a professional level—most of them knew her only as 'Wasp' and did not know who she was or where she lived—Mikael Blomkvist was the only one who had stumbled on to her secret. He had come to her because she made a blunder that not even a twelve-year-old would commit, which only proved that her brain was being eaten up by worms and that she deserved to be flogged."

The minimum skill set needed to "crack" a computer system is simply the ability to read English and follow directions. Neophyte crackers (or newbie hackers) often glean the information they need from books or the internet. Launching a more sophisticated crack attack against a "hardened," or protected, target requires the following knowledge base: three to four years of practice in computer languages like C, C++, Perl, and Java; general UNIX and systems administration theory; LAN/WAN theory; remote access; access and common security protocol information; and a lot of time. Also, there are certain social engineering skills that have to be acquired, which is often achieved through online interactions with the more talented and seasoned hackers.

How did Lisbeth Salander view herself as a hacker? When Blomkvist asks her this very question, Lisbeth replied, "I'm probably the best in Sweden. There may be two or three others at about my level."

Finally, like most hackers, Lisbeth is self-taught. "What could she say?" she wonders in response to Blomkvist's question about how she had taught herself hacking. "I've always been able to do it" (*The Girl with the Dragon Tattoo*).

Lisbeth embraces her identity and skills as a hacker, and so, through it, we are able to gain insight into her psyche. By understanding hackers in general, and how Lisbeth compares, we can better understand Lisbeth herself.

The Psychology of Hackers

There has been little psychological research done on hackers, largely for the reasons I mentioned previously. But results from three studies my colleagues and I conducted on hacker-conference attendees over the last decade help shed light on hackers generally, and Lisbeth specifically.

The first study focused on the demographic, behavioral, and psychological myths held by mainstream society about hackers; the results were examined in my first book on the subject, *The Hacking of America*.

The second study focused on whether hackers are as strange behaviorally and psychologically as the media and the public believe them to be. If asked to describe the traits of hackers, most people in mainstream society would probably suggest that hackers have a low tolerance for

business suits and business attire, preferring to wear clothes optimizing comfort, function, minimal maintenance, and a rebellious attitude. Onlookers in the mainstream would also likely add that hackers are obviously more "connected" to their computers than to people, perhaps even being addicted to their machines. And in terms of religion and self-control, most mainstream onlookers might suggest that hackers would probably describe themselves as agnostics, atheists, or followers of Zen Buddhism or Taoism. Finally, when hackers communicate with others, they tend not to make direct eye contact, a trait often diagnosed in persons with autism. To analyze these assumptions, this second study included detailed findings on hackers' autism-spectrum traits and on their self-reports about whether they believe their somewhat odd thinking and behavioral patterns help them be successful in their chosen field. The results were recently published in *Corporate Hacking and Technology-Driven Crime*.

The third study (completed in 2010 and whose results are first reported here in this essay) focused on the self-reported levels of *alexithymia* among hacker conference attendees; alexithymia is a difficulty in not only identifying and describing one's own feelings but in distinguishing between feelings and bodily sensations. Individuals with high levels of alexithymia are also said to experience a paucity of fantasies and to be preoccupied with external events.

By examining Lisbeth's patterns of thought and behavior while keeping in mind the results of these three studies, we can see how her identification as a hacker lets us understand her in a new way.

Lisbeth Salander: "Weird" Computer Hacker?

Throughout the three novels, Lisbeth Salander is repeatedly described by others as "weird," particularly when it comes to her social interactions. She seems to prefer the company of her computer to that of other people, and indeed, if forced to make the choice between developing an intense relationship with computers or with people, many hackers would choose the former over the latter. (Research has shown that, often, this is due to a lack of trust in people that is rooted in psychologically traumatizing events in childhood. Lisbeth certainly experienced trauma during her childhood, including the abuse by her father toward her mother. Research also suggests that the thrills of computer hacking provide a nice antidote to the pain caused by her understandably little trust in human relationships—but I'll talk more about that shortly.)

An interesting incident occurs when Salander risks a visit to Advokat Nils Bjurman (who had abused her during previous visits) because she needs to purchase a new computer after her favorite one, hidden in her rucksack, was run over by a car in the parking lot at work. While use of a computer is necessary for her job, her feelings appear to go beyond necessity. The loss of her computer causes Lisbeth to remark that she has "an urgent desire to kill someone" (*The Girl with the Dragon Tattoo*). The purchase of a first computer is typically an extremely significant experience for computer hackers, and the object itself holds much meaning—not unlike how young teens idolize their first human lover.

Lisbeth reflects on the destroyed computer in detail: we learn it was a white Apple iBook 600, with a twenty-five-gig hard drive and 420 megs of RAM, manufactured in January 2002 and equipped with a fourteen-inch screen. When Lisbeth bought it, it was the most recent and technologically advanced computer that Apple offered. Though Salander does not perceive herself as materialistic (and does not appear to be), her computers are always upgraded with the very latest and, sometimes, most expensive configurations. State-of-the-art computer equipment is the only extravagant entry on her "must-have" expenses list. Lisbeth also admits that though the loss of her first computer upset her immensely, it was not the end of the world, since she "had an excellent relationship with it during the year she had owned it" (*The Girl with the Dragon Tattoo*).

In short, Lisbeth thinks of her computer less as an object and more as a companion with whom she has formed a special relationship. She needs a new, fast machine, even if getting one means having to submit to physical and sexual abuse at the hands of her perverted guardian. This close relationship seems also to extend, to a degree, to hackers who have the same tech interests as she does. Like other hackers attending hacker conferences, Lisbeth tends to like or trust only those who are "different," like her.

Lisbeth also seems somewhat more comfortable with those who dress in their own unique styles, demonstrating her further affiliation with those outside of mainstream society. For example, Armansky sees Salander in a cafe with three girls and a boy, all dressed similarly to Lisbeth. Though she seems to be as reserved around her friends as she is at work, Lisbeth actually almost smiles at a story shared by one of her companions, who has purple hair—a style not common at the time in mainstream society. Armansky wonders how she would react if one day he came to work with green hair, worn-out jeans, and a leather jacket covered with graffiti and rivets instead of business clothes—if he looked less mainstream.

As far as those in mainstream society are concerned, hackers seem to be behaviorally and psychologically "different." This perception is a common first impression by many who meet Lisbeth in all three installments of the Millennium series. Even Mikael Blomkvist has this initial reaction. Blomkvist openly admits that he cannot figure out Salander, who is "altogether odd." She has long pauses in her conversations and her apartment is messy—even bordering on chaotic. Her kitchen hasn't been cleaned in ages, she has bags stuffed with newspapers in the hallway, and clothes are heaped on the floor rather than placed in a closet. She has love bites on her neck from an obvious recent sexual encounter, numerous tattoos all over her body—including a dragon tattoo on her shoulder blade—and two piercings on her face. In other words, summed up simply: "She was weird."

However, many in mainstream society simply have difficulty seeing the special gifts that hackers possess, such as thinking creatively and seeing patterns in information. And though to the outside world Lisbeth looks as if she is out of control and messy, that isn't actually the case. As is typical of hackers who are intensely involved in finding patterns and solutions to challenging problems, she simply places a higher priority on accomplishing objectives other than cleaning kitchens, placing discarded newspapers neatly in the trash container, and hanging clothes in the closet. This same kind of seemingly misplaced attention is also not uncommonly found in writers engaged in penning a new novel. So are computer hackers like Lisbeth Salander really all that "different" from the rest of us?

Prior to 2000, the literature on hackers painted a rather bleak and abnormal picture of their behaviors and thinking patterns. Taken as a   241 composite, the studies suggested that hackers under age thirty reported and/or exhibited many short-term stress symptoms like anxiety, anger, and depression. These symptoms were linked to things such as psychological pain rooted in peer teasing and harassment during childhood; introverted behavior and thinking tendencies that maintain a strong inward cognitive focus; anger that parents and others in mainstream society misunderstand or denounce their inquisitive and exploratory nature; educational environments that do little to sate high cognitive and creative potentials, resulting in high degrees of boredom and the pursuit of stimulation and a fear of being caught, charged, and convicted for hacking. Hackers use their exploits to fill some, if not all, of the voids created by these factors.[3]

Given that this composite was put together largely from studying young males charged with computer crimes, White Hat hackers complained in the early 1990s that such a profile, as depicted in the mental health literature and in the popular media, may not hold for the majority of hackers.[4]

In an effort to address this shortcoming, my colleagues J. L. Dodge, S. S. Moutsatsos, and I released our research findings from a comprehensive survey of the behaviors, motivations, psychological predispositions, creative potential, and decision-making styles of over 200 hackers (male and female) attending the 2000 Hackers on Planet Earth (HOPE) conference in New York City and the DefCon 8 hacker conference in Las Vegas. We found that whereas some previously reported findings and perceptions held about those in the Computer

---

[3] R. Blake, *Hackers in the Mist* (Chicago: Northwestern University, 1994).

M. Caminada, R. Van de Riet, A. Van Zanten, and L. Van Doorn, "Internet Security Incidents, a Survey Within Dutch Organizations," *Computers and Security* 17 (1998).

E. D. Shaw, J. M. Post, and K. G. Ruby, "Inside the Mind of the Insider."

http://www.securitymanagement.com/library/000762.html (1999).

[4] R. Caldwell, "University Students' Attitudes Toward Computer Crime: A Research Note," *Computers and Society* 23 (1993).

R. Caldwell, "Some Social Parameters of Computer Crime," *Australian Computer Journal* 22 (1990).

Underground (which we called *myths*) could be found in some hacker conference participants, others could not.

Our findings revealed that, contrary to the suggestion in popular and academic literature that only males are active hackers, there are also female hackers—though they made up only about 9 percent of the study's participants. Also, contrary to the myth that those in the hacker world are typically students in their teens, the findings revealed a broader hacker conference participant range, with the youngest respondent being fourteen years of age and the eldest being sixty-one years of age. The average age for respondents was twenty-five years—right around Lisbeth's age in the Millennium trilogy.

Contrary to the belief that hackers tend not to be gainfully employed, the 2002 study findings revealed that, unless they were currently in school, the hackers who were nearing or over age thirty tended to be gainfully employed. The largest reported annual income for a hacker conference attendee was $700,000. The average salary reported for the 190 male respondents was about $57,000; the average salary for the eighteen females was about $50,000. One other gender difference found in this study was that male hackers preferred to work for larger companies, while female hackers preferred working for smaller ones. Lisbeth is more like the females in our study than the males since, by her mid- to late-twenties, she is working for a small firm, Milton Security and earning more than 160,000 kronor a year (roughly $25,000) working part-time. If she worked full-time and accepted all the assignments Armansky offered her, she still would likely only make the average female salary.

Other key findings from this study that are relevant to Lisbeth Salander include the following:

1. Almost a third of the hacker respondents reported that they had experienced childhood trauma or significant personal losses, but the majority of hacker respondents did not make such claims. Significantly, of those hacker conference attendees who reported troubled childhoods—like Lisbeth—just over 60 percent of them said that they knew these events had a long-term adverse impact on their thoughts and behaviors—and on their relationships with others. We

can imagine Lisbeth reporting something similar, were she willing to answer such a survey.

2. Based on self-reported indicators of stress, the hackers experienced only mild, rather than pronounced, stress presentations, a finding that runs counter to common beliefs about hackers. In *The Girl with the Dragon Tattoo*, Lisbeth Salander admits, for example, that it does no good to cry; this is an example of a survival skill that she learned early on. Moreover, she learned that every time she tried to make someone aware of something in her life, the situation grew worse. Consequently, she decided it was up to her to solve her problems by herself, using whatever methods she deemed necessary. This kind of thinking-behaving mind-set indicates an individual who is able to maintain control in a stressful environment.

3. Those hackers who were more hostile (as assessed through a self-report measure) were also more sensitive to perceived and actual slights, referred to as *interpersonal sensitivity*. On numerous occasions, we see signs of interpersonal sensitivity in Lisbeth Salander. For example, in the closing of *The Girl with the Dragon Tattoo*, when Lisbeth sees Blomkvist in a romantic position with Erica Berger, the pain Lisbeth experiences is so immediate and so fierce that she stops midstride, incapable of movement. Feeling rejected, she becomes filled with anger, part of her wanting to rush after them. Though she doesn't act, she even thinks about taking the metal sign and using the sharp edge to cleave Berger's head in two.

4. During times of high distress, the hacker respondents noted that they generally appear to others to remain relatively calm and poker-faced rather than emotionally expressive. The same could be said about Lisbeth. For instance, people meeting her for the first time typically describe her as emotionless. When guardian Bjurman blasted Lisbeth with a series of questions about her sex life in *The Girl with the Dragon Tattoo*, Salander blurted out, "No, it's not particularly nice to be fucked in the arse—but what the hell business is it of yours?" But this was the *only* time that she outwardly

lost her temper. Otherwise, she intentionally kept her eyes on the floor so that they would not betray her discomfort or distress.

5. During the data analysis phase of our study, the long-term health prognosis, or Type scores, of the hacker respondents were placed on a continuum from the "self-healing, task-and-emotion-balanced" end—typically describing healthy, "self-healing" Type B individuals—to the "disease-prone" end—typically describing heart disease–prone Type As (who tend to prioritize tasks) and the cancer-prone Type Cs (who tend to prioritize emotion). Contrary to prevailing myths about hackers having strong Type A predispositions, the researchers found that the most frequent Type scores for hacker conference attendees—both male and female—were in the self-healing Type B category. A seventy-item self-report personality inventory developed by researchers Ronald Grossarth-Maticek and Hans Eysenck that categorizes respondents into "types" was used for this study. On each type score, the maximum obtainable was 10. The hacking respondent's highest score represents his or her strongest predisposition, the second-highest score represents his or her next strongest predisposition, and so on. Any score meeting or exceeding a critical level of 5 is considered to be a significant predisposition toward a certain Type. The highest score in the hacker study group was 7 and represented the Type B category. Given the depictions of Salander in all three novels as a person with a quiet demeanor who remained expressionless during times of upheaval, it is very like that she, too, is a Type B individual. After all, Lisbeth is a survivor who, despite repeated abuse, lives a productive life after horrible trauma. Someone who survived all that would have to be an effective self-healer.

6. The hackers, on average, scored in the "high" range on a questionnaire assessing creative potential. Lisbeth is also a highly creative individual. Through her hacking exploits, she discovers that Harriet Vanger is alive and well and living in Australia after going missing forty years before—a task that required a kind of creativity: seeing special patterns in data

that others could not detect. Salander discovers this after numerous talented others in mainstream society had failed, including the police.

Lisbeth Salander: An Individual with Asperger's?

Lisbeth Salander is described by her boss Armansky as being a very thorough researcher who submits painstakingly detailed, accurate, insightful, and scientifically precise reports with footnotes, quotations, and source references. We learn that Lisbeth chose not to communicate with her boss about her findings until the end of an investigation, at which point she would do so without any evident emotional involvement in the subject. Later, we watch Blomkvist observe some of Lisbeth's hidden talents—such as seeing patterns and understanding abstract reasoning where other people only perceive white noise—and suggest that Lisbeth Salander has Asperger's syndrome.

Though Blomkvist's off-the-cuff remark isn't backed up in Larsson's writing with iron-clad evidence, it's worth considering for a moment whether, in fact, Lisbeth exhibits traits that would be in keeping with a diagnosis of Asperger's syndrome. This disorder is a neurological condition considered to be on the autistic spectrum. Autism is defined as individuals' manifesting rather severe abnormalities in social and communication development, marked by repetitive behaviors and a limited imagination. Asperger's syndrome, on the other hand, is characterized by milder dysfunctional forms of underdeveloped social skills, repetitive behaviors, difficulty communicating, and obsessive interests. People diagnosed with the milder forms of Asperger's syndrome also seem to possess functional traits like high intelligence, exceptional focus, and unique talents in one or more areas, including creative pursuits.[5]

---

[5] S. Baron-Cohen, S. Wheelwright, R. Skinner, J. Martin, and E. Clubley, "The Autism-Spectrum Quotient (AQ): Evidence from Asperger's Syndrome/High-Functioning Autism, Males and Females, Scientists and Mathematicians," *Journal of Autism and Developmental Disorder* 31 (2001).

To put Asperger's syndrome in an everyday living perspective, individuals like Lisbeth Salander, who likely have this syndrome in milder or intermediate forms, tend to learn social skills with the same difficulty that most people learn math, but they learn math with the same ease that most people learn social skills.[6] However, it is important to note that most people who are very bright, have exceptional focus, and lack certain social skills do not have Asperger's. What distinguishes people with Asperger's is difficulty decoding subtle shades of meaning in language; many take words literally. Moreover they march to a different drummer, not because they choose not to adhere to social convention but because they don't understand social conventions.[7]

Because hackers in general have been thought to have higher degrees of Asperger's symptoms than most people in mainstream society, June Melnychuk and I studied whether this perception was valid in a sample of computer hacker attendees at the DefCon and Black Hat conferences in Las Vegas in the summer of 2007. The researchers' survey included the Autism-Spectrum Quotient (AQ) inventory of fifty self-report items, with the hacker respondents being asked to respond to the items using a "definitely agree, slightly agree, slightly disagree, and definitely disagree" scale. Ten of these questions assessed each of the five domains relevant to the autism spectrum—social skills or a lack thereof, attention switching, attention to detail, communication with others, and imagination. The findings indicated that the majority—about two-thirds of the 133 hacker conference respondents—had AQ scores in the intermediate range (scores from seventeen through thirty-two, inclusive). Of note, there were more males than females who scored in the *high* category of the AQ test, while there were more females than males who scored in the *low* category.

B. H. Schell, and J. Melnychuk, "Female and Male Hacker Attendees," In *Corporate Hacking and Technology-Driven Crime: Social Dynamics and Implications*, eds, T. J. Holt, and B. H. Schell (Hershey: IGI Global, 2001).

[6] B. H. Schell, and J. Melnychuk, "Female and Male Hacker Attendees," in *Corporate Hacking and Technology-Driven Crime: Social Dynamics and Implications*, eds, T. J. Holt, and B. H. Schell (Hershey: IGI Global, 2001).

[7] *Editors' Note*: For additional opinions on whether Lisbeth Salander has Asperger's, see essays in this volume by Hans Steiner and Robin Rosenberg.

Does Lisbeth Salander have Asperger's? While she does exhibit some of the symptoms such as high intelligence, repetitive behaviors, exceptional focus, and unique creative talents, she doesn't exhibit others, such as an inability to communicate effectively with peers interested in the same subject areas as she or adults in her workplace. She, like the majority of the hackers, would likely fall in the intermediate score range.

Lisbeth Salander: An Alexithymic Individual?

Finally, might Lisbeth be classified as someone who is alexithymic—and might this label be attributable to hackers, in general? Alexithymia refers to difficulty identifying and describing one's feelings, as well as distinguishing between feelings and bodily sensations. Individuals high in these traits are also said to experience a paucity of fantasies and to be preoccupied with external events.[8]

To get a better understanding of hackers and alexithymia, I asked attendees at the 2010 DefCon and Black Hat hacker conventions in Las Vegas to complete a self-report survey. Included in the survey was the Toronto Alexithymia Scale, or TAS.[9] Individuals scoring 74 or higher on the TAS are considered to be classified as alexithymic. In all, 156 males completed the survey, as well as five females. The study revealed that the hacker conference respondents had an average TAS score of 54, indicating that, as a group, male and female hackers seem not to suffer from alexithymia. Lisbeth doesn't exhibit alexithymia either. Though she may not voice her feelings, the inner life Larsson gives her shows she is very capable of identifying them (aside, of course, from her delay in realizing she is in love with Blomkvist). She also repeatedly shows signs of being able to distinguish between feelings and bodily sensations. For instance, she never feels something and cannot determine whether the source of her distress is internal and emotional or an external sensation like cold.

---

[8] G. J. Taylor, D. P. Ryan, M. A. Doody, and P. Keefe, "Criterion Validity of the Toronto Alexithymia Scale," *Psychosomatic Medicine* 50 (1998).

[9] Ibid.

Moreover, those hacker respondents with higher scores on the TAS (i.e., scores exceeding the critical cutoff score of 69) reported less ability to cope with stressors, had worse professional relations with peers, and had poorer personal relations with people in general. Most of these problems are not typical of Lisbeth and thus provide further "evidence" that she is not alexithymic: although Lisbeth's relationships are few, they are largely positive; she has excellent working relationships with both Armansky and Blomkvist and is well respected by her fellow hackers.

Also of note, from that same 2010 survey, though unrelated to alexithymia: the hacker respondents had relatively high scores on "conscientiousness" and "being open to new ideas when solving problems"—two traits that apply equally as well to Lisbeth, and are on display during every investigation she undertakes during the trilogy. Her conscientiousness keeps her pursuing the truth long after others have stopped, and her openness to new ideas lets her see possibilities that others do not.

Complex Gifts

Lisbeth Salander, though fictional, has much in common with real-world hackers. In both, what is often perceived as "weird" is instead a particular set of compensatory gifts not so readily grasped by others. Lisbeth is portrayed as possessing an incredible and creative problem-solving capability—not unlike gifted mathematics and science professors (many of whom have been found to have intermediate scores on Asperger's syndrome diagnostic tests, as I believe Lisbeth would). Contrary to mainstream belief, both Lisbeth and most of her fellow hackers use those gifts not to damage society, but to contribute to it. And what looks like distance from others and a lack of emotion or caring is in many cases a high level of sensitivity to other people's feelings and to rejection that they have simply learned to hide.

Lisbeth, it appears, is an excellent representation of the hacker community. Rather than furthering stereotypes, Larsson has provided a nuanced portrait of a talented, complex young woman that is consistent with what we know of real-life hackers. The saying "Don't judge a book by its cover" applies equally as well to Lisbeth and to the hacker community in our world.

 BERNADETTE SCHELL is Vice-Provost of Laurentian University in Ontario, Canada. She has written a number of journal articles, chapters, and books on hackers, including *The Hacking of America: Who's Doing It, Why, and How*; *Internet and Society*; *The Webster's New World Hacker Dictionary*; *Cybercrime*; and *Corporate Hacking and Technology-Driven Crime: Social Dynamics and Implications*. She was also the Founding Dean of the Faculty of Business and Information Technology at the University of Ontario Institute of Technology (UOIT) in Canada.

We like Lisbeth Salander because we can identify with her—and because she is so outrageously different from us. She embodies certain sentiments with which we're all familiar: everyone knows what it feels like to be misunderstood, to feel like an outsider, or to question our faith in others. But not many of us know what it feels like to crack decades-old murder cases, have a "photographic memory," succeed in a crusade to stop women from enslavement in a prostitution ring, or battle for our lives against a deranged ex-Soviet spy who happens to be our father. Lisbeth possesses extraordinary traits and characteristics that might lead us to wonder: Is she something more than the Millennium trilogy's heroine? Could she, in fact, be a superhero? Considering everything from her appearance to her intellect to her personal goals, Robin Rosenberg makes a convincing case that Lisbeth Salander might indeed be just that.

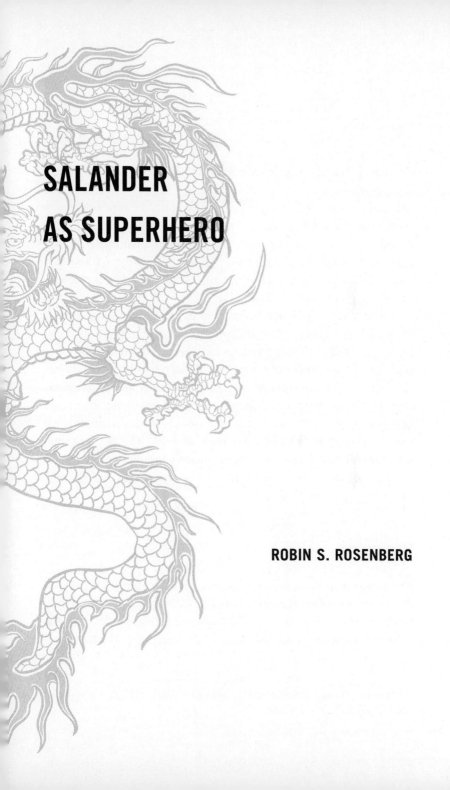

SALANDER
AS SUPERHERO

ROBIN S. ROSENBERG

Lisbeth Salander is a captivating protagonist. Her appearance and demeanor lead us—and the characters in her world—to make assumptions about her, to pigeonhole her as a Goth, a slacker, a rebel. Over the course of the first novel and the trilogy, Stieg Larsson upends our analysis of her character as he reveals her inner life, her outward behavior, and the choices she's made. We can't help but admire her grit and persistence, her inner strength and commitment, her strong moral code, and her adherence to it.

There's a sense in which Salander is an action hero, even though the action isn't generally hitting, punching, or kicking (though she engages in some of those actions, too). Rather, she engages in hacking, researching, and other uses of her substantial intellect and emotional strengths. Her heroism is demonstrated mentally as well as physically. I'll go one step further: I think that Salander is a *superhero*. She has the three most important characteristics typical of a superhero: a *mission*, (super)*powers*, and a superhero *identity*.[1] The fact that she's not explicitly labeled as a superhero—and that we only subliminally come to understand her as one—adds to her appeal. Let's explore these characteristics in more detail.

The Mission

Every superhero has a mission. Batman seeks to avenge his parents' deaths by "spending the rest of my life warring on all criminals."[2] Spider-Man's mission is to use his spider-like powers to help others. Superman fights for truth, justice, and—until recently—the American

---

[1] P. Coogan, "What Is a Superhero?" in *Superhero: The Secret Origin of a Genre*, eds, R. Rosenberg, and P. Coogan.

[2] *Detective Comics #27*, 1939.

way.[3] Most superheroes don't begin with those missions, though. Their missions arise as a response to events in their lives—most frequently traumatic events. These events steer the protagonist to dedicate him or herself to a (superheroic) cause. The murders of Bruce Wayne's parents steer him to train and study for years and then don the Batsuit in order to reduce crime in Gotham City. The murder of Peter Parker's Uncle Ben leads the newly spider-powered adolescent to dedicate his life and powers to protecting others rather than pursuing fame and glory as an enhanced being. Clark Kent's questions about his place in the world steer him toward his mission as Superman.

Salander, too, has life events that steer her toward a mission. At the beginning of Larsson's trilogy, Salander's work as a private investigator is a job: she does the work she's hired to do and doesn't get involved in her investigations beyond what is required. She doesn't yet have a mission in the heroic sense, but when investigating Mikael Blomkvist for Dirch Frode (Henrik Vanger's attorney), the pieces don't all add up and she's intrigued. Mikael Blomkvist plans to go willingly to jail without disclosing the sources for his inaccurate reporting on Wennerström. Salander welcomes the opportunity to be paid to find out more about Blomkvist.

During this same general time period that Blomkvist begins looking into Harriet's disappearance, Salander undergoes a new traumatic experience of her own that involves secrets, surviving injustice, and being disempowered: she is coerced into performing oral sex on her new guardian, Nils Bjurman—a man in a position to destroy her life and autonomy. Salander is not willing to remain subjected to Bjurman's torture, so she sets out to entrap him by filming him when he next demands oral sex. He demands more than that, though, and he brutally rapes her.

After being taunted by others and witnessing abuse in her home as a child, as an adult Lisbeth places a high value on being in control of her life—and Bjurman's brutal assault made her feel out of control. Although she gains a hold over him by filming the rape and thereby securing evidence of his crime, this hold came at a great personal cost.

---

[3] In *Action Comics* #900 (2011), Superman renounces his American citizenship and declares himself a citizen of the world.

Salander is not someone who likes feeling powerless. (As we learn in the second novel, when she was strapped down in the seclusion room as a child, she'd calm herself by imagining being in control—by being able to act on her own behalf.)

It is in the aftermath of her experience with Bjurman that she discovers Blomkvist's new project: to find out what happened to a young woman, Harriet Vanger, who went missing decades ago. When Blomkvist asks Salander to research the case and track down old murders that might correspond to selected biblical passages, Salander is intrigued.

It is while hunting for the details of that first murder case—in which the woman was bound and tortured—that Salander seems to develop the stirring of purpose that Blomkvist already possesses. For her, the investigation shifts from an interesting puzzle that slakes her intellectual curiosity to one of a *mission*—to uncover the truth and see justice done. Blomkvist's mission becomes her mission, though they have different ideas of what justice might ultimately mean. Salander turns up additional murders that were not on Harriet's list. And when the job for which she was hired is over (but the killer not yet discovered), she wants to continue. Blomkvist says he'll pay her but she would have done so for free.

As she and Blomkvist find and put together the pieces, she also sees Blomkvist's burning passion to discover the person who sadistically murdered young women. Based on her own experience with Bjurman (and as we find out in the subsequent stories, her experiences with child psychiatrist Teleborian), she can identify with these dead women—these victims—and no doubt views Blomkvist's goal and efforts to solve their murders as heroic. She is transformed by watching him and by taking part in the cause for truth and justice, just as sidekicks are transformed by their mentors (as Robin was by Batman, for instance).[4] We see her channel her sense of agency and *self-efficacy* (her belief that she can do what she sets out to do), into a desire to fight for justice as she interprets it.[5]

---

[4] Although Lisbeth may start out as a sidekick, that's not to say that Blomkvist is a superhero. He's not: he has a mission—as many kinds of heroes do—but he doesn't have superpowers nor does he have a superhero identity.

[5] *Editors' Note*: See Mikhail Lybansky's essay on justice for more about this.

Transformation can also arise in response to trauma. In my formulation, Salander's experience of being raped was the turning point that steered her to her mission. Like other survivors of trauma, Salander found a way to make personal meaning of her traumatic experience. Salander's transformation as a result of her traumatic experience is consistent with the findings of an area of psychological research referred to as *posttraumatic growth*, in which the stress of trauma challenges people's beliefs—about themselves, the world, and their place in it—and induces them to grow in positive, meaningful ways.[6] (A minority—about 20 percent—-of people who experience a trauma go on to develop posttraumatic stress disorder [PTSD]; they may not experience posttraumatic growth while their PTSD symptoms are prominent and chronic.) Trauma can leave the survivor wondering, "Why did this *happen?*" and when the trauma has a personal element, such as with rape and assault, the survivor may wonder, "Why did this happen to *me?*"

As survivors struggle to answer that question, over time most report feeling stronger for having come through their traumatic experience. They make sense of their (senseless) traumatic experience and newly discovered strength by committing themselves to helping others. Sometimes survivors work to prevent what happened to them from happening to others. Candy Lightner and Sue LeBrun-Green, who lit the fire of awareness about drunk driving when they started Mothers Against Drunk Driving (MADD), are perfect examples of this. The seeds of MADD were planted in 1980 after Lightner's thirteen-year-old daughter, Cari, who was walking to a church carnival, was hit and killed by a drunk driver.[7] Another person who made meaning of family trauma is William Minniefield, an African American man whose brother died waiting for a kidney transplant and whose other brother is waiting for one still. Organ donation by minorities is less common and leads to even longer wait times for organs that are the best match for African Americans. Minniefield

---

[6] P. A. Linley, and S. Joseph, "Positive Change Following Trauma and Adversity: A Review," *Journal of Traumatic Stress* 17 (2004).

[7] Go to http://www.madd.org/about-us/history/madd25thhistory.pdf for more information about the history of MADD.

founded the Minority Organ Donation Education Program to educate minority populations about organ donation, and to try to prevent what happened in his family from happening to others.

Other survivors may develop missions to help people like themselves—survivors after the fact. After David Schury's recovery from the burns that covered over 30 percent of his body, he and his wife, Michele, started the From Tragedy to Triumph Foundation, which provides support to burn victims and their families.[8]

In a sense, Salander develops a mission after her experience with Bjurman: to use her talents and abilities to figure out who abused, tortured, and murdered young women. Her answer: Gottfried and then Martin Vanger. Like other trauma survivors, Salander acts to prevent further victims. She prevents Blomkvist from being another of Martin's victims, then injures Martin and chases him on her motorcycle at which point Vanger decides to kill himself, steering his car directly into an oncoming truck.[9] Martin Vanger isn't able to harm any more women because of her intervention.

It is during the period of Blomkvist's helplessness—when Martin Vanger holds Blomkvist hostage in the basement room and is about to kill him—that Salander transforms from Blomkvist's sidekick to a (super)hero in her own right. Like any superhero, she saves him at risk to her own life. She's dedicated. Her sense of purpose is so great, in fact, that she becomes a moral leader with a clear vision of the correct path ahead. When she later explains to Henrik Vanger's attorney, Dirch Frode, what was really going on with Martin Vanger, Frode—temporarily unable to decide among untenable moral choices about what to do about Martin's basement torture chamber, how much to tell the police, and what to reveal about Martin's misdeeds—realizes that "here he was taking orders from a child [Lisbeth]."

---

[8] Go to http://www.ftttf.org/davesstory.html for more information about their story.

[9] In the Swedish film version, Salander has a more direct hand in Martin Vanger's death: he doesn't drive in front of a truck, but ends up accidently driving down a hillside. He remains alive but trapped; he asks Salander to help him get out. Salander refuses and his car (and he) ignites and goes up in flames.

Salander even espouses to Blomkvist the superhero's credo—that people have a choice in how to behave, even if they had a bad childhood. She challenges him by stating, "So you're assuming that Martin had no will of his own and that people become whatever they've been brought up to be," and, "Gottfried isn't the only kid who was ever mistreated. That doesn't give him the right to murder women. He made that choice himself. And the same is true of Martin" (*The Girl with the Dragon Tattoo*).

As with other superheroes, part of Salander's mission is to see that justice is served for others—in this case, the dead women—at least as much as it can be. She wants Frode and Henrik Vanger to do their best to identify the victims and provide their families with "suitable compensation." She also wants them to donate two million kroner each year, in perpetuity, to the National Organization for Women's Crisis Centres and Girls' Crisis Centres in Sweden. Her transformation to hero/moral arbiter is complete. She has made meaning of her own traumatic history and seeks to prevent what happened to her from happening to others.

The first novel is Lisbeth's "origin story," a story that explains who she was "before" (before the events that began her transformation) and who she becomes; superhero origin stories document transformations of personal growth, typically in response to some type of trauma or crisis. This transformation, reflected in her attire and behavior, is clear at the beginning of the second book, *The Girl Who Played with Fire*. She no longer dresses to give off an angry attitude, and during the beginning of the Caribbean hurricane she put her own life at significant risk to find her young lover George Bland and bring him to safety. On their way back to the hotel, Salander again puts herself at risk to prevent Richard Forbes from killing his wife. Deviating from her normal snarky or defensive attitude, she is polite to the local police investigating Richard Forbes' disappearance, answering their questions without malice. She even allows strangers to touch her without giving them a look or biting their heads off![10] This is a

---

[10] In *The Girl Who Played with Fire*, Salander allows the Nobel Estates realtor to "kindly put his arm around Salander's shoulders, escorting her to the door" (p. 89), an action unthinkable at the beginning of the first novel.

different Salander than we are introduced to at the start of the first book. She is no longer someone who wants to be left alone and who interferes in other people's lives only through her computer, and only when paid or for her own personal ends. She has become a protector and avenger.

Powers

The "powers" of superheroes (that is, *superpowers*) are generally considered to be powers, skills, and abilities that are beyond that of the average person. Salander has several that could be considered superpowers—skills and abilities that are far enough above average that they are fantastical in the same way that Batman's abilities are. [11]

Hacking

Salander's most impressive superpower is probably her hacking ability.[12] It is fantastical and, to people who are not tech savvy, borders on magical. Salander's hacking saves the day and without it Blomkvist's mission would likely come to naught. He didn't have enough powers to achieve the mission on his own.

Salander's hacking is also instrumental to her transformation into a superhero; over the course of the trilogy she uses this power to "do good" for others, selflessly and at personal risk, in order to reveal the truth about the bad guys (and thus protect others from future harm), as well as to save herself.

---

[11] Although some superheroes are very intelligent—such as Bruce Wayne or Tony Stark—I don't consider intelligence *per se* to be a superpower. In our world, highly intelligent people, as a group, don't seem to be superpowered. Rather, I propose that for a talent, skill, or ability to be considered a superpower it must border on the fantastical. A superpower may be related to aspects of intelligence, such as Tony Stark's inventing ability, but it doesn't have to be.

[12] *Editors' Note*: See Bernadette Schell's essay on hacking for more information about this.

The Ability to Delay Gratification and Regulate Emotions

Salander also has some of the less obvious but still typical superhero powers. One of those powers is her remarkable ability to delay gratification: to put off a "reward" in the short term for a larger "reward" in the longer term.[13] As her first guardian, Holger Palmgren, taught her, she gives careful consideration to the long-term consequences of her actions and is *remarkably* able to forgo the momentary satisfaction of lashing out at the villains of the story in order to reap a more lasting protection later. She bides her time for events that may take weeks to bear fruit, as she did when she sets up her plans to divert money from Wennerström at the end of the first book, opening banking accounts and obtaining false IDs. Another example can be found in the last book: rather than impulsively try to use her hacking skills to get short-term revenge on her enemies, she spends weeks obtaining and organizing information for Blomkvist's book and for her own legal case.

Children who are better able to delay gratification go on to be adults who are better able to regulate their emotions.[14] You may feel that Salander didn't delay gratification when she was a child—she fought back when bullied and she refused to answer questions she didn't want to answer. I argue, though, that these acts of apparent rebelliousness weren't *gratifying*. She fought back in the hopes that the bullies would learn not to mess with her, and she didn't answer the teachers' questions because she didn't understand the point in doing so. Like children who can delay gratification, Salander became better able to regulate her emotions. Consider that in the second novel, we learn that beginning during her childhood, when she feels out of control and panicky, she imagines herself in a situation in which she is in control. Such mental distraction by imagining situations in which

---

13 W. Mischel, E. B. Ebbesen, and A. Raskoff Zeiss, "Cognitive and Attentional Mechanisms in Delay of Gratification," *Journal of Personality and Social Psychology* 21 (1972).

14 Y. Shoda, W. Mischel, and P. K. Peake, "Predicting Adolescent Cognitive and Self-Regulatory Competencies from Preschool Delay of Gratification: Identifying Diagnostic Conditions," *Developmental Psychology* 26 (1972).

she can be in control is very adaptive, and helps calm her and make her feel stronger.

Photographic Memory

What about her other superpower—the "photographic memory," her ability to "see" accurately in her mind's eye things that she's seen before? Guess what? Salander's photographic memory is as much a fictional superpower as is Superman's X-ray vision and Spider-Man's spider-sense. If only it were possible! Psychologists who have investigated the possibility of this type of memory study *eidetic imagery*—the experience of, after looking at a scene or object, being able to conjure up accurately and vividly in the mind's eye an image of what was previously seen. Whereas normal visual images are typically experienced as arising in the mind, people who claim to have eidetic imagery report that those images seem as if they are projected outside, even though they know the images are not real.[15]

Eidetic imagery isn't "photographic" memory, though. No memory is truly photographic, but rather is a function of what we perceive—what we pay attention to and how we organize that information. Thus these memories can't be 100 percent accurate, since we can't pay attention to everything happening around us (using all five senses) and be thinking about it at the same time. People who are reported to have particularly good eidetic memory still make errors when reconstructing what they saw, and these visual images stay relatively sharp only for a few minutes. People who seem to have good visual memories, perhaps even approaching Salander's apparent talent, are likely using mnemonic techniques to help them memorize what they are seeing. Acronyms are an example of a type of mnemonic (such as ROYGBIV to remember the colors of the rainbow).[16]

---

[15] For more information, see http://plato.stanford.edu/entries/mental-imagery/quasi-perceptual.html. Also R. N. Haber, and L. Haber, "Eidetic Imagery," in *Encyclopedia of Psychology*, vol. 3, ed. A. E. Kazdin, (Washington, DC: American Psychological Association, 2000).

[16] For an article debunking "photographic memory" read:
http://www.slate. com/id/2140685/ and http://www.psychologytoday.com/articles/200603/the-truth-about-photographic-memory.

Salander never says that she has a photographic memory, though. It is Blomkvist who labels her ability in that way. In the first novel, Blomkvist tells Salander how fantastic a researcher she is. Salander replies,

"That's just how it is. I know computers. I've never had a problem with reading a text and absorbing what it said."

"Your photographic memory," he said softly.

"I admit it. I just have no idea how it works. It's not only computers and telephone networks, but the motor in my bike and TV sets and vacuum cleaners and chemical processes and formulae in astrophysics. I'm a nut case, I admit it: a freak."

Salander seems to emphasize that she's *absorbing* the information (that is, mentally processing and then understanding the complex phenomena that she sees), whereas Blomkvist focuses on her visual memory as being like a camera, which it clearly isn't. (Also, even if you can remember something accurately, you don't necessarily understand what you're seeing. Where Blomkvist must labor days or weeks to understand Wennerström's financial transactions, Salander unravels and understands them in much less time.)

Further evidence that she doesn't have a photographic memory is found in the second novel, where Salander refers to having *memorized* the multiplication tables and the three-line mathematical formula in *Dimensions in Mathematics*. Although it's possible that her use of the term *memorize* is a Swedish-to-English translation error, I don't think so. So another way of understanding Salander's apparent visually related superpower is not that she has a photographic memory, but that she's very good at making sense of complex visual information, and very good at memorization. That is, she's smart (like many superheroes—think Batman, Iron Man, Spider-Man), but she has a particular set of intellectual smarts. She's very good at analyzing and understanding what she sees, whether it's reams of financial documents, computer code, or social cues.[17]

---

[17] Some characters in the trilogy wonder whether Salander has Asperger's syndrome because she doesn't reciprocate the everyday social niceties such as making

Superperseverance

Salander has one more superpower: Like all superheroes, she keeps going despite setbacks and hardships, including physical pain. For instance, in the second novel, she's like the Energizer bunny: despite being shot in the hip, back, and *brain* and then being buried in an unmarked grave, she just keeps on going. In that scene, she is clearly like a superhero under vicious attack who won't go down; in such scenes in superhero stories, the villain sometimes utters remarks to the effect of, "Why won't you just die?" We can only marvel at her ability to survive and persevere.

Salander is more than a hero; she possesses powers that are beyond those of most mortals. Does she have the third characteristic—a superhero identity?

Identity

Most superheroes have two identities; their superhero identity and their "civilian" identity. The superhero identity typically has two elements—a code name and a costume. The *code name* conveys something about the character and his or her powers. Salander's code name is Wasp; this is the name under which she "operates" as a cyber(super) hero. How did she get this name? When she was boxing—with men much bigger than she—she fought admirably; in fact, boxing with her was "like scrapping with a hornet," a type of wasp. The name *Wasp* also conveys other information about Salander. According to Webster's unabridged dictionary, the wasp has a narrow waist (true of Salander), and the female has a stinger. Salander may not have a physical stinger coming out of her body, but over the course of the first book she sets up a "sting" operation (on Bjurman). Moreover, like a

---

eye contact, or returning a greeting or smile; they think it's because she doesn't understand these social conventions. I propose that Salander does *not* have Asperger's; she *understands* normal social conventions, but chooses not to conform to them (this lack of conformity gave her strength during her years of incarceration in a psychiatric hospital). In fact, Salander is a very astute observer of human nature and understands what motivates a given person.

wasp, when Salander sets her sights on someone, she can be annoying or even cause pain. The dictionary also gives a second meaning to the word—someone who is petulant or snappish, and that is certainly a characteristic of Salander as well. More about wasps: according to Wikipedia,[18] wasps prey on pest insects and so are used as a form of pest control. How appropriate, since that is exactly what Salander tries to do!

Among superheroes, a code name also serves to separate the two identities and thus protect the superhero's civilian identity, as it does in Salander's case. Because her hacking is illegal, and Salander is a very private person, she hacks under the name "Wasp" and thus protects her civilian identity.[19]

The second identity characteristic of the typical superhero is a *costume*. Usually a superhero's costume stands out and announces to the world the superhero's status; if you see a person dressed in tights and a mask, you'll think "superhero" (or supervillain, but you'll think super-something). Bruce Wayne realized the power of a costume; before he became The Batman he contemplated what costume to wear when fighting criminals in order to "strike terror" into their hearts. Inspired by a bat that happened to fly into his house at the right moment, he dresses in a batlike costume. Salander's costume—the Goth one that she wears at the beginning of the trilogy—also has a goal that serves the purpose of announcing her status as different. As Blomkvist notes in the third novel, "Salander always seemed to mark her private space as hostile territory" with the "rivets in her leather jacket as a defense mechanism, like the quills of a hedgehog. To everyone around her it was as good a signal as any: *Don't try to touch me—it will hurt.*"

It's not simply that Salander's costume consists of black leather. The X-Men wear black leather, too (at least in films), as do other superheroes such as the Punisher. Salander's costume also consists of body piercings, tattoos, and a coif that together scream "Goth" and don't inspire the sense of security that tights and a cape do. Blomkvist's

---

[18] http://en.wikipedia.org/wiki/Wasp.

[19] Lest you are asking yourself which identity is the "real" Salander, the short answer is that both identities are "real"—each is a different facet of her, and each serves a purpose.

analysis about Salander's costume is correct. Salander knows that people make inferences about her; she chooses to dress that way because she wants people to form a certain impression of her.

That's why Salander is a *sleeper* superhero: she intentionally projects an appearance that camouflages her true intents to do good in the world. We make inferences about people based on their appearance and dress—though our inferences aren't always accurate. Salander's costume leads us to think that she'll be a troublemaker, not a savior. Regardless of fairness or accuracy, we are all guilty of making inferences about others based on appearance.[20] In one study, college students were shown photographs of teenagers and were asked to give their impressions about the people in the photographs. In some photos, the teens were wearing T-shirts with alcohol-related ads on them, whereas other photos showed teens in plain T-shirts. Teens who wore alcohol-related T-shirts were judged to be less honest, less responsible, less likely to be punctual or do well in school, and more likely to be a "party animal," to drink, and be a risk taker.[21] Wow! The only difference between the two groups of teens in the photos was the presence or absence of alcohol-related content on the T-shirts.

Salander's attire, and the impression she makes, transforms over the course of the trilogy as she transforms. As she becomes less interested in thumbing her nose at others and more interested in uncovering truth and justice, she ditches her Goth accoutrements one by one. By the time Salander and Blomkvist track down the site of the first Vanger murder, Salander's has done away with her mohawk and wears no makeup or leather. In fact, Salander puts on "regular" clothes and covers up her tattoos, takes out her bodyware, and passes as a lady when it suits her purposes, as she does when she visits banks to set up the fund transfer from Wennerström's accounts into her own accounts. Subsequently, she only puts on her full Goth regalia when it

---

[20] K. K. P. Johnson, and S. J. Lennon, eds, *Dress, Body, Culture. Appearance and Power* (Berg Publishers, 1999).

[21] J. E. Workman, N. E. Arseneau, and C. J. Ewell, "Traits and Behaviors Assigned to an Adolescent Wearing an Alcohol Promotional T-Shirt," *Family and Consumer Sciences Research Journal*.

is part of her legal strategy in *The Girl Who Kicked the Hornet's Nest* to appear as an extreme version of the apparently rebellious young woman she was at the beginning of the series. (Her transformation is even more noticeable in the films.)

One of the fascinating aspects of Salander's character is that her appearance belies her strength and morality. Her Goth attire initially leads us (and the other characters that encounter her in the trilogy) to assume that she is a slacker, a troublemaker, and a rebel, just as participants in the study about alcohol content on T-shirts assumed certain characteristics of the photographed T-shirt wearers. Salander's costume and demeanor mask or hide how smart and capable she is. Moreover, her petite, androgynous physique leads us to assume that she's no real threat, just as people do with Clark Kent in his bumbling persona. And just as Clark Kent is in fact more powerful than people know, so, too, is Salander. As the stories unfold, Salander's true character—her mettle, her personality, her motives—is revealed to us. And we are surprised. Like Holger Palmgren, Dragan Armansky, and Mikael Blomkvist, we are impressed by her superpowers as we get to know her, but also by her independence, her inner strength and conviction, and her moral code. She can hide her strength completely when she needs to, though, like Clark Kent and Peter Parker. She does when she first meets Nils Bjurman, her new guardian.

And She Battles a Supervillain!

There's one more characteristic of a superhero that Salander shares: she must battle a supervillain. Her supervillain is her previously unknown half brother, Ronald Niedermann, whose superpowers include an inability to feel pain, plus superstrength and a superstrong skeleton, making him practically invulnerable (as noted in the second novel). His inability to feel pain is a genetic abnormality that makes him a mutant, and an evil one at that. (Some might say that he's a henchman for his father, but Niedermann is a villain in his own right, making his own decisions and plans, though he is not as effective a villain as is his father.)

The Girl with the Dragon Tattoo: The Novel versus the Swedish Film

A few words about the first novel versus the first Swedish film (okay, maybe more than "a few" words):

The first film deviates from the first novel is two ways that amplify Salander's superhero-ness: 1) In the film, Salander inserts herself into Blomkvist's investigation into Harriet's disappearance by sending him an anonymous email with the solution to the code. In the book, Blomkvist asks Frode to recommend a research assistant to help him with the archival research and Frode recommends Salander. 2) The film has Salander make many of the crucial connections that in the book are made by Blomkvist, including the cracking of the numerical code in Harriet's diary and the meaning of religious passages associated with each victim. With these differences, the film creates a Salander who is initially more preoccupied with the case than the Salander in the book (thus revealing her with a sense of mission earlier on), and amplifies her powers (code cracking gets added to the list); moreover, in the films her interest in the case is timed to coincide with the *immediate* aftermath of her rape by Bjurman so that the link between her rape and her desire to see justice done is more apparent.

The Unconscious Becomes Conscious

We like the Larsson books because they surprise us. We become intrigued by Salander just as Blomkvist (and Palmgren and Armansky) are intrigued by her. We may be surprised by her character and some of her actions, but I propose that we also unconsciously recognize the familiar elements of the superhero genre as we get to know Lisbeth Salander over the course of her stories, and we come to see her as a superhero.

How would we come to see her as a superhero without consciously being aware of doing so? Through a psychological phenomenon called *priming*, which occurs when a preexisting memory (or combination of memories, such as the memories of characteristics associated with superheroes) is activated and that activation lingers and influences us. Here's how it would work: as we learn of Salander and her adventures, we associate the descriptions of her with superhero characteristics. We realize that, like superheroes, she:

- develops a mission (to find the murderer of the young women associated with Harriet Vanger's disappearance). We cheer for her and her mission, just as we do for Batman and Iron Man and other heroes who serve their own form of justice.
- has extraordinary abilities ("powers"): hacking, emotional regulation, photographic memory, superperseverance. We marvel at these powers just as we do at Spider-Man's spider-sense and strength and Superman's and Supergirl's X-ray vision and superhearing.
- has a "dual" identity—captured in her code name and her costume.

As these elements—mission, powers, and identity—converge, we then come to associate Salander *herself*, and not just the individual elements, with the concept of "superhero." Even though those elements of her character are never explicitly named as superhero elements, the odds are that most of us "got" the superhero aspects of her character. She's a superhero for a new set of readers and viewers.

ROBIN S. ROSENBERG, PhD, is a clinical psychologist. She is series editor of the Oxford University Press *Superhero* books, author of *Superhero Origins: What Makes Superheroes Tick and Why We Care,* blogger for the *Huffington Post* and *Psychology Today,* and coauthor of *Introducing Psychology: Brain, Person, Group* (introductory psychology textbook) and *Abnormal Psychology* (abnormal psychology textbook). She is a Fellow of the American Academy of Clinical Psychology. Dr. Rosenberg has taught psychology courses to college students. Her first foray into applying psychological theories and research to popular culture figures was for *The Psychology of Harry Potter;* she is the editor of the anthology *The Psychology of Superheroes.* Her website is www.DrRobinRosenberg.com.

Deciding who should punish whom—and how—is one of the central themes in the Millennium trilogy. It's also one of Lisbeth Salander's primary obsessions. She has found herself on both sides of the justice equation, as someone who has been persecuted and someone who avenges the persecution of others; through her experiences we see justice gone horribly wrong—as when the state failed to protect her as a child—and we also see her mete out justice in some . . . unusual ways. Is Lisbeth a righteous avenger or an out-of-control vigilante? Mikhail Lyubansky and Elaine Shpungin tackle the question of whether Lisbeth's ends justify her means, philosophically *or* psychologically.

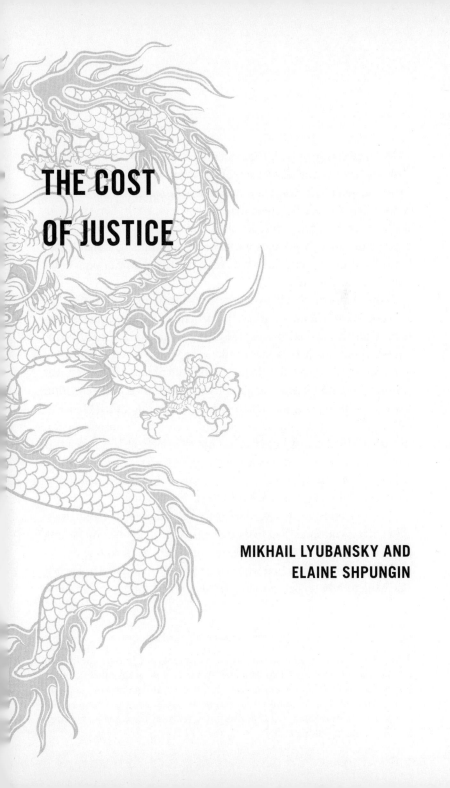

THE COST
OF JUSTICE

**MIKHAIL LYUBANSKY AND
ELAINE SHPUNGIN**

Stieg Larsson's Lisbeth Salander is a unique and compelling heroine who, as Niels Arden Oplev, director of the Swedish film version of *The Girl with the Dragon Tattoo,* told Charlie Rose[1], refuses to become a victim no matter what happens to her. Haunted, resilient, savvy, dark, unpredictable, and endlessly resourceful, she delivers ingeniously planned and colorful acts of "vigilante justice" to the irredeemable criminals who have the misfortune or poor judgment to cross her path.

Following in the footsteps of previous superheroes—she does, after all, take on evil villains—Lisbeth is a female David to all the misogynistic Goliaths in Sweden. She's the ultimate underdog: abused, abandoned, disenfranchised, and waif-like in appearance. And we love her, not despite her anger and violent potential, but because of it. Her anger is righteous. Her violence, apparently justified. After all, we neither mourn for the monsters that heroes kill, nor question their choice to kill the monsters. Killing and being killed are what monsters are for. But what are the costs to Lisbeth—and to society at large—for this violent brand of vigilante justice? And, given the exact circumstances at hand, was there anything she might have done instead that would have served both her and society better?

These questions are not posed solely for the sake of a fictional analysis. Though less common than in works of fiction, vigilantes—including female vigilantes—exist in the real world, too, as of course do the inhumane individuals upon whom the vigilantes exact their revenge.[2] The Millennium trilogy presents fertile ground for exploring these

---

[1] Charlie Rose interview, Season 18, episode 75, April 20, 2010.

[2] Consider, for instance, the case of Kimberly Cunningham. In 2003, she learned that her then fourteen-year-old daughter, Amanda, was (at age nine) raped on two occasions by the girl's uncle, Coy Hundley. Cunningham bought a gun and confronted Hundley at his place of work. When Hundley did not deny the allegations, Cunningham shot him five times, reloaded the weapon, and fired five more rounds, killing him.

questions. Lisbeth may be a fictional character, but the world she inhabits is very much like the one that Larsson actually occupied and seemed to clearly want to illuminate and critique. In the words of Larsson's lifelong partner, Eva Gabrielsson, "Stieg Larsson's actions, and his views of the world, can mainly be understood from a perspective of women's rights . . . The Millennium crime novel trilogy is a new way of making discrimination and violence against women visible."[3] By giving the reader glimpses of her tragic life and the multiple abuses endured by her and other women at the hands of these men, Larsson sends Lisbeth forth as his personal angel of justice. In this context (as social commentary), Lisbeth seems to represent one way that real justice can be achieved—not just in Larsson's world of hopelessly twisted men and broken justice systems, but also in our own. Before examining this idea further, let's take a few moments to unpack the meaning of the word justice.

Doing Justice

Justice is defined by Dictionary.com as "the quality of . . . righteousness, equitableness, or moral rightness," while "doing justice" is defined as "acting or treating fairly." This intertwining of the concepts of fairness, moral rightness, and deserved punishment is at the heart of what is most confusing about the idea of justice: Fairness by whose standards? Rightness according to whose morals? Deserving according to what criteria?

The implied answer to all these questions is "according to the law of the land." Indeed, in democratic states like Sweden[4] and the United

---

[3] From a 2009 speech to Observatorio contra la Violencia Domestica y de Genero, http://www.thefirstpost.co.uk/54145,people,news,stieg-larsson-remembered-by-eva-gabrielsson#ixzz1To21EaHn.

[4] Sweden is technically a constitutional monarchy, with King Carl XVI Gustaf as the head of state, but, as in most contemporary constitutional monarchies, royal power in Sweden is limited to ceremonial functions. Notably, Sweden is currently ranked fourth on the Democracy Index (9.5 on the 10-point scale), an index compiled by the Economist Intelligence Unit that claims to measure the state of democracy in 167 countries. The United States, with a score of 8.18, is ranked seventeenth.

States, the country's laws are considered to constitute a social contract in which the people select representatives (i.e., legislators) to make the law and then are morally and legally bound to follow it. In this context, justice becomes equated with compliance with the law and "doing justice" becomes operationalized as the legal process of determining who broke the law and how to punish the "offending" person(s).

In this way, the concepts of justice and punishment are so thoroughly intertwined that it might initially be difficult to even conceive of the former without the latter. Yet there are, in fact, a variety of legitimate answers to the questions above other than "according to the law of the land." Religious teachings (which vary according to the religion in question), philosophical ideas (e.g., Kant's categorical imperative), political ideologies, and cultural frameworks all influence both individual and community notions of justice. The complexity and disagreement inherent in different answers to these questions explain, in part, both the multiplicity of "justice systems"[5] in existence among human societies and the frequent dissatisfaction with the extent to which these systems bring about desired outcomes. While a comprehensive review of such systems is beyond the scope of this essay, a bird's-eye view of some ways in which they differ will help us examine the underlying justice themes in Larsson's world, and our own.

One way of looking at justice systems is to examine where they may land on the "punitive" to "restorative" continuum. Generally speaking, the more punitive a justice system, the more it is concerned with what rule was broken, who is to blame, and what punishment would best match the severity of the rule-breaking. Examples of justice systems encompassing this approach are Old Testament justice ("an eye for an eye") and vigilante justice—both practiced to some extent by our heroine—as well as by what we typically see in the formal, Western criminal justice system, as represented by police,

---

[5] We use "justice system" to refer to an institutionalized process for dealing with rule violations and/or conflict in a given community. In addition to the formal criminal and civil justice systems, schools, workplaces, and families all also have institutionalized ways of "doing" justice.

attorneys, judges, and mandatory sentencing laws that treat crimes as having been committed not against individuals or communities but against the state.

On the other end of this spectrum, the more restorative a justice system, the more it is concerned with what harm was done, who was impacted by the harm, and what action would best address (restore, repair) the harm to all parties.[6] Examples of such systems include victim-offender mediation,[7] family group conferencing,[8] and restorative circles.[9]

We all operate under some form of justice system—in our families, workplaces, relationships, and communities—even if we are not fully aware of the systems we follow (many of which we have simply inherited without examination). Thus, one of the benefits of examining justice systems this way is to make visible that which is often invisible. Doing so allows the community in question (and the individuals in those communities) the possibility of choosing a way of doing justice that is more closely aligned with its values, rather than merely going along with a system that may not actually be serving those values.[10] To make such choices, community members must be aware of what they

---

[6] H. Zehr, *The Little Book of Restorative Justice* (Intercourse, Good Books, 2002).

[7] A process in which the victim of a crime and the person who has taken responsibility for committing that crime have an opportunity to talk to each other (usually face-to-face) with the help of a trained mediator. In the meeting, the offender and victim typically talk about what happened and the impact the event had on their lives. Sometimes there is also the additional step of agreeing on a plan to repair some or all of the damages.

[8] A restorative approach that is designed to have child and adult family members solve their own conflicts, instead of involving courts or other professionals.

[9] A restorative practice developed in Brazil that seeks to engage conflict without preidentifying offenders and victims (because those roles are seen as dynamic) and that involves both those who directly participated in the conflict and the community members who are impacted.

[10] The possibility of choosing how to do justice comes from the work of Dominic Barter, who, with his associates, developed (in the favelas of Brazil) a restorative practice called Restorative Circles. See http://www.restorativecircles.org.

value as a community[11] and realize that the different justice systems have very different implications for those we label "victims", those we label "offenders", those empowered to decide how justice will be administered (e.g., judges, peers), those who carry out the administration of justice (e.g., prison corrections officers, community members), and the community itself.

Despite the mainstream justice system's hegemony in both Sweden and the United States, the alternatives are real, not hypothetical. This is most obvious in US tort law,[12] where the individual harmed has the choice of addressing the harm by filing a lawsuit (i.e., engaging the mainstream justice system) or engaging an alternative justice system such as mediation, arbitration, or a restorative process. However, even in criminal law, in which the breach of a duty is considered to be against the state rather than an individual,[13] those involved in or impacted by the alleged criminal behavior have the option of asking the District Attorney not to file criminal charges (though the D.A. may file them anyway), as well as engaging an alternative justice system (e.g., a restorative system, vigilantism) that would operate parallel to—and often independent of—the criminal proceedings.

The Millennium series presents one such alternative to conventional justice in the form of Lisbeth's response to the violence she

---

[11] This is both an individual value and a group process, as communities (e.g., municipalities, school districts) are comprised of individuals who must reach some consensus regarding what kinds of justice systems will be available to the community.

[12] A tort is a common law term used to describe a breach of any civil duty (other than a contractual duty) owed to someone else. It is differentiated from a crime, which involves a breach of a duty owed to society in general. Examples of torts include auto accidents, defamation, product liability, environmental pollution, and any intentional act that could reasonably be predicted to result in harm to an individual.

[13] Thus, if John brutally beats Nathan, who dies from the injuries, John's crime, according to criminal law, is against the state (for violating the state's prohibition against battery and homicide) not against Nathan. The implication of this distinction is that the wishes and needs of the so-called "victim" are not prioritized and sometimes completely ignored. Thus, in a homicide case, the District Attorney may ask for the death penalty (and the judge may grant it), even against the wishes of the victim's family.

encounters. In Gabrielsson's words, "Larsson believed in 'an eye for an eye, a tooth for a tooth.' He never forgave and he was very clear about this: to get revenge, or avenge your friends, is not just a right, but an absolute duty."[14] However, the Millennium trilogy takes this Old Testament model of justice one step further. It seems to advocate for vigilante justice,[15] an approach that, by definition, bypasses the formal criminal system and thrusts the responsibility of judge, jury, and executioner solely into Lisbeth's hands.

A Response to the Concept of a "Broken" Criminal Justice System

The notion behind vigilante justice is that sometimes it is necessary for citizens to dole out justice on their own, because the formal criminal justice system, government, or other institutional authority is hopelessly limited in its ability to deliver true justice by the presence of bureaucracy, incompetence, and/or corruption. This is evident throughout the trilogy, but especially in regard to Wennerström, the Millennium series' unseen symbol of financial corruption. In Larsson's words, "The Wennerström empire of obscure companies was linked to the heart of the international Mafia, including everything from illegal arms dealing and money laundering for South American drug cartels to prostitution in New York, and even indirectly for child sex trade in Mexico" (*The Girl with the Dragon Tattoo*). Thus, Lisbeth's actions (e.g., toward Wennerström) are offered, in part, as a critique of the corruption and biases that Larsson believed ran rampant throughout the Swedish justice system and, more broadly, Swedish society. It's a valid critique, and one that is equally applicable to the US criminal justice system and society.

---

[14] From Gabrielsson's memoir *"There Are Things I Want You to Know" about Stieg Larsson and Me* as quoted in the 2-18-2011 issue of the Daily Mail, http://www.dailymail.co.uk/femail/article-1358412/Revenge-girl-dragon-tattoo.html.

[15] An alternative reading is that it is Blomkvist's style of justice that the novels condone. Either way, as our editor correctly pointed out, what a man advocates for in fiction is not necessarily the same as what he advocates for in real life.

For instance, despite the fact that studies consistently show that people in different racial groups use and sell illegal drugs at highly similar rates, in some states black men have been incarcerated on drug charges at rates twenty to fifty times greater than white men.[16] Nationally, the *Miami Herald* reports that "African Americans, who are 12 percent of the population and about 14 percent of drug users, make up 34 percent of those arrested for drug offenses and 45 percent of those serving time for such offenses in state prisons."[17] If anything, the data are even more discouraging when we examine the outcomes for the most severe crimes. In 2003, then governor of Illinois (where we currently reside) George Ryan commuted the sentence of every one of the 167 inmates on the state's death row. His decision was not the result of popular pressure,[18] nor did it come from a deep personal conviction.[19] Rather, Ryan was reacting to some shocking numbers: in the twenty-three year period from 1977 to 2000, DNA and other evidence exonerated more inmates than were executed, and it is unknown whether some of those who were executed may also have been innocent of those crimes.[20]

Lisbeth has good reasons for taking justice into her own hands. Given the biases inherent in the formal criminal justice systems,[21]

---

[16] M. Alexander, *The New Jim Crow: Mass Incarceration in the Age of Colorblindness* (New York: The New Press, 2010).

[17] "Five Myths About Incarceration," *Miami Herald*. June 23, 2011, http://www.miamiherald.com/2011/06/23/2281985/five-myths-about-incarceration.html.

[18] Though down from a 1994 high of 80 percent, 67 percent of Americans still supported the death penalty in 2003.

[19] Ryan was a Republican and lifetime supporter of capital punishment who, even as he was calling for a moratorium on the death penalty, remarked, "I still believe the death penalty is a proper response to heinous crimes."

[20] U. Kukathas, *Death Penalty (Contemporary Issues Companion)* (San Diego: Greenhaven, 2007).

[21] The issues are not just fictional. In the United States, for example, the real criminal justice system has been rightly criticized because of the racial profiling among some portion of law enforcement personnel, the re-victimization and retraumatization of victims from having to provide in-person testimony under cross-examination, and the relationship between the defendants' financial resources and trial outcomes.

along with Lisbeth's manipulated mental health history and Bjurman's exalted status as an attorney, the likelihood that her accusations in a court of law would lead to meaningful consequences for Bjurman is quite low, whereas the costs to her of either filing a formal grievance or not taking any action are both quite high.

In this context, in which the formal system is both incapable of delivering "eye for an eye" justice at all to the likes of Bjurman and unwilling to deliver it in full[22] to men such as serial kidnapper, rapist, and murderer Martin Vanger, it seems reasonable to have a capable vigilante dole out the justice. Thus, as a result of Lisbeth's willingness to act outside the formal justice system, Bjurman gets to experience all that his actions have created for Lisbeth: the terror and pain of being tied and raped, the helplessness and powerlessness of having one's reputation and status hang on the actions of another (his reports; her video tape), and the frustration and shame of trying to have relationships with others while being "labeled" as dangerous and less than human (her mental status; his tattoo).

A Response to the Concept of Broken Men

In addition to being a response to a broken criminal justice system that is not seen as capable of delivering the "right" eye-for-an-eye punishment, vigilante justice also seems to involve personal and societal protection stemming from a need for safety. The latter introduces an element of subjectivity that creates considerable moral complexity. For example, it is notable that Lisbeth chooses to dispose of some criminals (e.g., the motorcycle gangsters sent to burn down Bjurman's home) by turning them in to the formal system, rather than disposing of them through her own means. In this way, the reader is intended to understand that not all criminals (and not all criminal acts) should be treated in the same way—that some criminals are not so much "inhumane monsters" as simply humans gone awry, while others are cold-blooded, irredeemable monsters whose only functions are to do monstrous things and then be killed (or be set ablaze or hacked with

---

[22] The death penalty in Sweden was repealed in 1921.

an axe) for doing those things. This is an important distinction. The Millennium novels are not about humans gone awry; they are about the monsters.

Yet, as already mentioned, the Millennium novels are not typical monster stories. We know that Larsson intended them as social commentary on the real Swedish underworld and on men's inhumanity toward women more globally. Martin Vanger, Bjurman, and the rest of the monsters in the stories may be fictional, but they are supposed to represent real-world criminals like serial killer Ted Bundy who, like Martin Vanger, also targeted women.[23] Like Larsson's villains, many true-life serial killers seem outwardly functional and "normal." "Most serial killers are white, male, above average in intelligence, and adroit at wearing a mask of charm and sanity," wrote journalist Myra MacPherson.[24] She was writing about Bundy, but the words are equally applicable to Vanger, Bjurman, and Teleborian. Yet, there is something else that the killers all have in common, and it is the exact same characteristic that Larsson's villains share: they all lack empathy.

If this seems banal and inconsequential, it is neither. The lack of empathy—defined as the ability to identify with or vicariously experience the feelings, thoughts, or attitudes of another—seems to be the defining characteristic of a personality disorder called psychopathy and, according to psychologist Simon Baron-Cohen's book *The Science of Evil*, is the very essence of evil.[25]

It is this lack of empathy that sets Martin Vanger, Bjurman, Alexander Zalachenko, and Teleborian apart from the garden-variety criminals that Lisbeth (and Larsson) is willing to feed to the law. At least in the present moment, there is no effective treatment for psychopathy, no drug, psychotherapy, or social intervention. Left to their own devices, these men (and they almost always are men) will harm others, again and again and again. Thus, Lisbeth takes justice into her

---

[23] We deliberately picked Bundy as someone that American readers are likely to recognize, but for each celebrity there are many more, like Javed Iqbal Mughal, whose names and stories are less well known.

[24] MacPherson's article appeared in the May 1989 issue of *Vanity Fair*.

[25] *Editors' Note*: See the essay on psychopathy by Stephanie Mullins-Sweatt and Melissa Burkley in this book for more on psychopaths in the Millennium trilogy.

own hands in cases where, according to the data, there seems no hope that the perpetrators will ever regret their actions, much less repent or change their ways.

Given this, Lisbeth not only delivers the "right" amount of vigilante justice but also exorcises their type of "evil" from the earth. That is, not all criminals who have killed someone (e.g., the motorcycle gangsters) receive the death penalty from her. Rather, we are left with the sense that it is not simply the fact they have killed that propels Lisbeth to go after Vanger, Zalachenko, and Niedermann, but rather an extra element, perhaps a lack of capacity for empathy,[26] that suggests they must be completely eradicated.

Given the "broken system and broken men" argument presented by Larsson, the reader feels strongly compelled to agree with Lisbeth's approach to justice. The benefits of such an approach include a kind of efficiency, effectiveness, and "equality" in punishment that a formal court of law cannot approach, as well as a measure of safety for Lisbeth and other potential victims. Such safety is rarely guaranteed by a formal criminal process, even in the case of life sentences—complications to this may include the reduction of sentences for "good behavior," the victimization of others within the prison system, and the "long distance" orchestration of harm to those involved in "putting someone away."

However, as stated previously, all justice systems have both costs and benefits to those involved. What are the costs, then, to Lisbeth and to society at large, for the kind of vigilante justice Larsson seems to advocate?

The Cost of Vengeance

In Satyagraha Leaflet No. 13, Gandhi wrote: "Victory attained by violence is tantamount to a defeat, for it is momentary." Gandhi was not speaking out of a starry-eyed idealism, but out of the conviction that violence would continue to beget a further and escalating cycle

---

26 The biker gang didn't show any empathy for their victims, but they seemed to care about each other.

of violence, and that the de-escalation of this cycle begins with individual acts of *Satyagraha*—a refusal either to bend to the violence of the other or bend to the idea that the other is less human than you are. In this vision—shared by other spiritual leaders, sung and unsung—it is the ability to see one's "enemy" as human that allows us to become more human ourselves, for one of the costs of living only with hatred and fear is a blunting of our own sense of humanity and life force. The idea here is not for Lisbeth to forgive Vanger or Zalachenko or Bjurman, but rather to find a way to meet their lack of compassion with an inner compassion born not of fear or weakness but of the strength it takes to see all human life—even life that has done monstrous things—as sacred.

In this view, Lisbeth's brutal behavior prevents her own healing process, for according to Gandhi's philosophy, if we do a monstrous thing to "right" someone else's monstrous behavior, our hands are still stained with blood and our hearts with the inner conviction that a piece of the monster lives in us as well. As Nietzsche wrote in *Beyond Good and Evil* about those who fight monsters, "If you gaze for long into an abyss, the abyss gazes also into you." Lisbeth might be safer for the moment, but she is not left living in a "safe" world or one in which she has reprieve from her inner nightmares and demons.

There are considerable costs for the vigilantes, but perhaps theirs is a sacrifice made for the greater good. After all, by slaying the dragons, doesn't Lisbeth create a safer kingdom for the rest of us? The answer, as previously, is that alongside the seeming benefit of safety, vigilante justice also holds costs for the rest of us.

First, like the current criminal justice system, vigilante justice precludes the voices of all who are impacted from being weighted in the justice. No human is really an island. Both the actions of Lisbeth and the men involved impact numerous people around them, including other victims and their families. At its most basic, the actions of a single vigilante remove the possibility of having other victims participate in the justice process, at best leaving them with a distant vicarious sense of justice being done. What crime victims often long for, and report finding helpful, is being heard and seen for the fullness of what they endured and having their "why" questions about the harmful action answered.[27] This kind of result is far more likely to occur in a more restoratively oriented justice process.[28]

Even if their complete lack of empathy precludes the possibility of men like Bjurman and Teleborian from taking any responsibility (i.e., showing an understanding of how their actions impacted others) or showing any remorse, it is still often a powerful and healing experience for their victims and/or the victims' families to confront their attackers and have their painful experiences (and the consequences of those experiences) heard and acknowledged. In fact, while it is ideal that the understanding and responsibility come from the offender, victims who have participated in restorative processes—like restorative circles and family group conferences—report that simply having others in their community hear and understand their pain and the impact of the actions on them also has a supportive quality.[29] In addition, a process in which voices of multiple affected people are included (e.g., the offender's family) and agreements are allowed to emerge that are satisfying to all of these parties tends to be perceived as both more just and more humane than a process in which justice is carried out by either the state or by independent vigilantes.

We come now to the final, and perhaps most important, question: Even if a more "humane" action may have some benefit for Lisbeth, would it not simply increase the likelihood of cruelty and abuse by

---

[27] L. W. Sherman, and H. Strang. *Restorative Justice: The Evidence* (London: The Smith Institute, 2007).

[28] Unlike conventional (punitive) approaches to justice—which ask who is at fault and what is the appropriate punishment—restorative approaches ask what harm was done (to all parties) and how the parties to the conflict might repair the harm. While the criminal courts in both Sweden and the United States discourage contact between the so-called offender and the so-called victim, the restorative process deliberately creates a safe space where those parties can come together and, with the help of a facilitator, work toward mutual understanding (including an empathic understanding of the victim's experience) and voluntary agreements about how to move forward.

[29] L. W. Sherman, and H. Strang, *Restorative Justice: The Evidence*.

S. Gillinson, M. Horne, and P. Baeck, *Radical Efficiency: Different, Better, Lower Cost Public Services* (London: NESTA report, 2010).

current and future offenders? The argument (we believe it is originally from the Talmud) is often phrased something like this: *If we are kind to those to whom we should be cruel, we will ultimately be cruel to those to whom we should be kind.*

The words seem eminently reasonable. We can well imagine the first part leading to the second[30] but, as dichotomous options almost always are, the choices are false. Our choices are not limited either to being cruel or being kind. Thus, in the cases of Vanger, Niedermann, and Teleborian, our choices are NOT either to kill them or to buy them lunch and send them on their way. Both Sweden and the United States have a due process that allows an impartial body to determine culpability. If these men are determined to be guilty, we can incarcerate them for life or otherwise limit their freedom—not to punish them (because the goal of punishment is to discourage future similar behavior and we know such men cannot be discouraged), but to ensure our own safety. We should limit their freedom but treat them humanely. Though they might have done monstrous things, we don't need to be monstrous in turn. Despite whatever corruption and bias might exist in the formal system, we should treat these offenders as human beings. The bias and corruption are not irrelevant, and we don't intend to suggest that either should be ignored. Rather, our point is that a broken justice system does not psychologically or ethically justify Lisbeth's cruelty any more than Martin Vanger's painful and abusive upbringing justifies his.

The Talmud quote also suggests that cruelty is a necessity. We don't agree. We don't want to choose between being cruel to someone who deserves it and being cruel to someone who doesn't. Sure, that's an easy choice, but it's set up that way to justify being cruel to *someone*. This same logic is at the heart of Larsson's novels. Lisbeth's actions of setting her father on fire and sodomizing Bjurman are undeniably cruel, but they are supposedly justified on the grounds that

---

[30] The quote suggests that if we treat psychopaths kindly (i.e., withhold severe punishment), we increase the likelihood that they will harm innocent others (i.e., those who deserve our kindness) in the future.

Zalachenko and Bjurman deserved them. We reject the dichotomous options; we don't want to be intentionally cruel to anyone.

We reject, as well, the word "kindness" in this context. Opponents of the death penalty are not advocating kindness; they're advocating fairness and compassion, the not-so-radical idea that this person who may have done some terrible things (let's assume that, as in the Millennium novels, the person's innocence is not in dispute) is still a human being who, like Martin Vanger, may have experienced profound neglect or abuse.

Compassion is not forgiveness, and it certainly is not a lack of accountability. It just means that we believe that no one is born wanting to rape and kill[31] and the fact that some person has done so—perhaps multiple times—likely means that his or her life has been filled with so much abuse and pain that he or she was moved to violence. We don't condone or excuse such a person's choices[32] and we don't want to do anything to compromise the safety of others but, along with revulsion, disgust, and fear, we also feel compassion. Consider Martin Vanger. No doubt his genes alone placed him at high risk for deviant criminal behavior—and he did ultimately make the choice to follow in his father's footsteps—but we doubt he would have become the sadist he was if his father hadn't abused him.[33]

---

[31] Though psychopathy may seem like an exception, it isn't. Not all people who lack empathy rape or kill, and studies show that the heritability of most psychopathic characteristics is in the moderate range (h2=.50 to .67) for most people who meet the criteria for psychopathy, suggesting that unique life experiences do contribute to the development of antisocial behavior, even in cases of psychopathy. Data supporting this can be found in C. Patrick's *Handbook of Psychopathy*.

[32] We really do see them as choices. Though much of the variance in deviant criminal behavior can be accounted for by genetics and immediate familial environment (two lotteries Martin Vanger clearly did not win), the data suggest that even this highly combustible combination of risk factors does not guarantee deviance. Martin Vanger's sister Harriet, as well as Lisbeth herself, are proof that Larsson didn't think so either.

[33] *Editors' Note*: For a discussion about the propensity for violence, see Joshua Gowin's essay in this book.

We are NOT advocating putting the "perpetrator's" needs and welfare before that of the person or persons who were harmed. As readers, we care more about Lisbeth's welfare than about Bjurman's or Niedermann's or Teleborian's. Obviously! The same would be true in a real-life situation. But empathy and compassion are not about priorities, nor are they about compromise.

To be compassionate is to recognize everyone's humanity and value everyone's needs. This works because compassion is not a zero-sum game. Feelings of compassion for one person do not lessen one's ability to feel compassion for another.[34] To the contrary, our personal experience is that, when we are in a more compassionate and loving space, we have more to give to everyone around us.

Compassion is also a choice. When we act without compassion (and we sometimes do), it is usually because we have given ourselves permission to do so. When this happens, we almost always later regret it. One reason for this is that our lack of compassion rarely results in outcomes we enjoy. Another reason is that compassion is not charity. To be sure, it can be a tremendous gift to another, but it is a gift to ourselves as well. Just as torture and other acts of cruelty dehumanize both the person tortured and the torturer, so do compassion and empathy reconnect us to our own humanity. As we pointed out earlier, Lisbeth pays a price for her vigilantism. The price is hard to see because, by the time we meet her, she is already hardened and emotionally damaged by her history of abuse and trauma. She has paid a price nevertheless, and the nightmares, the emotional detachment, and the social isolation may only be the tip of the iceberg.[35]

Ultimately, however, our society's priorities probably come down to safety. Whether we're talking about terrorists, murderers, or rapists, as citizens we want some assurance that those who have hurt us or others before will be unable (or unwilling) to do so again. The safety

---

[34] M. Rosenberg, *Nonviolent Communication: A Language of Compassion*, 1999.

[35] In the case of Kim Cunningham, she does express regret about taking the matter into her own hands even though she continues to maintain that Hundley deserved to die, "As I fired that gun," she explains, "all I wanted to do was protect my family, but I ended up damaging it instead."

needs are legitimate, but will cruelty really contribute to our safety? Though the question continues to be debated, there is no compelling evidence that either torture or the death penalty increase safety. To the contrary, in many cases (psychopathy may be an exception), restorative processes can better meet society's (and the victims') safety needs than incarceration or other punishments, which address neither the contextual nor interpersonal factors that contributed to the violence in the first place.

Larsson stacks the deck in Lisbeth's favor. He pits an incompetent, morally corrupt system against a highly competent moral authority. Lisbeth's judgment of the villains' guilt is not in dispute. Her revenge-taking seems appropriately measured. Her priorities seem beyond reproach. We can live with her choices. They are just and motivated primarily by safety needs. But they are not without cost and, ultimately, are unsustainable. Larsson created a memorable heroine. Would that he had also created a memorable justice system that could replace the one that's broken or have her focus her efforts on system reform rather than circumvention. *The Girl Who Kicked the Hornet's Nest* was a step in that direction, but ultimately stopped short[36] when Lisbeth again turns to vigilantism to dispose of Niedermann. In the process, Lisbeth makes a fine superhero but a poor model of real-world, sustainable, compassionate justice. We can enjoy the former as a harmless fantasy, just as long as we also recognize the latter.

MIKHAIL LYUBANSKY, PhD, is a member of the teaching faculty in the Department of Psychology at the University of Illinois, Urbana-Champaign, where he teaches *Psychology of Race and Ethnicity* and *Theories of Psychotherapy*. His writing, which

---

[36] *The Girl Who Kicked the Hornet's Nest* is the last novel of the Millennium series, but there is evidence that Larsson planned to continue the series and presumably would have, if not for his untimely death. It is possible, given this novel's focus on systemic problems, that Lisbeth might have eventually moved away from vigilantism in favor of systemic change. Unfortunately, those stories will continue to be untold.

usually focuses on race relations and restorative practices, appears in his Psychology Today blog, *Between the Lines*. He is currently continuing his learning of Restorative Circles and working on a book about socially responsible psychology. Follow him on Twitter: @MikhaiLL.

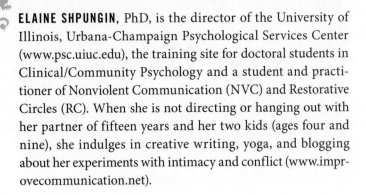

ELAINE SHPUNGIN, PhD, is the director of the University of Illinois, Urbana-Champaign Psychological Services Center (www.psc.uiuc.edu), the training site for doctoral students in Clinical/Community Psychology and a student and practitioner of Nonviolent Communication (NVC) and Restorative Circles (RC). When she is not directing or hanging out with her partner of fifteen years and her two kids (ages four and nine), she indulges in creative writing, yoga, and blogging about her experiments with intimacy and conflict (www.improvecommunication.net).

ABOUT THE EDITORS

ROBIN S. ROSENBERG, PhD, is a clinical psychologist. She is series editor of the Oxford University Press *Superhero* books, author of *Superhero Origins: What Makes Superheroes Tick and Why We Care*, blogger for *Huffington Post and Psychology Today*, and coauthor of *Introducing Psychology: Brain, Person, Group*, (introductory psychology textbook) and *Abnormal Psychology* (abnormal psychology textbook). She is a Fellow of the American Academy of Clinical Psychology and has a clinical practice in Stanford, CA. Dr. Rosenberg has taught psychology courses to college students. Her first foray into applying psychological theories and research to popular culture figures was for *The Psychology of Harry Potter*; she is the editor of *The Psychology of Superheroes* anthology. Her website is DrRobinRosenberg.com.

SHANNON O'NEILL is an editorial consultant for a prominent literary agency in Washington, DC. She evaluates and edits manuscripts and proposals and guides authors through the publishing process from beginning to end. She holds a Master's degree in writing from Johns Hopkins University, teaches composition at American University, and occasionally guest lectures at local and national literary events.

More Psychology of Titles

The Psychology of The Simpsons
D'oh
EDITED BY ALAN BROWN, PHD, WITH CHRIS LOGAN

Psychologists turn their attention to *The Simpsons*, one of America's most popular and beloved shows, in these essays that explore the function and dysfunctions of the show's characters.

9781932100709 • TRADE PAPERBACK • $17.95 US/$19.95 CAN • MARCH 2006

The Psychology of Harry Potter
An Unauthorized Examination of the Boy Who Lived
EDITED BY NEIL MULHOLLAND, PHD

Harry Potter has provided a portal to the wizarding world for millions of readers, but an examination of Harry, his friends and his enemies will take us on yet another journey: through the Muggle (and wizard!) mind.

9781932100884 • TRADE PAPERBACK • $17.95 US/$19.95 CAN • MAY 2007

The Psychology of Survivor
Leading Psychologists Take an Unauthorized Look at the Most Elaborate Psychological Experiment Ever Conducted … Survivor!
EDITED BY RICHARD J. GERRIG, PHD

From situational ethics to tribal loyalties, from stress and body image to loneliness and family structures, *The Psychology of Survivor* is a broad look at cutting-edge psychological issues viewed through the lens of *Survivor*.

9781933771052 • TRADE PAPERBACK • $17.95 US/$19.95 CAN
AUGUST 2007

The Psychology of Joss Whedon
An Unauthorized Exploration of Buffy, Angel, and Firefly
EDITED BY JOY DAVIDSON, PHD

Revisit the worlds of Joss Whedon … with trained psychologists at your side. What are the psychological effects of constantly fighting for your life? Why is neuroscience the Whedonverse's most terrifying villain? How can watching Joss' shows help you take on your own psychological issues?

9781933771250 • TRADE PAPERBACK • $17.95 US/$19.95 CAN
DECEMBER 2007

Even More Psychology of Titles

The Psychology of Superheroes
An Unauthorized Exploration
EDITED BY ROBIN S. ROSENBERG, PHD
In *The Psychology of Superheroes*, almost two dozen psychologists get into the heads of today's most popular and intriguing superheroes.
9781933771311 • TRADE PAPERBACK • $17.95 US/$19.95 CAN • MARCH 2008

The Psychology of Dexter
EDITED BY BELLA DEPAULO, PHD
Seventeen psychologists and devoted *Dexter* fans take on the show's psychological complexities, analyzing not just the title character but also his family, coworkers, and even his viewers. Think you know *Dexter*? *The Psychology of Dexter* will make you think again.
9781935251972 • TRADE PAPERBACK • $14.95 US/$18.95 CAN
SEPTEMBER 2010

The Psychology of Twilight
EDITED BY E. DAVID KLONSKY, PHD, AND ALEXIS BLACK
Explore the minds and motives of Bella, Edward, Jacob, and more with a deeper look at the series that's captured the hearts—and psyches—of millions.
9781936661121 • TRADE PAPERBACK • $14.95 US/$17.50 CAN
OCTOBER 2011

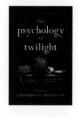